To William,

Hope there's something of interest
for you herein

best,

Andrew

RELIGION, LAW AND TRADITION

What sort of legal traditions exist in the world? What are the similarities and differences between Old Testament, Jewish, Canon, Islamic, Chinese, Hindu and Buddhist Law?

These so-called 'religious laws' apply to over half the world's population. Do they, as lawyers have assumed, form a coherent group that can be contrasted with the 'secular laws' of European states? The contributors to this volume agree that they do not. In the seven chapters devoted to each 'religious law' they explain why not, and offer expert and up-to-date descriptions of each tradition. The remaining chapters offer new legal taxonomies and new approaches to comparing the world's legal systems. Through discussion of the connections between religion, law and tradition, this volume contributes to our understanding of comparative religion as well as comparative law.

Andrew Huxley was a barrister in the London criminal courts for some years. He has taught law at Oxford, in Barbados and Hong Kong and, since 1984, at the School of Oriental and African Studies, London. He writes on the laws of Southeast Asia, on Buddhism and on the legal mechanisms of globalisation.

RELIGION, LAW AND TRADITION

Comparative studies in religious law

Edited by Andrew Huxley

RoutledgeCurzon
Taylor & Francis Group

First published 2002
by RoutledgeCurzon
11 New Fetter Lane, London EC4P 4EE

Simultaneously published in the USA and Canada
by RoutledgeCurzon
29 West 35th Street, New York, NY 10001

RoutledgeCurzon is an imprint of the Taylor & Francis Group

© 2002 Edited by Andrew Huxley

Typeset in Times by
Integra Software Services Pvt. Ltd, Pondicherry, India
Printed and bound in Great Britain by
Antony Rowe Ltd, Chippenham, Wiltshire

British Library Cataloguing in Publication Data
A catalogue record for this book is available
from the British Library

Library of Congress Cataloging in Publication Data
A catalog record for this book has been requested

ISBN 0–7007–1689–0

In memory of

DAVID DAUBE

scholar and teacher
(1909–1999)

CONTENTS

CONTENTS

CONTRIBUTORS

Calum Carmichael teaches in the Department of Comparative Literature, Cornell University. He has published extensively on the Bible as literature.

David Daube (1909–1999) taught at Berkeley, Oxford, Constanz and Aberdeen. Among his many books (listed at p. 87ff of ed. Calum Carmichael 1993 *Essays on Law and Religion, the Berkeley and Oxford Symposia in honour of David Daube*) are *Studies in Biblical Law* (1947), *Roman Law: Linguistic, Social and Philosophical Aspects* (1969) and *The New Testament and Rabbinic Judaism* (1973). His contribution to this volume has not hitherto been published.

Silvio Ferrari teaches at the Instituto di diritto ecclesiastico canonico, Milano and writes [mainly in Italian] on comparative canon law issues. He has also published in English in international journals.

Andrew Huxley teaches at the Law Department, School of Oriental and African Studies, London. He edited the book *Thai law: Buddhist Law* (1996) and has published several articles on Buddhist law and Southeast Asian law.

Bernard S. Jackson teaches at the Centre for Jewish Studies, the University of Manchester. He was previously a Professor of Law at Liverpool University. He is a publisher of legal journals, as well as a prolific author on law and semiotics.

Werner Menski teaches at the Law Department, School of Oriental and African Studies, London. Among his recent books are *South Asians and the Dowry Problem* (1998) and *Muslim Family Law* (1998) (co-authored with H.H. Judge David Pearl).

Randall Peerenboom teaches at the Law School, U.C.L.A. and practices in Beijing. His book *Law and Morality in Ancient China* (1993: State University of New York Press) is a classic.

Jacques Vanderlinden teaches at the *Institute pour l'étude du common law en français*, the Université de Moncton, Nouveau Brunswick. For many decades, he was Professor at the Law Faculty of the Université Libre de Bruxelles and President of the *Société Jean Bodin pour l'histoire comparative des institutions.* Among his many books are *Anthropologie juridique* (1996) and *Comment comparer les droits?* (1998).

Lynn Welchman teaches at the Law Department, School of Oriental and African Studies, London. She has recently published *Islamic Family Law: Text and Practice in Palestine* (1999).

ACKNOWLEDGEMENTS

Like so many other of London's recent contributions to legal scholarship, this volume owes its existence to the W.G. Hart Bequest. We are grateful both to W.G. Hart himself, and to his trustees for agreeing that the 2000 Workshop should be devoted to Comparative Law. Thanks to Belinda Crothers for organising and administering the *W.G. Hart Workshop on Comparative Law in the 21st Century* and to Lord Goff of Chieveley for delivering the keynote address. Jonathan Price of RoutledgeCurzon has smoothed the publication process. I have been able to carry out my editorial tasks amid the sylvan beauty of Rockbridge County, Virginia. For this I must personally thank Frances Lewis and the Law School of Washington and Lee University.

But the greatest debt owed by an editor of a volume such as this is to the contributors. For lending their expertise to this volume, I thank Professor Calum Carmichael of Cornell University, Professor Bernard S. Jackson of the Centre for Jewish Studies, Manchester University, Professor Silvio Ferrari of the Institute of Ecclesiastical Canon law, the University of Milan, Professor Randall Peerenboom of the University of California at Los Angeles, Professor David Daube, late of the University of California at Berkeley, Professor Jacques Vanderlinden of the Université Libre de Bruxelles and the Université de Moncton, Nouveau Brunswick, and my colleagues in the SOAS Law Department, Lynn Welchman and Werner Menski.

Exposition Universelle de 1900

1

INTRODUCTION

Andrew Huxley

This volume started as one of the panels at the *W.G. Hart Workshop, 2000*.[1] Lawyers from SOAS and the University of Glasgow jointly convened the workshop in order to commemorate the centenary of the *International Congress of Comparative Law*, Paris 1900. The *International Congress*, which was held as part of the Paris *Exposition Universelle*, is a significant event in Comparative Law's development. Richard Hyland sees it as a *rite de passage*, the culmination of 'the initial phase of modern comparative scholarship'.[2] Peter de Cruz sees it as the transition from dreamtime to modernity, when 'the first serious attempts were made to formulate the functions and aims of comparative law'.[3] A century later, how much has changed?

We can estimate the degree of change by comparing Comparative Law's buzzwords then and now. In 1900, the key concepts were *unification, evolution* and *taxonomy*. In 2000 they seem to be *globalisation, transplants* and *incommensurability*. In 1900 the young discipline was confident that the comparative method would transform our knowledge of law, as it had already transformed our knowledge of language and biology. In 2000 comparative lawyers are 'shaken by deep theoretical malaise'.[4] They need a 'radical revision of [their] modes of thought'.[5] The mainstream of academic comparative law scholarship 'is an exhausted *genre*'.[6] Starting from the bright, confident morning of Paris 1900, the discipline stumbled into London 2000 in a late night angst of failed aspirations. This volume focuses on one particular failed aspiration. Since 1900, Comparative Law has aspired to offer a world-wide picture of law through its taxonomy of families of law. Even though the bulk of twentieth-century work has focused on law in Europe and North America, the legal families' approach has enabled the discipline to claim that it provides a full global coverage. Most of the taxonomies that Comparative Law still takes seriously invoke a family of religious laws. The general approach is that European law can be divided according to political ideology (Marxist or non-Marxist law) and dependence on Roman Law (civil or common law), while non-European law can be divided into written law (which is religious) or unwritten law (which is custom). The purpose of this volume is to examine the concept of a family of religious laws.

I invited two groups of specialists who otherwise rarely meet each other to discuss these issues together. One bundle of invitations went to experts on Judaism, Christianity and Islam who, if not enthusiastic about the label *religious law*, have at least grown used to it. Another bundle went to experts in the legal traditions of China, India and Southeast Asia, who find the label more problematic. In my call for papers I asked them to consider three questions:

1   Is it useful to classify the world's legal phenomena into families?
2   If so, should one of the families be labelled as *religious systems*?
3   If so, which of Eurasia's written legal cultures should be included with the *religious systems'* family?

Familiar problems with timing and funding meant that some of the invitees were unable to attend the Workshop. I am delighted that, nevertheless, they have succumbed to my pestering and produced chapters for this volume.

Chapters 2–5 – Carmichael on the Old Testament, Jackson on the Jewish tradition, Ferrari on Canon law and Welchman on Islamic law – examine the law that has emerged out of the theistic religions of the Middle East. Bernard Weiss is surely right in his claim that these religions share a distinct relationship with law:

> Law, it seems, is integral to monotheistic religion. The world's sole creator is necessarily by right its sole ultimate ruler, legislator, and judge. All law worthy of the name must therefore originate with him.[7]

Chapters 6–8 – Peerenboom on Chinese law, Menski on Hindu Law and Huxley on Buddhist law – concern the legal traditions of South and East Asia. I am implying a geographical distinction between Near and Far East, but it is not that Orient v. Occident division about which Edward Said has warned us.[8] When discussing religions, we should look east and west from the 60°E line of longitude that descends from the Urals to the Iran–Afghanistan border. To the west the 'religions of the book' developed, with their common approaches to the divine and their common mythologies of Abraham and Moses. To the east developed several approaches to the sacred, different both from the Abrahamic religions and from each other. Whether Buddhism, Hinduism, Daoism and Confucianism should be labelled as a *religion*, rather than a philosophy, or a health programme, are controversial questions explored in the following chapters.

At the very least, I hope that twenty-first century taxonomists of law will pay more attention to this definitional problem than their predecessors did. This would encourage them to measure the respective contributions made by Christianity and Classicism to the civil and common law: Do European lawyers today descend more from Gratian and Aquinas, or more from Cicero and Ulpian? My next best hope is that twenty-first century comparatists should include *taxa* from either side of the Urals in their *phyla* and *genera*. 'Eastern' Chinese law and 'Western' Canon law, for example, share a positivist, hierarchical approach to legislative power.

2

While 'Western' Islamic law and 'Eastern' Buddhist law share the belief that ultimate power over law lies with this generation's interpretive community. The concept of *religion* alone does not help us analyse these similarities. We need a more detailed examination of how the authors of the law-texts (the Brahmin exegetes, the Muslim *'ulama,* the Chinese erudites, the Jewish rabbis, the Buddhist *vinay-adhara* and the Christian canonists) related to political structures, and to their own tradition and to their own public. The first seven chapters provide thick descriptions of these issues. To encourage comparatists to read them, I shall abstain from the usual editorial practice of giving a half-page summary of each chapter. I am judging you by my own low standards: Whenever I come across such an introduction, I xerox it and leave the rest of the volume unread.

In Chapter 8, the *Panel Discussion*, the contributors talk informally about the methodological issues at the heart of this book. We who study classical legal traditions, whether written in Chinese, Sanskrit or Hebrew characters, acquire a professional deformation, a bashfulness about speculating in print on areas outside our expertise. Because we know all too well how easy it is to draw wrong conclusions about our own area, we avoid commenting on territories about which we know little. Yet we must overcome this reticence if we classicists are to make any contribution to Comparative Law's debates. When comparing the tradition we know with another, we step down from our podium of expertise into the floor-level debate. We do this regularly anyway – when asking questions at Law Faculty seminars, when dashing off emails to colleagues at the end of a long workday, when pontificating over a pint – but seldom in print. The *Panel Discussion* has been stitched together from such shreds and patches. I recommend it to readers who assume that specialists in our abstruse fields must inhabit a distant methodological planet. Mildly eccentric we may be, but the intellectual world we inhabit is much like yours: in order to understand law, we read the same people – Marx, Weber, Hart, Dworkin – as everybody else.

Chapters 9 and 10 have a different aim. Chapters 1–8, taken as a whole, offer a destructive analysis of the category *religious legal systems.* But none of us has our foot in your door, trying to sell you an alternative legal taxonomy as if it was cheap double-glazing. This is bad news for readers like myself, who can only construct their own schemes through criticising other peoples'. In Chapters 10 and 11, David Daube and Jacques Vanderlinden remedy this deficiency by offering their own approaches to the macro-comparison of religious legal systems. They have rather different sales techniques. Vanderlinden goes for the hard sell: after knocking the competition and flourishing a bit of logic, he shows us charts and examples that illustrate the subtleties of his scheme. Daube preferred to illuminate the big questions by shining a focused beam of intelligence on points of detail. His sales-pitch is so soft that we may wonder what he is selling until the moment we sign the cheque. Given these differences in approach, it may be helpful to introduce Chapters 9 and 10 with a paragraph apiece.

David Daube (1909–1999) taught at Cambridge, Aberdeen, Oxford, Constanz and Berkeley. Among his students were three of the present contributors. He was no stranger to SOAS, having delivered there some of his most important contributions on the common intellectual background to Roman and Jewish law.[9] In 1983 he addressed an audience in Toronto on the *Jewish and Roman philosophies of law*. This hitherto unpublished lecture (which is included by kind permission of Daube's literary executor Calum Carmichael) fits the themes of this volume perfectly. That it is the first of his posthumous publications is a mixed blessing indeed. Like the other contributors, Daube belittles the 'time-hallowed contrast between societies where law is a branch of religion and societies where it is independent'. But then he goes on to describe 'fundamental down-to-earth dissimilarities' between the world of the *Talmud* and that of the *Corpus Iuris*. I take this to be his double-glazing scheme: as an indispensable preliminary to confident taxonomising, we must make systematic comparisons, one on one, between Roman law and Jewish law, Canon law and Chinese law, Hindu law and Islamic law, and so on. The final sentence of his lecture draws a moral to which we must all strive to adhere: 'Don't drive a camel with flax through a narrow street on Hanukkah.' If I dare point a moral to Daube's moral, it is that, when we apply our heads to the nebulous questions of law worldwide, we must ensure that our feet don't lose contact with the muddy ground of legal detail.

Jacques Vanderlinden's friendship with SOAS Law Department goes back to the 1960s when he, Tony Allott and Jim Read succeeded for a while in making African law into a glamorous, cutting edge discipline. For an all-too brief term in 1974 he joined us in the Department. During the 1980s he steered Europe's leading inter-disciplinary comparative forum, the *Jean Bodin Society for the Comparative Study of Institutions*, away from Eurocentricity towards serious intellectual engagement with the rest of the world. For the last decade he has been attached to the world's only *Centre for the study of common law in the french language*. I am indebted to him for various kindnesses that far exceed the normal academic courtesies. I regard Chapter 10, in which he blends points made by the panellists into a palatable dish, as another personal kindness. He, in turn, wishes to acknowledge some editorial assistance 'in rendering my Belgian porridge palatable to English *fins becs*'. Vanderlinden's approach to taxonomy depends on classifying the sources of law, and in particular, 'how the sources are perceived by those inside the legal system.' At first sight, his approach might seem to echo those twentieth-century comparatists, such as René David and Konrad Zweigert, whose taxonomies this volume has denounced. On closer reading, his approach is quite different, because his traditional emphasis on sources is combined with a radical pluralist approach to laws, norms, ethics and etiquette. This approach of running with the hare and hunting with the hounds (I use a metaphor that may soon be consigned to history) leaves him open to criticism from both traditionalists and radicals. The Vanderlinnaean taxonomy has been in a state of development since 1995: no doubt it will be further refined to meet the criticisms that this latest statement of it will attract.

So much for the contents of this book. For the rest of this introduction, I offer some of my own answers to the questions with which it is concerned. I have a double glazing scheme of my own, which might, dear sir or madam, be of some interest to you. If you'll just stand patiently by the door for a minute or two, I can show you how to save real money on those winter heating bills...

WHAT DISCIPLINE DO WE PRACTICE?

With one obvious exception,[10] we contributors would not label ourselves as comparative lawyers. We prefer to identify ourselves with disciplines such as Legal Semiotics, Legal History, Law and Narrative and Asian Legal Studies. Not that what we choose to call ourselves makes much difference to our perceived identity. In law faculties we will always be known, Welsh village style, by our specialism: Evans the Postman, Jones the Driver, Jackson the Judaist and Menski the Hinduist. We can hardly complain about this nomenclature, since we spend half our time writing for such journals as *The Jewish Law Annual, Asian Culture Quarterly* and *Buddhist Forum,* and attending conferences on Islamic, Classical or Indological Studies. We can relax in the company of fellow specialists: we don't have to explain our basic vocabulary at the start of each lecture, and we know that the editor will be able to provide that special font we need. In such company we can pick interdisciplinary brains. However good our linguistic skills, we can always learn more about legal vocabulary by talking to the experts in our language. However good we are as legal historians, we can always learn more from listening to the generalist historians. We swap notes with economists ('Have you heard the latest gossip from Delhi?'), with anthropologists ('Is that new publishing house in Bangkok any good?'), with sociologists ('Can you get a decent pizza anywhere in Tel-Aviv?') and with political theorists ('Does the hotel at Dun Huang take American Express?'). This half of our life is irrepressibly interdisciplinary.

At the risk of sounding smug, while comparative lawyers were calling for a multi-disciplinary approach,[11] we have just gone out and done it. Perhaps that is why Comparative Law has begun to show some interest in us. Ugo Mattei wants to incorporate our observations 'within the mainstream of comparative law to avoid [our] marginalisation into area studies'.[12] What an invitation! He sounds to my ears as if he were saying 'You few non-European specialists are marginalised in your sturdy lifeboat: come and join the rest of us on our sinking raft'. I would prefer to see our relationship to Comparative Law like this: We live in the no-man's-land beyond Comparative Law's borders. We make our living smuggling understanding across the frontiers of several disciplines. Occasionally we visit the comparatists to try and sell them a sparkling nugget of analysis. But you're more likely to find us selling our wares in the bazaars of Religious Studies, Area Studies, History and Philosophy. In this volume we have come together as friendly outsiders to offer a diagnosis of Comparative Law's illness and to suggest some roots and herbs that might alleviate the symptoms.

How would we describe ourselves? Certainly not as experts in *religious law*. If you applied that label to David Daube you might capture his work on the *Talmud* and the *New Testament*, but you would have missed his work on the *Corpus Iuris Civilis*. Unless you would like to refer to Roman law as a religious system? There were, of course, Graeco-Roman gods who lived on Mount Olympus, but Hans-Georg Gadamer reminds us how un-religious they were: 'The question of faith is entirely avoided by the life forms of Greek religion. Obeying the cult's laws and honouring the gods can even accord with atheistic doctrines'.[13] The European legal tradition is rooted in both 'religious' Jewish law and 'cultic' Roman law. At what point in the last 2000 years did European law stop being religious? To answer such a question requires a whole book. Likewise, comparatists need at least book-length knowledge of Hindu or Chinese law before assigning them to the religious or traditional phylum.

There are several similarities between the seven legal traditions examined herein: All are at least a thousand years old. All are written traditions, structured as exegesis of an old text containing timeless truth. All emanate from Eurasia. And all continue to influence twenty-first century legal behaviour. If the label *religious* cannot capture these common elements, what label will? Mattei refers to the *radically different legal cultures*,[14] apparently without realising how eurocentric this label is. Since every comparison is reversible,[15] it is from the Chinese lawyer's point of view, modern European law which is *radically different*. We need a label that applies as well to European law as to Chinese and Islamic law. The best label I can come up with is to describe the subject matter of this book is the acronym *OWL*, which stands both for *Old World Lawtexts* and for *Obsolescent Written Law*. I emphasise the 'O' word in both these formulations: what critically differentiates these seven systems from the normal Comparative Law fodder is oldness, obsolescence or, if you prefer, history. If we OWL experts have anything to offer Comparative Law, it is not an expertise in comparative religion, but an awareness of how legal traditions change through time. Those European lawyers who share this approach are historians of the legal tradition which they practice, men like Franz Wieacker, Harold Berman and Peter Stein. What these three have in common with us can be summed up in five letters – Weber.

The grand Montesquieu, Marx and Maine nineteenth-century comparative tradition culminated in Max Weber. But to an astonishing extent, twentieth-century Comparative Law has lost contact with its forebears:

> ...literature on comparative legal culture is a literature of gaps and of hopes...Max Weber is part of the grand tradition; Weber's ideas and schemes have had great influence among law and society scholars, though not, unless I am badly mistaken, among comparativists.[16]

The exception proving Lawrence Friedman's rule is Mirjan Damaska, whose adaptation of Weberian techniques to illuminate comparative legal procedure seems to me the only work of genius that twentieth-century Comparative Law has produced.[17] If, however, we wish to read treatments of such Weberian themes as the sociology of the legal profession, we must walk out of the Law Library into the sociology section of the main library.[18] We OWL experts, on the other hand, are steeped in Weber. Whether we agree with him or not, we cannot avoid engaging with him, since it was he who set our twentieth-century syllabus. Consider the following Weberian questions: Did Islam change from a religion of conviction to a legalistic, feudal religion? Was Confucianism only of interest to the bureaucrat literati who governed China? Was Buddhism so preoccupied with conscience and ritual formalism that it could scarcely develop a specialised legal learning? Weber's answers rested on an inadequate factual base, and we have had to spend much of the last century marshalling the detailed evidence to confirm or rebut them. More generally, Weber taught us to do more than simply understand the *Torah*, the *Hadith, Manusmrti*, the *Vinayapali*, the *Codex Iuris Canonici*, the *Corpus Iuris Civilis* and the *Han Codes*. We have to understand and sympathise with the scholarly communities that preserved these texts and the interpretative traditions they applied to them. Once we know how these legal scholars think, we try to compare levels of sophistication as between them and us. To do so, we must find a way to scramble round Weber's most problematical legacy, his understanding of rationalisation as what 'the systematic thinker performs on the image of the world: an increasing theoretical mastery of reality by means of increasingly precise and abstract concepts'.[19]

Because of our daily engagement with Weber, we OWL experts have never been allowed to forget the big questions. Mary Ann Glendon rightly stresses the role these questions play in attracting new students: 'What gets a scholar hooked on comparative legal studies, I believe, [is]...the unrestricted desire to know.'[20] But will the newcomers stay hooked if, as William Ewald contends, the mainstream's animating spirit is 'the Muse *Trivia*, inspirer of stamp collectors'?[21] When I addressed UK comparatists under the title 'The future of comparative law: back to the nineteenth century',[22] I was urging a reconnection with this tradition of big questions. Something got mislaid as we passed from the nineteenth to the twentieth century. Let's go back to Paris 1900 and see if we can relocate it.

PARIS 1900

The comparatists of 1900 talked of *unification*: we talk of *globalisation*. For Edouard Lambert, the general reporter of the Paris Congress, Comparative Law was a 'unifying force' that would result 'in the progressive effacement of the accidental diversity that prevails among legal systems located in countries of similar development and economic condition'.[23] Once the whole world had caught up with modernity, it could be governed by universal legal principles. For Lambert, no less than for Marx, history told a big story with a happy ending: thanks to the beneficent intervention of Europe in the rest of the world's affairs, mankind would one day be governed by universal legal principles.[24] Let's place this universalism in its context: Between 1890 and 1914 the world much resembled today's global market. 'There were few borders that mattered. Money, goods and people flowed freely ... [Since 1878] an international financial system came into existence which limited the economic autonomy of national governments.'[25] To remind us that the comparatists of 1900 were as globally-minded as ourselves, I have reproduced the *globe celeste* (mascot and logo for the *Exposition Universelle*) as the frontispiece of this volume.

Admittedly, their attitude to the globe was different from ours. Their wish for legal unification was a corollary of their imperialism. In 1900 France was still acquiring its worldwide empire. Whatever the delegates knew of the non-European OWLs, they had learnt in a colonial context. Pondicherry, with its Hindu population, was ceded to the French in 1674. Tunisia, with its Muslim population, became a French protectorate in 1881. Laos, with its Buddhist population, was not to be fully incorporated into Indochine Française until 1904. Though European imperialism dragged on until the 1970s, most lawyers had by then consciously adopted post-colonial attitudes. Does anyone still open the dusty volumes of colonial law reports? Does anyone (other than stamp collectors) remember the old colonial geographies: French Indochina, the Dutch East Indies, the Central African Federation, and so on? In 2000 even the Parisians would scarcely dare to categorise the *Code Napoleon* as being better than the *Le Code* of fifteenth-century Vietnam. We have repressed 1900's dream of *unification* so as to make room for 2000's dream of *globalisation*. We claim nowadays that the *lex mercatoria*, as conceived in Washington, should be adopted, not because it is better than its local alternatives, but because it is more convenient. Instead of universal legal principles, *globalisation* has given us universal market principles. We are, as Lambert hoped, 'progressively effacing ... accidental diversity', with reference not to Statutes but to fast food, computer games and sports footwear. Paris 1900 envisaged a legal globalisation based on European law; in 2000 we are getting an economic global- isation based on European market institutions.

The comparatists of 1900 talked of *legal evolution*: we talk of *legal transplants*. According to Jerome Hall:

> Many of the participants in the 1900 meeting stated that the function of these disciplines was to trace the evolution of various societies and, finally, of all mankind through a series of definite stages.[26]

It was the English delegate, Frederick Pollock,[27] who most explicitly treated imperialism and Darwinism as mutually supporting creeds. One of Pollock's inaugural lectures starts with a paean to Darwin and to the historical method which 'is nothing else than the doctrine of evolution applied to human societies and institutions',[28] then proceeds to illustrate the survival of the fittest by invok- ing English rule over India. Why do the colonised not rise up against their rulers? Because:

... our rule is better in the estimation of the majority of the dwellers in India than any other rule which they could probably look for in our absence ... It signifies that our empire is not of brute force, but of judgement and righteousness; in one *[sic]* word – for I will not shrink from being bold in my office – that it is an empire of law.[29]

Pollock's Dworkinian cadences offer us a version of consumer choice: by refraining from slaughtering our army of occupation, the Indians signify their preference for our common law tradition. Once the last of the world's savages has opted for English judgement and righteousness, the world will be united under Queen Victoria's empire of law. Say what you like about this argument, Pollock at least offered a testable definition of what the survival of the fittest means in a legal context. Pollock persuaded himself that what was fittest coincided with what was most English. Today it is not quite so obvious that Evolution would dress herself in the cricket jumper and frayed bespoke shirt that bespeak an English gentleman.

Rather the contrary. Evolution appears to us as a cruel, mindless, stochastic process. *Cruel*, because for every successful adaptation, a hundred more are doomed. *Mindless*, because there is no purpose to evolution, nor even a trend towards greater complexity. Some species, after all, display secondary simplification: that is they change 'back' to simpler forms. *Stochastic*, because the criteria which species have to meet are subject to random change. If a large chunk of comet happens to land on our planet, then it's goodbye dinosaurs, hello mammals. We have lost Pollock's faith in evolution as progress. It is all too easy to imagine cockroaches emerging as the fittest species to a post-nuclear world, or the protozoa as the fittest phylum in a post-greenhouse world. This helps explain why Alan Watson's coinage – the *legal transplant* – has filled some of the space vacated by social Darwinism. *Transplants* evoke a world of human agency in which lawyers do what they have always done best, which is to pass off someone else's thoughts as their own. If we talk about transplants 'succeeding' or 'failing', however, we do so unscientifically, since there is no control group against which we can check social change.

For example, the transition from socialism in 1990s Russia was a very crude transplant indeed. I could understand anyone who said it has proved a failure, and that Russia would have done better to transplant a different set of market institutions. But this is not a scientifically testable proposition which we can link to other proven facts in order to produce inductive knowledge. I cannot share Lord Goff's vision of the as-yet-unwritten essential texts of comparative law: 'In the end, they have to be works of synthesis, which compare and select in a Darwinian exercise of the survival of the fittest ...'[30] Only if we can foresee the future, do we have criteria by which to judge fitness. Next year a chunk of comet might fall on Hamburg and wipe out the Max Planck Institute. In 2003, Elvis Presley might return from the moon to lead a World Government. In 2004, barristers might be allowed to remove their wigs on exceptionally hot afternoons ... Those who coopt Darwin to describe social processes will be overtaken by unforeseen events such as these.

Pollock's empire of law has gone where the woodbine twineth. In a few decades noone left alive will have directly experienced European colonialism. I hope that Darwinian metaphor in the social sciences shares its fate. Steve Jones' *aperçu* is a *koan* on which we should meditate until enlightened: 'Evolution is to allegory as statues are to birdshit.'[31]

The comparatists of 1900 talked of *taxonomy*: we talk of *incommensurability*. In 1900 they saw legal history as the springboard into a better future: once the whole world reached the final, that is European, stage of development, it would share a global, that is European, law. In 2000 we see legal history as a drag on such progress. We associate the long-standing legal traditions of China, India or the Middle East with the failure of transplants and resistance to globalisation. The Parisian delegates thought of Darwin as having built on the work of Linnaeus. Evolutionary theory had added an historical dimension to biological taxonomy *per species et genera*. Hence, they felt, establishing a legal taxonomy was the necessary step towards identifying the laws of legal evolution.

The first of their taxonomies was Esmain's division of 1905. He divided the world's laws into five families – Romanistic, Germanic, Anglo-Saxon, Slavic and Islamic. Note the absence of any legal family east of the Urals: he omitted them, I surmise, because any law that existed outside Europe and the Mediterranean was either unwritten (and therefore dismissable as custom) or written (and therefore dismissable as religious law). Esmain (and the many taxonomers from Levy-Ullman to René David who have adapted his basic scheme) seems actually to be classifying law texts. Far from reflecting plain facts about the present population of legal systems, his taxonomy reflects the rhetoric by which lawyers justify their legal cultures. Instead of asking the question *What is French law like?* He asks *What do French lawyers look to as their founding document?* Each of his five legal families would give a different answer – the *Corpus Iuris*, the *Leges Barbarorum*, Coke's *Institutes*, the *Kormchaia Kniga* and the *Qu'ran*.

The *donnée* for Sauser-Hall's classification of 1913 was the *ad hoc* division of humanity into races: he divided world law into Aryan, Semitic, Mongolic and that of barbarous people. We no longer regard such treatment of human diversity as scientific, indeed we pass it by in embarrassment. We should, however, linger long enough to appreciate just how far colonial legal attitudes were permeated by race. I commend this remark by a Burman born in 1864 in free Burma. His father sent him down to colonised Burma to be educated by the English, and he graduated from Christ's College, Cambridge in 1893. Here he offers reasons why the colonial government should not pay attention to the Buddhist law texts:

> The rulings in the *Dhammasats*, which were never issued as imperative law by sovereign authority, are in the main a foreign importation, an Aryan source representing an ideal state of society, which has developed under Brahmanical and Buddhistical influences, and they are but a veneer on the Mongoloid people of Burma.[32]

I've never understood why racial determinism prevented the Mongoloid Burmese from appreciating Aryan Buddhist law, while allowing them to appreciate Aryan English law.

Back in the early nineteenth century, the Brothers Grimm had been the Darwin of their day and linguistics provided the best model of scientific taxonomy. The Indo-European language family gave Henry Maine a ready-made field of comparative legal study, but the first general taxonomy inspired by language classification was that of Arminjon *et al.* in 1950. It results in seven families: French, German, Scandinavian, English, Russian, Islamic and Hindu. The Indo-European language family is indeed spoken by more people than any other. Nonetheless, it is surprising that it should provide six out of the seven categories here, while Sino-Tibetan, the world's second most spoken language family, receives not a mention.

In 2000 taxonomy's value is no longer taken for granted. Some comparatists flirt with the notion of *incommensurability*. If there is no common scale of measurement by which the taxa (legal traditions) can be weighed and evaluated, then we cannot say which level of classification our taxon should occupy. Is the common law a phylum, a genus or a species? At its extreme, incommensurability leads to the *Rudyard-Lyotard Conjecture* that there is a theoretical limit on the understanding different traditions can have of each other. Jean-François Lyotard suggests this,[33] and Rudyard Kipling versifies his conjecture:

Oh, East is East and West is West,
and never the twain shall meet...[34]

Nowadays incommensurability is preached on both sides of *la Manche,* that notorious barrier to understanding.[35]

Since the OWLs are so often taken as the epitome of otherness, OWL experts must take this conjecture seriously. Europeans have long shuddered at the alterity of Jews and Muslims. During the last two centuries, Europeans discovered hitherto unsuspected dimensions of otherness from China to Peru. Can Europeans ever truly understand the law of the Incan Empire? Probably not, since they swiftly extirpated the society in which it had flourished. Can Europeans ever truly understand Chinese law? Well, at least it remains unextirpated. There's nothing to stop us moving to a new life in Shanghai. We can negotiate contracts and play golf with Chinese lawyers by day. We can practise calligraphy, drink rice-wine and watch *kung-fu* videos from Hong Kong in the evening. Maybe after twenty years of this, we would not yet have reached true understanding of Chinese law. But how do we know unless we try? Incommensurability is an empirical question. Some Europeans – like Joseph Needham – may understand China as well as the Chinese do. Some Asians – like the Dalai Lama – may understand Europe as well as we do. It seems rude to set any theoretical limit on their understanding unless we claim to know as much as they do. What will my Southeast Asian friends think if I solemnly declare that I shall never get to know them properly? Until our friendship has lasted a lifetime, its potentialities have not been fully tested. Never-the-twain-shall-meetism is not as reprehensible as racism or colonialism, but it is a junior member of the same family of sins. Richard Rorty's refutation of it depends on the image of an open-ended conversation:

> Hermeneutics sees the relations between various discourses as those of strands in a possible conversation, a conversation which presupposes no disciplinary matrix which unites the speakers, but where the hope of agreement is never lost so long as the conversation lasts.[36]

In real life, the context in which such an open-ended conversation can thrive is that of a life-long cross-cultural friendship, such as that between René David and John Merryman.[37] Returning to Kipling's *Ballad of East and West*, we can label this as the *Rortyo-Rudyardian refutation* of incommensurability: 'When two strong men stand face to face, though they come from the ends of earth'.

WHAT PURPOSES DOES TAXONOMY SERVE?

The *Encyclopedia Brittanica* warns us that 'A classification or arrangement of any sort cannot be handled without reference to the purpose or purposes for which it is being made.'[38] Because Ugo Mattei is explicit about the purposes his taxonomy is designed to fulfil, I shall use him to represent other recent legal taxonomies, such as those of Masaji Chiba,[39] Patrick Glenn,[40] William Twining,[41] and Werner Menski.[42] Mattei wants his taxonomy to answer big comparative questions, such as why and how legal systems change, why some transplants are successful and others not.[43] Samuel Krislov once remarked that 'Taxonomies are ... proto – theories',[44] but Mattei wants taxonomy to aspire to become fully-elaborated theory. Did any scientific taxonomy achieve as much as Mattei hopes for? The *Periodic Table* was a very successful taxonomy, but it did not answer any big questions. The big question (why the various taxa fitted as they did into the Table) could only be answered after the atom had been split. By reminding ourselves how scientists have actually used taxonomy, we may acquire a lower expectation of what it can achieve in comparative law.

The point at which biological taxonomy began to emerge from its Aristotelian stupor was when John Ray (1627–1705) turned away from the more obvious aspects of living things (such as colour and habitat) in favour of structural elements like vertebrae and toes. It takes a certain chutzpah to ignore the zebra's stripes in favour of counting its teeth, but that proved to be the high road to successful biological taxonomy. I strongly suspect that Comparative Law has not yet met its John Ray. We are still admiring law's stripes when we should be counting law's teeth. While his predecessors had worked top-down, Linnaeus (1707–1778) approached his task from the bottom-up, beginning with the *species*, and organising them into larger groups or *genera*, then arranging analogous *genera* to form families, *phyla* and kingdoms. I suspect that – if we ever identify law's teeth – we must then build our schemes upwards from them, Linnaeus-style. By trying to divide the world's law up into kingdoms, we are starting where we should end. Biologists have reached their present state of taxonomic enlightenment in several stages. They agreed on labels for the various levels from kingdom down to individual. They adopted naming conventions based on these levels. They developed tests to check the accuracy of how a taxon had been classified. And, even after all this, they accepted that taxonomy is a matter of judgement, not proof. Zoological taxonomy remains controversial, especially, as we shall see, at its topmost level of kingdoms.

Linguistic taxonomy borrows its terms from biology. Thus the language with which I struggle is classified as Sino-Tibetan *phylum*, Tibeto-Burman *family*, Burmish *division*, Burmese *language*. A classification like this does not answer any big questions, but it can suggest new areas worth investigating:

> What has emerged from recent work in typology is that certain logically unconnected features tend to occur together, so that the presence of feature A in a given language will tend to imply the presence of feature B. The discovery of unexpected implications of this kind calls for an explanation and gives a stimulus to research in many branches of linguistics.[45]

We can imagine legal taxonomy throwing up this kind of opportunity. We might find some unexpected legal correlation (for example, the more clauses in the Constitution, the higher the clear-up rate for reported violent crime). We could then have fun dreaming up linking explanations. In cases like this taxonomy is helpful, but I do not think that it is theoretical. I cannot find a scientific taxonomy that performs as Mattei wants legal taxonomy to perform.

Let us take a less ambitious function, that of providing a simple, first-approximation list of what the world contains. There's something very satisfactory about dividing the global population into units that we can count with our fingers. Thus we divide the world up into two hemispheres, three political-developmental 'worlds', four quarters, five continents and seven oceans. When looking up into the sky, we don't mind using a couple of toes as well: Earth's night sky, seen from the temperate zones, is divided into the twelve signs of the zodiac. This educative function is a perfectly proper one for taxonomy to fill, but it may not be achievable scientifically: modern astronomy does not give its blessing to the signs of the zodiac. Nor, at its most general level, is the taxonomy of languages scientific. To provide an overview of Earth's linguistic diversity, the *Encyclopedia Brittanica* has to divide the world into nine arbitrary but convenient regions (six in Eurasia, plus Africa, Oceania and the Americas). The non-arbitrary, scientific classification into language family starts at the next level down. It is the same in biology, where the highest level classification is neither arbitrary nor settled.

While our parents were confident that the global population of living things divides between the animal and the plant kingdom, the matter is nowadays controversial. One common approach involves adding an extra rank:

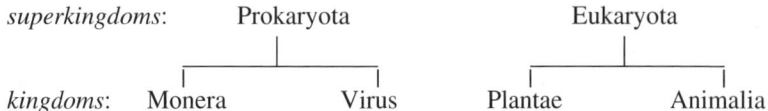

superkingdoms: Prokaryota Eukaryota

kingdoms: Monera Virus Plantae Animalia

We have no idea as yet whether the highest level of legal taxonomy will prove to be arbitrary or scientific. But, at least for the purposes of our introductory lectures, we need a legal equivalent to the five continents, the seven oceans and the twelve constellations. I propose that we use alphabetical order.

AN ALPHABETIC TAXONOMY OF LAW

Instead of offering a taxonomy of law, I am offering one of *written* law. Following the example of my students, I am answering the question to which I have an answer, rather than the question set. Historians will always be interested in *unwritten* law, or custom, or habitus. But to what extent does it continue to play a role in the contemporary legal scene? Donald Kelley's rider to Jacques Derrida reminds us that European lawyers are reluctant to even consider law in its unwritten form:

> 'The concept of writing should define the field of a science' … and this has been conspicuously true for the science of law.[46]

And who can say that Derrida and Kelley are wrong? In Papua and Amazonas a few preliterate cultures still survive. But surely by 2020 globalisation will have turned them into impoverished, alienated semi-literates? I regret the fact that these changes are underway: I would prefer the world to retain enough diversity to support both literate and pre-literate societies. However, this does not seem a likely outcome.

The classical legal systems with which this book is concerned (along with one which we have omitted) can each be assigned to its own writing system:

Chinese law:	*Chinese* ideographs
Hindu law:	North Indian *Devanagri* alphabets
Buddhist law:	South Indian *Pallava grantha* alphabets
Jewish law:	*Hebrew* alphabet
Byzantine/Slav law:	*Greek/Cyrillic* alphabets
European laws:	*Roman* alphabet
Islamic law:	*Arabic* alphabet

Which means that two Eurasian cultural phenomena, legal tradition and writing system, cut at the same joints: There is no member of the (Pali) Buddhist legal tradition who doesn't use a *Pallava Grantha* based alphabet. There are no *shar'ia* experts who don't use the *Arabic* alphabet, no Chinese lawyers who prefer to read their sources in Roman script. There are many more than seven writing systems in the world (most of them invented in Eurasia). But the seven best known Eurasian legal traditions each employs its own writing system. If we need a taxonomy for that introductory lecture to our Comparative Law course, then this alphabetical order is better than most. We talk of seven seas, seven ages of man and seven types of ambiguity. Let's also talk of the seven legal traditions enshrined in their seven alphabets.

Alphabetical taxonomy has the advantage of drawing attention to aspects of tradition that are often overlooked: how is thought nudged and constrained by the writing system used to express it? The Hebrew, Arabic, Greek and Roman alphabets are ordered in a straight line from *Alpha* to *Omega*, while all of the Indian alphabets are ordered in a two dimensional matrix. No doubt this difference nudged Greeks in the direction of geometry and Indians in the direction of algebra. But how did it affect the organisation of law-texts? And is there any way in which China, which came very late to its equivalent of alphabetic order, can be brought into the comparison? My alphabetic approach assumes that the classical lawtexts inhabit the 'domain of Gadamer's *sprachlichkeit* linguisticality, subject to the play of forces that constitute our experience as human beings'.[47] Islamic lawyers would reject my approach in favour of a hermeneutics that focuses on authorial intent. Brahmans, Buddhists, and Rabbis deploy other hermeneutics of their own. Those of us who use the alphabetic approach must, therefore, acknowledge that it is not an eternal truth since the dawn of time, but something pragmatic that happens to work in the year 2000.

To ask the questions posed in the last paragraph is to assume that writing systems get things done, each in their own way. Thomas Pynchon in *Gravity's Rainbow* plays this theme for laughs. He describes how the Soviets brought the New Turkic Alphabet to Central Asia in the 1920s:

> Native printers get crash courses from experts airlifted in from Tiflis on how to set up that NTA. Printed posters go up in the cities, in Samarkand and Pishpek, Verney and Tashkent. On sidewalks and walls the very first printed slogans start to show up, the first Central Asian fuck you signs, the first kill-the-police-commissioner signs (and somebody does! this alphabet is really something!) ... [48]

But the same theme can be treated as deadly serious. In his scary novel *The Names*, Don DeLillo draws our attention to the sacredness of writing systems, the numinosity of alphabets. Like prayer, like sacrifice, like meditation, epigraphy can make things happen:

> The mystery of alphabets, the contact with death and oneself, one's other self, all made stonebound with a mallet and chisel. A geography, a gesture of the prayerful hand.[49]

The writing hand is a prayerful hand. In other words, the look-and-feel of alphabets seeps into religion just as it seeps into law, and into every other corner of the written culture. DeLillo helps us appreciate this look-and-feel: 'If Greek or Latin characters are paving stones, then Arabic is rain.'[50] And on the Devanagri family of scripts: 'The letters, attached to top-strokes, were solid, firmly stanced. It was as though the sky and not the earth offered ultimate support, the only purchase that mattered.'[51] Near the climax of his novel, DeLillo moves us beyond writing systems to confront language itself. The hero has been living in Athens for some months before he visits the Acropolis. When he does, he finds himself:

> ...listening to people read to each other, listening to the guides speak German, French, Japanese, accented English...I move past the scaffolding and walk down the steps, hearing one language after another, rich, harsh, mysterious, strong. This is what we bring to the temple, not prayer or chant or slaughtered rams. Our offering is language.[52]

Elsewhere he reduces this meditation to six words: 'The river of language is God.'[53]

As legal academics, we label one stretch of the river of language as 'religion' and another as 'law', so as to debate which flows into the other. But, to the eye of Shiva, our efforts are nugatory. We can never step twice into the same river, neither can we subdivide its flowing waters.

NOTES

1 *Comparative Law in the 21st Century* held at the Institute for Advanced Legal Studies, London, 4–6 July, 2000.
2 Richard Hyland, 'Comparative Law' 184–199 of ed. Dennis Patterson *A Companion to Philosophy of Law and Legal Theory* (Oxford: Blackwell Publishers, 1996), 184.
3 Peter de Cruz, *A Modern Approach to Comparative Law* second edition (Deventer: Kluwer, 1999), 15.
4 Ugo Mattei, 'Three Patterns of Law: Taxonomy and Change in the World's Legal Systems' *American Journal of Comparative Law* 45: 5–44 (1997), 11.
5 Pierre Guiseppe Monateri, cited in Mattei, *supra* note 4, at 11.
6 Pierre Legrand, 'John Henry Merryman and Comparative Legal Studies: a Dialogue' *American Journal of Comparative Law* 47: 3–66 (1999), 65.
7 Bernard G. Weiss, *The Spirit of Islamic Law* (Athens: University of Georgia Press, 1998), 1.
8 Edward Said, *Orientalism* (Harmondsworth, Penguin Books, 1985).

9 David Daube, 'Rabbinic Methods of Interpretation and Hellenistic Rhetoric' (1948), 333–355 of ed. Calum Carmichael *Collected Works of David Daube, Volume One, Talmudic Law* (Berkeley: Robbins Collection, 1992).

10 Jacques Vanderlinden, *Comparer les droits* (Brussels: Kluwer-Belgium, 1995). I note that when comparatists are talking to each other, they refer to him as an 'African legal scholar' – he appears to be merely a weekend member of the comparative law club: Mattei, *supra* note 4, at 24.

11 For instance, John Merryman's vision of a new paradigm: 'All approaches, from humanistic to scientific, and all disciplines, from philosophy, literature and history through sociology and economics, are in principle equally valid.' Legrand, *supra* note 6, at 66.

12 Mattei, *supra* note 4, at 8.

13 Hans-Georg Gadamer, 'Reflections on the Relation of Religion and Science' trans. Joel Weinsheimer 119–127 of *Hermeneutics, Religion and Ethics* (New Haven: Yale University Press, 1999), 121.

14 Mattei, *supra* note 4, at 8.

15 Chad Hansen has explained the reversibility of comparison as well as anyone: 'These observations about the differences between Chinese and English syntax explain (from a Chinese point of view) why *we* place so much emphasis on the sentence, or (from our point of view) why Chinese philosophers do not. Either of two morals can be drawn: Chinese thinkers have a blind spot or we have an obsession'. Chad Hansen, 'Chinese Language, Chinese Philosophy, and "Truth"' *Journal of Asian Studies* 44: 491–519 (1985), 500.

16 Lawrence M. Friedman, 'Some Thoughts on Comparative Legal Culture' 49–57 of ed. David S. Clark *Comparative and Private International Law: Essays in Honor of John Henry Merryman on his Seventieth Birthday* (Berlin: Duncker & Humblot, 1990), 55.

17 Mirjan R. Damaska, *The Faces of Justice and State Authority: a Comparative Approach to the Legal Process* (New Haven: Yale University Press, 1986). Others share my high opinion: Hyland, *supra* note 2, at 193; William Twining, 'Comparative Law and Legal Theory: the Country and Western Tradition' 21–76 of ed. Ian Edge *Comparative Law in Global Perspective* (Ardsley: Transnational, 2000), 75.

18 And there we should pick up: Elliot A. Krause, *Death of the Guilds: Professions, States, and the Advance of Capitalism, 1930 to the present* (New Haven: Yale University Press, 1996).

19 Max Weber, *From Max Weber: Essays in Sociology* (London: Routledge & Kegan Paul, 1948), 293.

20 Mary Ann Glendon, 'Why cross boundaries?' *Washington & Lee Law Review* 53: 971–980 (1996), 974.

21 William Ewald, 'Comparative Jurisprudence (1): What was it like to try a rat?' *University of Pennsylvania Law Review* 143: 1889–2149 (1995), 1892.

22 B.I.I.C.L. and U.K.N.C.C.L. joint meeting: *Theory and Method in Comparative Law* INSTITUTE OF ADVANCED LEGAL STUDIES, London, 11 December, 1997.

23 Lambert disagreed with Karl Marx's evolutionary materialism. Legal systems differ not only because of their stage of economic development but also for 'political, social and moral reasons'. Any legal differences that is not classifiable under these heads 'are due to historical accident or to transitory and superficial causes'. Lambert translated in Hyland, *supra* note 2, at 186.

24 John W. Cairns, 'Comparative Law, Unification and Scholarly Creation of a New *ius commune*' *Northern Ireland Legal Quarterly* 32: 272–83 (1981), 272–273.

25 John Gray, *False Dawn: The Delusions of Global Capitalism* (London: Granta Books, 1998), 61.

26 Jerome Hall, *Comparative Law and Social Theory* (Louisiana State University Press, 1963), 16–17.

27 Pollock's 'renown extended beyond his native land and made him a dominant figure at the first great Congress of Comparative Law held in Paris in 1900'. L. Neville Brown, 'A century of Comparative Law in England: 1869–1969' *American Journal of Comparative Law* 19: 232–252 (1971), 235.

28 Frederick Pollock, *Oxford Lectures and other Discourses* (London: MacMillan & Co, 1890). I am citing his inaugural lecture 20 October, 1883 at Corpus Christi, Oxford, titled 'English Opportunities in Historical and Comparative Jurisprudence', 41.

29 Pollock, *supra* note 26, at 53.

30 Lord Goff, 'The Future of the Common Law' *International and Comparative Law Quarterly* 46: 745–760 (1997), 748.

31 Steve Jones, 'Go Milk a Fruit-Bat!' *New York Review of Books* 17 July, 1997, 39–41, 40.

32 Taw Sein Ko, 'Introduction' vii-viii of U Gaung *Digest of the Burmese Buddhist Law concerning Inheritance and Marriage, Volume 1 Inheritance* (Burmese language edition) (Rangoon: Superintendent, Government Printing, 1899).

33 Lyotard's incommensurability oscillates between, at one extreme, an endless proliferation of private languages and, at the other, 'some fundamental East/West distinction.' John McGowan, *Postmodernism and its Critics* (Ithaca: Cornell University Press, 1990), 188.

34 Rudyard Kipling, *The Ballad of East and West,* quoted in *Oxford Dictionary of Quotations* Third edition (London: Book Club Associates, 1979), 297. Apparently Indian hemp's effect on Kipling was to alter his mental polarity: 'And the talk slid north, and the talk slid south/with the sliding puffs from the hookah-mouth . . .' *The Ballad of the King's Jest*, ibid.

35 On the relationship between Lyotard's incommensurability thesis and other Francophone postmodernisms (including those of Jacques Derrida, Michel Foucault and Pierre Bourdieu): McGowan, *supra* note 31, at 180–210. For discussion of Anglophone views (as espoused by Thomas Kuhn, Richard Rorty and Alasdair MacIntyre): Richard J. Bernstein, 'Incommensurability and Otherness Revisited' 85–93 of ed. Eliot Deutsch *Culture and Modernity: East-West philosophic perspectives* (Honolulu: University of Hawaii Press, 1991).

36 Richard Rorty, *Philosophy and the Mirror of Nature* (Princeton: Princeton University Press, 1979), 317.

37 Legrand, *supra* note 6, at 40.

38 *Encyclopedia Brittanica CD-Rom* (1995), *sub nom* Biology.

39 Masaji Chiba, 'Other phases of Legal Pluralism in the Contemporary World' *Ratio Iuris* 11: 228–245 (1998).

40 H. Patrick Glenn, *Legal Traditions of the World* (Oxford: Oxford University Press, 2000).

41 William Twining, *Globalisation and Legal Theory* (London: Butterworth, 2000).

42 Werner Menski, *Comparative Law in a Global Context: the Legal Systems of Asia and Africa* (London: Platinum, 2000).

43 Mattei, *supra* note 4, at 9.

44 Samuel Krislov, 'The Concept of Families of Law' 25–38 of ed. Adam Podgorecki, Christopher Whelan, Dinesh Khosla *Legal Systems and Social Systems* (London: Croom Helm, 1985), 31.

45 Encyclopedia Brittanica, *supra* note 36, *sub nom.* Linguistic Taxonomy.

46 Donald R. Kelley, 'Lord Deliver Us from Justice', *Yale Journal of Law and the Humanities* 5: 159–168 (1993), 159; quoting Jacques Derrida, *Of Grammatology* (1974), 27.

47 Weiss, *supra* note 7, at 69.

48 Thomas Pynchon, *Gravity's Rainbow* (London: Jonathon Cape, 1973), 355.
49 Don DeLillo, *The Names* (New York: Random House, 1982), 284.
50 id., at 137.
51 id., at 284.
52 id., at 330.
53 id., at 152.

2

RELIGIOUS CLAIMS ABOUT BIBLICAL LAW

Calum Carmichael

I will look at two biblical rules that critics commonly claim reveal a religious dimension in biblical law. In particular, they attribute a mysterious, non-rational dimension to the rules and assert that this element is religious in character, and is so ancient that it goes back to pre-Israelite times. Leo Strauss articulates this view that, in effect, takes literally the metaphoric equation of antiquity with the divine: 'The ancestors are superior, and therefore the ancestors must be understood, if this notion is fully thought through, as gods or sons of god, or pupils of god.'[1] I will reject both the religious claim and the related claim that we are touching on matters of great antiquity in the sense that biblical rules come from the very distant past. I will also touch on some larger issues about law and religion, law and storytelling, and the comparative approach to biblical law.

First, some general comments are useful as an introduction to the nature of biblical legal material. To formulate their laws biblical lawgivers focus primarily on Israelite national epics and legends. From their contemporary world the law-givers bring a variety of extant legal and ethical rules – in some shape or form not available to our scrutiny – and reformulate them in light of the epics and legends. Thus, only after contemplating problems that they encounter in mythical narratives about the origin of the world, the origin of the nation's ancestors and the origin of the nation itself, do the lawgivers proceed to commit laws to writing. An ancient and a modern parallel – they are no more than that – present themselves when we observe the biblical procedure.

The famous Greek tragedies of the fifth century BCE explore profound ethical and legal issues that come up in Greek mythology – that is, in ancient stories about Greek origins. The authors of the tragedies are familiar with the rise of the new craft of rhetoric for dealing with crimes that are far from straightforward. The craft itself was a product of the enormously complicated problems thrown up by the political turmoil in Sicily around 500 BCE[2]. An example of rhetoric used for legal purposes is when accused of a crime you plead that the wrong has been committed but argue that extenuating circumstances exist. The authors of the tragedies, in turn, are influenced by the new way of defending wrongdoing.

However, instead of turning to crimes in the society of their time they focus instead on wrongdoing in the mythical world of their ancestors. Clytemnestra assassinates her husband Agamemnon who has just returned from the Trojan War. While he was away, she had an adulterous relationship. Among other defenses she reminds her accusers that Agamemnon had sacrificed their daughter Iphigeneia and had a mistress in Cassandra. Oedipus slaughters his father and marries his mother but is he to be held guilty for monstrous deeds when he acted innocently? Oedipus's son, Polynices, dies in a rebellion and the ruler Creon denies him burial. His sister Antigone, however, feels compelled by a higher law to grant him it. The other sister Ismene demurs on the ground that women should not take it upon themselves to defy public authority. Sophocles explores the claims of the two competing authorities. Matters of great ethical and legal import are filtered through the doings of mythical personages. Biblical laws prove to be similarly mediated: the issues taken up derive from a searching inquiry of the epics of the past. It is not irrelevant that the laws are set in the midst of the accounts of these epics.

A modern parallel is the way in which students in an American Law School acquire rules – for example, about contracts or criminal intent. They are not told the rules directly but have to search for them by immersing themselves in cases, the equivalent of narratives.[3] The students have some sense of what the rules might be – general awareness, education to date, and so on – but only through a series of readings will they eventually emerge with formulations of rules that are more complete than the ones they worked with initially. The formulators of biblical rules similarly owe a great deal to the cases under review – i.e. to the narratives that constitute the history of disputes and problems associated with the nation's beginnings.[4]

I take up the first of the biblical rules with its alleged religious element. It is the decidedly strange rule about feeding the needy in Deut 24: 19–22:

> When thou cuttest down thine harvest in thy field, and hast forgot a sheaf in the field, thou shalt not go back to fetch it: it shall be for the stranger, for the fatherless, and for the widow: that Yahweh thy God may bless thee in all the work of thy hands. When thou beatest thine olive tree, thou shalt not go over the boughs again: it shall be for the stranger, for the fatherless, and for the widow. When thou gatherest the grapes of thy vineyard, thou shalt not glean it afterward: it shall be for the stranger, for the fatherless, and for the widow. And thou shalt remember that thou was a bondman in Egypt: therefore I command thee to do this thing.

The first part of the rule concerns a forgotten sheaf of grain at harvest time. Only if the farmer forgets that he has left the sheaf in his field, then remembers that he has forgotten it, has he to refrain from returning to fetch it. He has instead to leave it in the field to be picked up by the needy. But there is no guarantee that a farmer will forget the sheaf, much less that he will remember that he has forgotten. As a rule encapsulating the principle of solicitude for the poor this one would certainly be inadequate and the practice unreliable. No wonder that in Rabbinic literature we find statements such as, 'All the commands in the Torah were given us by God to be observed knowingly, but this one [the forgotten sheaf] we can observe only unknowingly. For if we seek to keep it deliberately, it cannot be kept, since it is ordained only for forgetfulness' (*T. Peah* 3: 8; *Siphra* 27a). What highlights the curiously impractical instruction about the grain is the fact that the rule goes on in a much more rational spirit to urge the farmer not to beat his olive trees a second time and not to glean his vines a second time. To refrain from doing so will guarantee that the needy can indeed take what is left of the olives and the grapes. Forgetfulness is not an element in these subsequent rules – which highlights all the more that some special feature to do with memory underlies the rule about the forgotten sheaf.

Critics who are alert to the puzzling feature of the rule resort to a religious explanation. The rule must preserve a matter of great antiquity that goes back to a time before the kind of Israelite religion found in the present books of the Bible. The claim is that a sheaf of grain was left in the field as a propitiatory offering to a god.[5]

The rule's odd feature, in fact, has nothing to do with remote antiquity in the sense that the critics assume. (Not to be denied is that the custom of giving to the poor is from time immemorial.) Rather, it is the lawgiver himself who exploits people's belief in the authority of the past – a quite different matter. I suggest that the rule harks back to the problem of famine in Egypt as described in the Book of Genesis. The rule's intent is to evoke the role of Joseph in obtaining food for the Egyptians and his own family in bad times. Recall that in the first of Joseph's dreams he sees himself at harvest time as a sheaf of grain surrounded by other sheaves, all of which bow down to him. Joseph's dreams are from God and refer to future developments. This dream points forward to the time when his brothers have to go to Egypt to obtain food because there are no longer any harvests. On the occasion they do indeed bow down to Joseph, the overseer of all the grain in Egypt (Gen 42: 6, 43: 26). The dream encompasses the entire history of Joseph in Egypt. In what is a standard procedure for this lawgiver, he turns to this particular story because it provides the first example in the nation's history when a policy was put in place to supply those desperately in need of grain.

The key to comprehending the law about the forgotten sheaf is the role of forgetfulness in the Joseph story. The law takes up the drama of how Joseph's dream about himself as the superior sheaf of grain is delayed in its fulfillment. Recall that the dream only begins to show promise of fulfillment when in prison Joseph under God's direction interprets aright the dreams of the butler and the baker (Gen 40: 8). Joseph appeals to the butler to remember him when he becomes the pharaoh's butler again (Gen 40: 14). However, the butler 'did not remember Joseph, but forgot him' (Gen 40: 23). Only when the pharaoh has his dreams about the harvests does the butler remember Joseph (Gen 41: 9–13). That development triggers Joseph's rise to preeminence, to a position from which he administers food stores on behalf of those who would otherwise go hungry.

The standing sheaf of the dream, Joseph, like the sheaf in the rule, is first forgotten, then remembered, and, he, like the sheaf in the law, is able to provide the needy with grain. The oddity in the law that the sheaf has to be forgotten is designed to arouse curiosity and engage historical memory. The rule is religious only in so far as it exploits a legendary story about the first time people were aided in obtaining food in times of hardship.[6] The view is that such a rescue is providential and the example from the past should be remembered and imitated at harvest time. Imitated in the sense that a harvester should indeed leave for the poor some of the fruits of the harvest. One would misunderstand the rule by taking it literally, reckoning that obedience to it was only possible should forgetfulness prevail. Just as Joseph is not literally a sheaf of grain, so the rule should not be read literally.[7]

The view of scholars that the forgotten sheaf was a relic of a remote time when it was left behind for a religious offering indicates that they perceive a problem. The Rabbis explicitly give expression to it. In effect, all commentators have been too quick to come up with a solution for a problem that they have not, or have not fully, formulated. I agree that the rule is ancient in character, because the practice of giving to the poor has existed from remotest times. The rule, however, focused as it is on a particular narrative, has a specific, not a hoary origin. While both the narrative and the rule are ancient from our perspective, this rule's origin can be specified and linked to a mythical series of events.

Both biblical lawgiver and modern interpreters share in common the desire to attribute the rule about the forgotten sheaf to a distant past that on inspection turns out to be mythical. The law is but one of many where we find such an attempt to appeal to past times. The example of the biblical lawgiver is especially interesting in that, living hundreds of years later and for the purpose of lending authority to his laws, he passes himself off as Moses who, in turn, appeals to the past in giving his judgments. What emerges from how both ancient and modern interpreters think about the religious dimension to law is that religion is less a matter of theological ideas and more something that is synonymous with a mythical past. Ancientness becomes a metaphor for the divine.[8]

I turn to an example of a rule universally thought to be religious, both in the sense of being ancient and involving the divine, but which on closer inspection, being also tied to a narrative, alters the sense of the ancient and the divine. A consensus prevails among scholars that the ritual for the Day of Atonement in Leviticus 16 contains major elements that come from remote antiquity, from pre-Israelite times. For example, they make that claim for the ritual whereby a live goat, bearing all the sins of the Israelites, is sent into the wilderness to a demonic being Azazel. Somewhat similar practices found in Hittite and Mesopotamian sources from times much earlier than the Bible have greatly encouraged the view that the goat ritual was ancient even at the time of Israel's beginnings.

Scholars who compare the biblical ritual with the parallel ones in the Near Eastern material think that the Israelites were more advanced in their religious thinking than their neighbors. These critics claim that the Israelites were freer of the world of demons and deities than their counterparts, although why that constitutes an advance is not spelled out. In the matter of Azazel the Israelites have removed its demonic character. By the time they incorporate Azazel no longer is he an angry deity that needs to be appeased – the goat sent to him is not a sacrifice – nor is he a desert demon that is the custodian of evil.[9] Why the feature of the ritual about Azazel showed up in Israelite culture is indeed seen by these same critics as a puzzle. The favored solution is the claim that religious ideas have their origin in the remote past, in times when the ancients had an uncanny sense of the world of the numinous. The biblical recorders of the pre-Israelite ritual retained something of its antiquity because they too were intent on giving expression to the religious notion of atonement for sin. Only, in line with their belief in the one God Yahweh, they depersonalized the figure of Azazel and rendered it virtually meaningless.

Here, then, we have critics who assume that, even if a holdover from a previous era, a religious idea about the need to appease a deity or to unload guilt infuses a biblical law. Only they lack the means whereby they can trace the different steps over a long period of time that led to the biblical ceremony. I wish to argue for a quite different understanding of the ritual. In some sense religion is involved but only in a universal desire that comes to expression in societies secular or religious, namely, the wish to evoke and overcome regret about wrongdoing. I also cannot accept the view that we are dealing with matters that were already of great antiquity to the Israelites. The ritual is, in fact, relatively easy to interpret. It is a product of the lawgiver's own inventiveness, and there is no need to think that the ritual has undergone different stages of development over many centuries.

I rate the religious dimension in the rule not much higher than its presence in contemporary American thinking about the need to introduce the notion of atonement for the commission of crimes. In a recent article Stephen Garvey argues for such a need in our treatment of criminals.[10] In the biblical rule the concern is much broader than with punishable criminal acts and encompasses all of the offenses, legal and moral, of the entire community.[11] One day a year its members have to acknowledge their offenses and be rid of them. It is the latter notion that is the odd one because, in the words of Lady Macbeth, 'What's done cannot be undone.'[12] Yet the wish to achieve the impossible is ubiquitous and around at all times, testifying to a deep-seated human need to salve conscience such that the past is not just feigned to disappear but is somehow wiped out.[13] How has the biblical lawgiver addressed the matter?

With his all-consuming interest in origins he returns, I submit, to the first occasion in the nation's history when there was just such an attempt by wrongdoers to expunge their offense. I refer to the brothers of Joseph who infamously try to conceal their treatment of Joseph by faking his death when they furnish evidence from which Jacob concludes that his son, their brother, has been torn to pieces by a wild animal. They kill a goat, dip Joseph's coat in its blood, and present it as evidence of Joseph's end. On the basis of their unacceptable efforts to absolve themselves of responsibility for Joseph's dire fate, the biblical lawgiver devised an acceptable means of wiping out offenses that would serve the later sons of Israel.

The ritual is fundamentally commemorative in function. It encapsulates Joseph's brothers' offense. Their story provides the first example in the nation's history when offenders experienced forgiveness for their wrongdoing. The brothers' fakery with the goat inspires the attempt to achieve the same end for all Israelites. The things the brothers did with the goat and its blood constituted an attempt to cover up an offense by transferring it to the animal. Eventually they confessed their wrongdoing and were forgiven. In the ritual, the Israelites' offenses are transferred to a goat and the people thereby receive forgiveness.

My interpretation of the ritual follows from observing how it reflects the brothers' machinations with the animal. The ritual picks up on both the factual and the fictional aspects of what they do. There are two goats in the ritual of Leviticus 16, one that is sacrificed as a sin offering to Yahweh, the Israelite god, and the other that is sent off live into the wilderness to the mysterious being, Azazel. The actual slaughter of one goat corresponds to the fact that the brothers did indeed kill a goat in order to use its blood to suggest that a wild creature had killed Joseph. Sending alive the other goat into the wilderness corresponds, in turn, to the fiction that Joseph died in the wilderness, the victim of a wild beast. The dispatch of this second goat to Azazel conveys, in line with the brothers' deception, the notion of an innocent animal undergoing transformation into a demonic creature capable of killing a human being.

Critics to date think that Azazel as he appears in the Bible is the remnant of some ancient demonic being that the precursors of the Israelites once recognized. The name does not occur earlier than the passage in Leviticus 16 so that no evidence exists for the claim. I, in turn, cannot claim that Azazel is not a figure who was recognized in some shape or form by the ancient Israelites and neighboring peoples. However, I am inclined to think that like the ritual itself the name is also meant to allude to the fiction that the brothers made up about Joseph's fate.

Baruch Levine argues that the name means 'mighty goat' and is made up of the term *'ez,* 'goat,' twice repeated along with the term *'el* used adjectivally meaning 'mighty.'[14] The term *'el* can be used of mighty things in nature, for example, 'mighty mountains' in Ps 36: 6. The longstanding meaning has been 'goat that has gone away [into the wilderness]' from *'ez* 'goat' and the verb *'azal* 'to go away.' My suggestion is that the sound of the name with its doubly repeated reference to a goat serves to draw attention to the brother's ploy.[15] The name is like the name Onan with its doubly repeated sound *'on,* 'virility' – 'the virile, virile one.' Recall that Onan spilled his seed on the ground in order not to give Tamar conception (Genesis 38). The name is a made-up one for the purpose of drawing attention to his deception. A non-biblical example of an artificial name that mocks someone's action is Humpty Dumpty who is not an egg but a *testudo,* 'tortoise,' the precursor of the modern tank. The sound of the name – Humpty Dumpty – evokes this engine of war with its turtle shape and wooden wheels. The name was specifically coined to poke fun at the unsuccessful attempt by King

Charles to take the walled city of Gloucester during the English Civil War in 1643.[16]

With the slaughter of the goat the brothers seek to cover up their transgression against Joseph. Blood is used to this end. In the rule, the slaughter of the goat serves to expiate all of the transgressions of all the Israelites, and the priest uses its blood to represent their atonement. In the story, by devising the fiction that a wild animal has mauled Joseph, the brothers transfer to an animal their wrong-doing. In the rule, the dispatch of the goat to an imaginary demonic being creates the legal or religious fiction that human malevolence can be transferred to an animal. The two actions with the two goats in the rule represent the *au fond* impossible task of wiping out the wrongdoing.

That the ritual is designed to remind us of past events is not surprising – memory is crucial for the purpose of confession. In the story, Joseph triggers his brothers' memory – and confession of wrongdoing – by creating a nasty fiction himself when he treats them as spies. An equally important point is that, because the rule targets everyone in the community, there is a need for a mechanism that will aid the individual in recalling the particularities of his own wrongdoing. An effective device is to dramatize the offense of the community's first ancestors. The brothers' particular action with the goat reminds one of just how many different offenses they commit against Joseph and their father. For example, they misuse the blood of an animal, they falsely suggest that Joseph has been killed when he has not, they dishonor a parent, and they conceal their wrongdoing. The variety serves as a prompt for later Israelites each to recall his own multifaceted record.

The power of imitation plays a considerable part in the ritual. An Israelite is to identify with his first ancestors in seeking to rid himself of wrongdoing. The ritual itself imitates their sleight of hand. We are, again, looking at a universal phenom-enon that is present at all times and places, and not a little of its appeal is indeed magical in character. In the Book of Genesis, Jacob cheats Esau out of the right of the firstborn son (Gen 25: 24–34; 27). He does so by acting the part of his elder brother and taking on his identity. He cooks a dish that Esau normally cooks, becomes hairy like him, and presents himself as Esau to his blind father. What we find is a belief in the power of impersonation such that by acting the part of another person somehow one becomes that person.[17] In both ancient Greece and Israel one became educated not by attending set, impersonal lectures, but by attaching oneself to an admired individual with whom one lived, and then copying his words and deeds. The aim was to become that person. In the early Rabbinic use of ordination an ordained Rabbi would lean his hands on the head of his disciple with a view to conferring Rabbinic authority on him. The underlying idea was that the Rabbi was pouring his personality into the disciple so that the disciple would acquire his wisdom and power.

The elements I have isolated for understanding the ritual of the Day of Atonement, commemoration of a significant moment in history and identification with the original players in it, are not special to this particular institution. A well recognized example is the ritual of the Passover in the Book of Exodus. That institution recalls the rescue of the Israelites from their enslavement in Egypt. In addition, the required ritual of remembrance involves taking blood from a lamb, bread that has not been leavened and bitter herbs so that the participants identify with those who experienced the original events (Exodus 12).

GENERAL OBSERVATIONS

I conclude with nine observations about the nature of law and religion in biblical material and also about the connection that I have emphasized between law and narrative.

First, like the contents of all biblical and ancient Near Eastern codes of law, the rule about the Day of Atonement is a hypothetical construction, not intended, at the time of its formulation, to be fulfilled in real life. The rule is born of the ambitious attempt by scribes to overview all of Israelite history up until the Babylonian exile and create a fiction about the origin of Israelite law.[18] In line with a common convention of their time, the lawgivers attributed their laws to a legendary figure of the past, Moses, in this instance. One indication of the hypothetical character of the law about the Day of Atonement is the impractical element that the second goat somehow remains in the wilderness. Later interpreters rationalize the problem of impracticality. Although the Targum (a translation of the Bible into Aramaic in the early centuries CE) has not reached that stage – it has the animal hurled down a precipice to its death by a gust of wind sent by God (*Targum Yerushalmi* on Lev 16: 21), the Mishnah (a codification of Jewish law written in Hebrew at the end of the second century CE by Rabbi Judah the Prince) has. The animal is led away by someone and pushed over a ravine (*mishnah Yoma* 6: 3–6). By the time of the Mishnah rules that originally did not have legislative authority, came to be treated as if they had. The development illustrates how misinterpretation, not re-interpretation, is often the engine that drives this and indeed any legal or religious system.

Second, the rule's fictional, story-like character explains, partly, why there is no attempt to make the historical episode at its core explicit. The quality that Walter Benjamin saw in storytelling applies also to this biblical rule (and to others): 'It is half the art of storytelling to keep a story free from explanation as one reproduces it.'[19] The lack of institutionalized lawmaking in the time of the scribes responsible for the presentation of biblical rules permits a more literary quality to enter into their formulations. The magic of the ritual that the critics perceive as religious and descended from the remote past is, I claim, a form of enacted coded communication. The supposed religious aspects represent sophisticated and imaginative thinking. The intent is to engage the creator of the rules and their recipients in a process of reflection on their history and, consequently, to come to realize from their past who they are, or should be, in the present. 'All rituals,' says Victor Turner, 'have this exemplary, model-displaying character; in a sense, they might be said to "create" society, in much the same way as Oscar Wilde held life to be "an imitation of art."'[20]

Third, David Daube's point may well apply to the willingness with which scholars postulate a religious dimension to the rules. He claims that two contradictory needs – 'to look down on the "primitives" from the height of our progress,' and 'to look up to them from the depth of our decadence' – often show up together when we examine the ancient world, the two needs regularly impairing research.[21] In this instance, from the idealizing perspective we envy the ancients their supposed intimacy with the world of spirits and the forces of nature, but from the deprecating perspective we also think that they lacked rational instincts. Scholars err in thinking that the ritual was a solemn exercise in credulity in which the goat was thought to carry off the people's offenses. The goat ritual is an acted out story. The fables of Greek and Hebrew antiquity similarly communicate messages about human affairs. It would not do to treat them as if they are about the magical world of talking animals. Just as the fables in antiquity functioned to transfer to an imaginary world what goes on in the human, so the two goats in the law serve the same end. In both fable and law it is the indirect nature of the communication that contributes to its effectiveness. Aside from the impossibility of wiping out past offenses, the scapegoat ritual is not illogical and mystical but makes as much sense in the contemporary world as it did in the ancient biblical one.

Fourth, the absence of hard evidence for the dating of ideas commonly leads to the attempt to correlate what is supposedly primitive with an early way of thinking and what is considered progressive with a later. Lon Fuller points out that a common but mistaken view of legal fictions is that they belong to a stage in the development of the law that is long passed.[22] Behind the error is the claim that such fictions are naïve. Scholars tend to see certain biblical laws along similar lines. On the one hand, they think that the laws contain very old religious ideas. On the other hand, they dismiss these ideas as belonging to a stage of development that has been superseded by more advanced ones. Thus they sometimes attribute to the formulators of the laws themselves the toning down or downright removal of old and primitive notions.

To be sure, the matter is complicated. David Daube claims that there is a general criterion that helps to make a judgment as to what is primitive and what is progressive. If an idea shows up in a source and strikes a modern reader as awkward it is likely to be ancient.[23] The judgment is comparable, he thinks, to the one that textual scholars typically make when they come upon two texts, one of which, the *lectio difficilior*, is more awkward than the other. They judge that the more difficult reading is likely to be the older one. The other's existence is explained on the grounds that a scribe has removed the awkwardness.

An example he cites of an idea that became less attractive is that in early laws on the subject someone converting to Judaism is exempt from the normal incest laws. The convert is new born in such a fundamental sense that he or she is no longer the same person as in the pre-conversion stage. Should a brother and sister convert, for example, they are no longer related biologically and, in principle, can marry. Daube claims that over time this religious doctrine about new birth caused the Rabbis discomfort. He finds indication of the discomfort in the Rabbinic decision that a union contrary to Gentile law cannot be entered into even though, because of conversion, all former ties the previously related couple had have disappeared. A further illustration of such discomfort is that for the past three hundred years Jewish scholars interested in a critical reading of Jewish sources looked away from the doctrine of rebirth because it clashed with their feeling that such a literal notion of rebirth could not be taken seriously. On the basis of such reservations Daube concludes that the idea of rebirth must be old and the discomfort with it belongs to a later stage – it is obvious in the case of recent scholarly attitudes – and represents more advanced thinking.

Doubtless, there is something in Daube's criterion but there are complications with it too. The ritual of the scapegoat illustrates the difficulties in making the judgment that he does. The universal sense of the ritual is that in origin it is primitive. That view translates into the chronological one that it is very old. In turn, scholars see progressive factors come into play in the law in Leviticus 16 when they claim that the Israelite lawgiver has watered down the significance of the demonic being Azazel. The law, they conclude, must then be much later than the original hocus-pocus with the goat. I do not think that any evidence, in fact, supports the judgments that critics make about which aspects are old and strange and which are enlightened. If there is any merit to the description of the origin of the ritual that I have laid out, the judgment about the primitive v. the progressive is beside the point.

Fifth, when Garvey argues that atonement has always been associated with religion and theology he is anxious to stress for modern readers of law journals that the notion should not be associated with religion alone. 'Atonement's theological antecedents are important and illuminating, but as a theory of punishment, atonement can stand on its own.'[24] There may be a hint in his statement that to re-institutionalize atonement in the contemporary world would constitute an advance on any preceding religious use of it. Yes, the ritual of atonement as it is written about in Leviticus 16 is religious in that the priests control it. One takes too limited a view, however, if one sees it as purely religious. The ritual is inspired by a great story and is itself an impressive contrivance to remind one of that story. Both are taken up with the thoroughly human enterprise of sin, confession, remorse, and forgiveness. Activities and institutions other than religious ones can most certainly take up such matters. In his discussion of Hindu law in this volume, Werner Menski makes the point that, certainly within a Hindu framework, the distinction between the religious and the secular is meaningless 'since all secular activities occur within a wider framework of religious assumptions.'[25] His inclination is to generalize this point.

Sixth, religious claims about biblical rules have one overwhelming characteristic. The religious aspect is associated with great antiquity. Although I think that critics are wrong in how they have worked out the religious dimension for the two rules I have examined, it is nonetheless true that the lawgiver is himself concerned with narratives that for him represent the earliest times. Antiquity adds the weight of authority to his pronouncements. In addition to the examples provided by the rules about the forgotten sheaf and the ritual of the scapegoat, there is the powerful convention whereby prophets, God and Moses included, speak after an event as though they are speaking before it. For example, God and Moses deliver many of their rules for situations that arise long after the time when they supposedly lay them down. What is behind this convention is again the attempt to lend authority to the pronouncements that are being made. The use of the past to bolster credibility turns up in different guises at different times. The disciples of Freud and Wittgenstein often attribute their own psychological and philosophical judgments to their masters. On closer inspection, however, their views are not to be found in the pertinent texts but the disciples genuinely believe that they are there.

Seventh, as David Daube points out in his contribution to this volume, the oldest etymology that we have for the term 'religion' comes from Cicero: *relegere*, to read over and over again. A short time after Cicero the great Rabbinic sage Hillel uses *shana*, 'to repeat', for to study. The sense seems to come from the constant repetition of orally transmitted teachings. If Cicero's etymology is accurate – and even if it is not, it would still be revealing – we again touch on the notion that what is handed down from the past is what is religious. Contemporary developments in the United States point to the same phenomenon. There is the perception that in a multicultural society different groups possess their own communal narratives that incorporate myths, histories, stories, textual traditions, and bodies of law special to each. Legal scholars claim that these various narratives should be taken into account when deciding legal issues, especially constitutional ones. A group's commitment to its story generates a set of moral ideals and its distinctive voice should be heard, for example, in the Supreme Court, which itself is an institution that possesses its own special narrative history and ideals.[26] An inspiration for the contemporary view of law tied to narrative is the enduring influence of the Bible. It presents a body of law inseparably attached to a narrative history, the story of the exodus, that has a profound impact on some of these groups, African American, Amish, Jewish, and Southern Baptist, for instance.[27]

Eighth, in the biblical example of narratives that mediate laws I wish to stress that the narratives by themselves are hardly inspiring. Often chicanery and corrupt ways characterize them. The laws, in turn, are not exactly uplifting either. Beside the sometimes obscure character of their contents, they can come over as dry as dust. What is inspiring is the way in which the lawgivers wrestle with the problems of human conduct in the traditions of their people and break through to rules that address comparable problems that might arise in their own time, or any time, for that matter. The amalgamation presents one of the most remarkable examples of how laws tied to stories can create a group's identity.

Ninth, one surprising result of an inquiry into biblical law is that it is not comparison with legal material from other Near Eastern cultures that proves particularly helpful but comparison with biblical literature itself. One consequence is that the nexus between the laws and the literary traditions permits us marvelous access to the imaginative processes of the lawgivers. So far as biblical material is concerned, the comparative method in legal studies can prove to be overly restrictive.[28]

NOTES

1 Leo Strauss, *The Rebirth of Classical Political Rationalism* (Chicago: University of Chicago Press, 1989), 254.

2 David Daube, 'Greek Forerunners of Simenon,' *California Law Review,* 68: 301–305 (1980).

3 Llewellyn, the founder of the school of legal realism, spoke about cases as dramatic tales: Karl Llewellyn, *The Bramble Bush: On our Law and its Study* (Dobbs Ferry: Oceana, 1960), 116, 152.

4 Compare Huxley's account of rules closely linked to narratives in Buddhist sources: Andrew Huxley, 'The Vinaya – Legal System or Performance Enhancing Drug?' *Buddhist Forum* 4: 141–163 (1996).

5 See Gerhard von Rad, *Deuteronomium* (Göttingen: Vandenhoeck and Ruprecht, 1964), 109; Anthony Phillips, *Deuteronomy* (Cambridge: Cambridge University Press, 1973), 166; J.H. Tigay, *Deuteronomy* (Philadelphia: Jewish Publication Society, 1996), 229, 390. They have to twist the meaning of the verb 'to forget' – 'to overlook' is favored – to support their interpretation.

6 It is a notable fact that when we inquire about the topic of human rights in biblical material – neither the term nor its equivalent occurs – those fundamental claims about fairness typically turn up in contexts that transcend national and ethnic concerns. Although the biblical rule about feeding the poor is indeed slanted to serve national needs, its inspiration comes from a concern for both Egyptian and Israelite poor.

7 For a fuller discussion of the rule, see Calum Carmichael, *Law and Narrative in the Bible* (Ithaca, Cornell University Press, 1985), 282–288.

8 If we pursue the question as to what gives a theological content to a religion, in the example of Christianity its missionary slant would be important. If one has to win over people to a certain point of view, it is necessary to spell out what one believes. Judaism provides a contrast in that its general unwillingness to pursue proselytizing leaves its fundamental beliefs largely unstated. A major motivation for an increasing interest in comparative legal studies in Europe is precisely the need for each member country of the European Union to spell out to the others the nature of its own legal system.

9 D.P. Wright, *The Disposal of Impurity: Elimination Rites in the Bible and in Hittite and Mesopotamian Literature* (Atlanta: Scholar's Press, 1987), 72, 73.

10 Stephen Garvey, 'Punishment as Atonement' *University of California Los Angeles Law Review* 46: 1801–1858 (1999). I do not wish to underestimate the role that religion plays in the American legal system. On various aspects of its role, see Walter Weyrauch, 'Aspiration and Reality in American Law' 221–226 of ed. Alan Watson *Law, Morality, and Religion: Global Perspectives* (Berkeley: Robbins Collection, 1996), 222. (Arguing that any legal system has aspirations rooted in commonly shared religious and moral precepts. The American system, in particular, has an extremely high level of aspiration. However, because of the impossibility of living up to the ideals there is a gulf between aspiration and reality such that an unacknowledged shadow legal system has developed. It is essentially a bargaining one that ignores the due process of law.) Walter Weyrauch, 'Law as Mask – Legal Ritual and Relevance' *California Law Review* 66: 699–726 (1978). (Arguing that the American legal system has magical and religious roots that we find difficult to reconcile with our belief that modern law is intrinsically rational. The system contains implicit values that function as masks because they serve a deeply felt inner need, probably religious in character. Their purpose is 'to invoke a higher authority in a dramatic ceremony, and to channel emotions and events into fixed styles of reasoning that are, regardless of their intrinsic truth, aesthetically appealing and per-suasive to the participants and the community' [at 725–26]). Markus Dubber, Director of the Buffalo Criminal Law Center, favors – perhaps not entirely seriously – a Presi-dential Commission on Scapegoating, 'charged with the promulgation of scapegoating

guidelines, including a proviso that no animals were hurt in the performance of the ritual, thus making explicit the fact that animals today have gained that membership in the empathic community of justice which is denied by many humans called criminals.' (letter of 5/26/199 on file). Dubber's major point is that criminals are consigned to the modern unregulated prison pit, to survive as best they can 'among [other] wild beasts.' In their analysis of the contemporary scene both Garvey and Dubber link atonement closely with punishment. It would lead too far afield to trace why that equation came to be made in western legal and religious thinking.

11 The term 'sin' would be an appropriate one if we resorted to its original meaning in Old English when the word included wrongdoing of any kind. The Bible seems to have provided the impetus that led to its being confined to the religious sphere.

12 *Macbeth*, 5.1.75

13 On laws that accomplish the impossible, see David Daube, 'Greek and Roman Reflections on Impossible Laws' *Natural Law Forum* 12: 1–84 (1967).

14 See Baruch Levine, *Leviticus* (Philadelphia: Jewish Publication Society, 1989), 102. He thinks that the form may have developed through a reduplication of the letter *zayin*: '*ez-'el*, 'mighty goat' first pronounced '*ezez'el* and finally '*aza'zel*. Those critics who drop the reference to a goat and suggest that '*z'zl* is a metathesis of '*zz-'l* 'fierce god' do so because of their view that Azazel was once a demonic figure 'who has been eviscerated of his erstwhile demonic powers by the Priestly legislators.' See Jacob Milgrom, *Leviticus 1–16* (New York: Doubleday, 1991), 1021. H. Tawil, 'Azazel the Prince of the Steppe: A Comparative Study' *Zeitschrift für die altestamentliche Wissenshaft* 92: 58 (1980) openly admits that this supposed development prompted his attempt to explain the etymology. The name of the original being, he postulates, was deliberately altered 'to conceal the true demonic nature of this supernatural being.' The fiction of the goat as the wild creature would explain why Wright finds Azazel in Leviticus 16 to be a figure devoid of personality, in contrast to the demonic figures that turn up in the Hittite and Mesopotamian sources: Wright *supra* note 9, at 72–73.

15 In the Hittite *Ritual of Hurwarlu* there is found the idea of transferring evil to a dog, which, for the purpose of aggrandizing its powers, is thought of as an ass bearing it away. See Milgrom, *supra* note 14, at 1076.

16 See David Daube, 'Nursery Rhymes and History, Humpty Dumpty' *The Oxford Magazine* 16 February, 1956, 272, 274.

17 What makes Jacob's cheating successful, because he does indeed win out, is the belief that an oath once stated binds absolutely (Esau's when he swears away his birthright to Jacob) and a blessing once uttered is beyond recall (Isaac's when Jacob in disguise as Esau stands before him). The belief that the animal in the scapegoat ritual bears away the people's sin is comparably inscrutable. This is not to say that in each instance the belief is irrational. Behind the sacrosanct nature of an oath and a blessing – valid even if they are obtained by deception – is the serious matter that in a society lacking the use of legal instruments a person's word is of enormous importance. What appears irrational from our perspective is quite rational within the one foreign to us.

18 The phenomenon whereby people create a myth about the origin of its legal system is a common one. For some other legal systems, see Andrew Szegedy-Maszak, 'Legends of the Greek Lawgivers' *Greek, Roman, and Byzantine Studies,* 19: 199–209 (1978); H. F. Jolowitz, *Historical Introduction to Roman Law* (Cambridge: Cambridge University Press, 1952), 4, 10; Hector L. MacQueen, 'Regiam Majestatem, Scots Law and National Identity' *Scottish Historical Review,* 74: 1–20 (1995), and Thomas Acton, Susan Caffrey, Gary Mundy, 'Theorizing Gypsy Law' *American Journal of Comparative Law* 45: 237–249 (1997), 247–249.

19 Walter Benjamin, *Illuminations. Essays and Reflections* (New York: Harcourt, Brace and World, 1968), 89. Writing about effective communication, the Greek philosopher

Heraclitus claimed that the great communicators of the past 'neither told, nor concealed, but indicated.' (Plutarch, 21.404 Df.).

20 Victor W. Turner, *The Ritual Process: Structure and Anti-Structure* (London: Routledge & Kegan Paul, 1969), 117.

21 See David Daube, *Ancient Jewish Law* (Leiden: Brill, 1981), 56; and *Aspects of Roman Law* (Edinburgh: Edinburgh University Press, 1981), 164–175, for his discussion of the misunderstanding of the role of intent in ancient law.

22 See Lon Fuller, *Legal Fictions* (Palo Alto: Stanford University Press, 1967), 93–94.

23 Daube, *supra* note 21, at 21.

24 Garvey, *supra* note 10, at 1807.

25 See Werner Menski in this volume.

26 Robert Cover, 'Foreword: *Nomos* and Narrative' *Harvard Law Review* 97: 4–68 (1983); S.L. Stone, 'In Pursuit of the Counter-Text: The Turn to the Jewish Legal Model in Contemporary American Legal Theory' *Harvard Law Review* 106: 813–876 (1993). Menski, in this volume, argues that Mrs Gandhi's suspension of the Indian Constitution in 1975 came from her commitment to the idea that she was not just Prime Minister of modern India but a successor to the ancient Hindu *raja*.

27 On the role of narratives in recent legal scholarship, for example, feminist narrative scholarship and critical race theory, see Kathryn Abrams, 'Hearing the Call of Stories' *California Law Review* 79: 971–1052 (1991).

28 The following three books serve as a useful introduction to the study of biblical law: David Daube, *Studies in Biblical Law* (New York: Ktav, 1969); Raymond Westbrook, *Studies in Biblical and Cuneiform Law* (Paris: J. Gabalda, 1988); Calum Carmichael, *The Spirit of Biblical Law* (Athens: University of Georgia Press, 1996).

3

JUDAISM AS A RELIGIOUS LEGAL SYSTEM

Bernard S. Jackson

I have relatively little to say on the general classificatory issues of 'legal families' and 'religious systems' within them. Andrew Huxley's Call for Papers has provided some of the scholarly background to these questions. There is, in fact, a significant difference between what David and Brierley have to say in the second edition of *Major Legal Systems in the World Today* (1978), based on the sixth French edition of 1974, as compared with their treatment of the issue in the original French edition of 1964 (*Les Grands Systèmes...*). In the latter, as Huxley reminds us, the fourth group (not regarded as a proper 'family') is classified as 'systèmes philosophiques ou religieux', whose members David was hesitant even to call laws. By 1978, however, this fourth group had become (merely) 'Other Conceptions of Law and the Social Order', the 'sole justification for grouping them together' being 'the fact that all of them are based upon conceptions of law and the social order which are altogether different from those prevailing in the West'.[1]

David and Brierley make a valiant effort to avoid imposing western notions upon non-Western systems. Neither institutional definitions (rules enacted by legislatures or applied by courts) nor 'Realist' (sociological) ones (laws observed in practice) are to be imposed: law may, rather, be viewed in terms closer to a natural law model (their comparison), as a 'model of ideal behaviour'.[2] Jewish law[3] belongs to a group of non-Western societies in which 'law is fully recognised as being of eminent value but the law itself is a different concept than it is in the West'.[4]

In seeking a neutral ground for the classification of legal systems into families, David rejected criteria based upon the content of rules and opted instead for the 'truly significant... characteristics' of a given system of law. These could be 'detected by examining those fundamental elements of the system through which the rules to be applied are themselves discovered, interpreted and evaluated'[5] – a test which we might view as essentially positivist, indeed as evocative of Hart's 'secondary rules'. But tests based upon the 'law's conceptual structure or on the theory of sources of the law' were not in themselves sufficient; they needed to be complemented by criteria regarding the 'social objectives to be achieved with the help of the legal system or the place of law itself within the social order.'[6]

Perhaps it was a feeling that 'Muslim, Hindu, and Jewish laws' not only had insufficient in common, in terms of these two criteria, to be regarded as a legal family, but also lacked sufficient institutional structure[7] and social purpose, that led David to express his doubts as to whether they should be regarded as law at all. Logically, perhaps, he might have constructed a family of 'religious non-law'!

I shall not attempt to escape from this obscurity. More significant, I would suggest, is the internal history of each system, and the tensions apparent within it between characteristics which, for David, are anticipated to be a marker of difference between systems, rather than within them. David's presentation of these systems presents them as both isolated from foreign influences and internally consistent, in both synchronic and diachronic terms. For Jewish law, at least, I would dissent. Jewish law has been, internally, a site of struggle and diversity between different conceptions of both structure and objective.[8] With the foundation of the modern State of Israel, such issues have come to the fore. There is a movement, particularly amongst the 'modern Orthodox', partially (I discuss the import of this adverb further below) to adopt traditional Jewish law as the law of the State. That has involved presenting Jewish law according to the model of a western legal system – i.e. in predominantly (but see further below) positivist terms: as a normative system defined by rules identifying 'legal sources'. Indeed, the leading exponent of this approach, Justice Menachem Elon, a former Professor at the Hebrew University of Jerusalem and ultimately Deputy President of the Israel Supreme Court, has gone so far as to adopt a *Grundnorm* theory as the conceptual structure of his *magnum opus* on Jewish Law.[9]

A MODERN POSITIVIST MODEL

Elon defines the 'legal sources' as 'the sources of law and means of creating law recognised by the legal system itself as conferring binding force on the norms of that system',[10] and his language implies an equation of 'binding force' with 'validity'. But whence do these sources of law which confer such validity on the substantive norms themselves derive their validity? Elon follows Salmond (but more importantly Kelsen) in asserting the existence of a 'basic norm' which gives authority to the sources of law. This 'basic norm', which he refers to in both Kelsenian and Hartian terms as either a '*Grundnorm*' or 'basic rule of recognition', is identified by Elon with 'the fundamental norm that everything set forth in the Torah, i.e. the Written Law, is binding on the Jewish legal system'.[11] We may note that if Kelsenian analysis is to be applied, this rule is *not* to be identified with the *Grundnorm*, but rather with the 'historically first constitution',[12] since something further, taken from outside the system itself, is required to give authority to it. The need for such a step is accepted by Elon: 'The source of authority of this basic norm itself is the basic tenet of Judaism that the source of authority of the Torah is divine command.'[13] This, for Elon, is the real *Grundnorm*.[14] This view of Jewish law, in terms of a hierarchy of authority deriving ultimately from God, may appear natural and unsurprising.

There is, however, a different aspect of positivism increasingly stressed by legal theorists – particularly by Kelsen[15] and Hart, though in different ways – that has proved particularly attractive to modern Jewish law scholars. It is the degree of discretion, exercised quite legitimately under a power conferred by the very hierarchy of authority of the system, which positivism claims is (and in some versions is necessarily) exercised by the legitimate institutions of the system for the purposes of legal clarification and development. Elon has stressed this factor in terms of the 'legislative' sources of Jewish law;[16] Lamm and Kirschenbaum have done the same in respect of judicial discretion.[17] The attractiveness of this model for modern Jewish Orthodoxy lies in its explanation of the legitimacy of legal *development*. The argument can be presented that Jewish law, just because it is a system of law, may be expected to possess such institutions; and it is not difficult to proceed from that point to illustrate their existence from the treasure-house of data of the history of Jewish law.[18] Legal development is itself regarded as a positive value, in the context of debates with ultra-conservatives who deny the *moral* authority of the current generation to initiate change. The debate then becomes centrally relevant to the issue of incorporation of Jewish law into the law of the State of Israel, since few would deny that a necessary precondition of such incorporation is a degree of clarification, restatement and development.

There are, however, flaws in the attempt to apply these positivist models to the Jewish legal system. One resides in the temporal status of the historically first constitution (Kelsen) or ultimate rule of recognition (Hart). Both these jurisprudential theories accept that such a basic norm, identified for Jewish law by Elon as the rule that everything stated in the Written Law is of binding authority, may indeed be changed by unilateral, revolutionary action of the subjects of the law. Secular jurisprudence thus accords the current constitution a merely contingent validity, until and unless a revolution occurs and succeeds; but such a possibility can hardly be accepted for Jewish law, wherein the basic law is eternal, or at least (even if we think of notions of *berit hadashah* or concepts of *Torah* in the messianic age) is not susceptible to change by unilateral action by its subjects. The covenant may be broken, but it cannot be unilaterally revoked by its subjects. This theoretical dissonance raises an important methodological question: how legitimate is it, or what ends are served, by importing part of a theory while neglecting some other part which, according to the tradition to which it belongs, may represent a central or crucial aspect of that very theory?

THE SOURCES OF LAW

I believe that scholarly accounts of the early history of Jewish Law have been much affected by the dominant legal positivism of the modern age, leading to an unreflecting importation of models of the operation of law and justice which are simply inappropriate. Jewish Law has come to be viewed by some scholars as a system of positive law, differing from secular systems only in three respects: first, in its authorship (God); second, in its claims to perfection – of both the draftsmanship of its biblical foundations, and the social and spiritual values which it embodies; third, in its scope – covering ritual as well as 'civic' matters.[19] I shall argue, however, that the religious character of Jewish Law[20] manifested itself in its origins in ways very different from those of a system of positive law, and that important features of this different form of law have survived, despite the increasing positivisation of the system.

Let me outline immediately the central feature of this increasing positivisation. Justice is originally conceived not as a function of a revealed text, but rather as the activity of an inspired judge. The judge is not, originally, an interpreter of texts; he is a doer of justice. The sacred texts do, indeed, have revealed status. But their function is primarily didactic, not normative. The audience is the community as a whole, not the judge as legal specialist. The texts may guide the judge; they do not determine his decision.

In a recent colloquium in Paris on 'L'Idée de Justice dans la Tradition Juive' (part of a series on 'Généalogies de L'Idée de Justice'), the 'présentation' (of A. Garapon) posed the question: 'Comment se représente-t-on la function du juge? Est-il un ministre de vérité investi d'un véritable sacerdoce, un technicien ou plus simplement un arbitre?' I believe the first description is the most accurate; in my view, the religious element has indeed been underestimated in much modern scholarship. The predominant view of the authors of the Hebrew Bible was that '*mishpat*' is divine: *ki hamishpat lelohim hu* (*Deut.* 1: 17). It may be very conveni-ent to modern sensitivities to interpret this as meaning that the administration of justice[21] is *on behalf of* God (just as, in England, we still speak of the 'Royal Courts of Justice', where justice is administered on behalf of the monarch). The original conception, however, seems to be very much more direct: not only are the revealed norms divine; so too is the administration of justice, in both of the aspects which today we customarily distinguish: fact-finding on the one hand, application of rules to those facts on the other. The Rabbinic development of these conceptions has been discussed by Justice Haim Cohn in terms of the 'secu-larisation' of divine law.[22] I shall argue that, despite this 'secularisation', the surviving religious element in Jewish law resists the imposition of a positivist model. The issue has assumed practical importance in the context of attempts to incorporate Jewish law within the law of the modern State of Israel.

First, we may ask what sources judges were supposed to use in coming to their decisions. Perhaps the most famous charge to the judges in the Bible is that of *Deuteronomy* 16: 18, where they are commanded to deliver a 'righteous judgement'. This is further explained in both negative and positive terms: negatively, that the judges must avoid both partiality and corruption; positively, that they must pursue 'justice': *tsedek (tsedek tsedek tirdof)*. But what is this *tsedek*? There is no suggestion that it consists in following the rules of a written law book; the noun *tsedek*, in its feminine form, *tsedakah*, means righteousness, and more concretely charity;[23] it is difficult to grasp the sense of *tsedek* without being sensitive to this connotation. So it is possible to take the term most centrally translated 'justice' as having a non-positivist biblical connotation: the judges are told to 'pursue justice', without any suggestion that justice consists in following the rules of a written law book. Indeed, the function of the written law book is described quite differently in the following chapter (*Deut.* 17): as a text which the king must have prepared for himself (whether for his general edification, or, more likely, as a reminder of the 'constitutional' restraints upon his power).

This division between written law and the administration of justice is echoed in other sources, most notably the two different aspects of the 'reform' of King Jehoshaphat (in the ninth century). On the one hand, he sends his officers with a book of the law to 'teach' the people (*2 Chronicles* 17). On the other, his charge to the judges he appoints (*2 Chronicles* 19) makes no reference to their using a written law book; rather, he tells them to avoid partiality and corruption (as in *Deuteronomy*) and that 'God is with you in giving judgement' (*ve'ima-khem bidvar mishpat*). In other words, judicial decisions were conceived to be inspired: this, we may understand as a legitimation of the intuitive sense of justice. It receives explicit expression in relation to royal adjudication: 'Inspired decisions are on the lips of a King; his mouth does not sin in judgement' (*Proverbs* 16: 10).

I believe that the original conception of the inspired judge should be seen as part of a wider picture of divine adjudication. The claim that justice 'is' divine, or 'belongs' to God – *ki hamishpat lelohim hu* (*Deut.* 1: 17) – has often been watered down in modern scholarship, into what I have described as a 'functional' model of divine adjudication, one which maintains that special divine procedures of adjudication (we think of cases of oracular consultation, oaths, the ordeal by bitter waters, etc.) are used *only* when the human rationality of the judge runs out, i.e. in cases of special evidentiary difficulty. This functional view, to which I myself once subscribed, now seems to me to reflect our modern perspectives, rather than what the Bible tells us. Recall the vivid picture in *Exodus* 18 of Moses as the overloaded first instance judge. The problem, Moses explains, derives from the fact that the people expect him, in dealing with each and every case, 'to inquire of God' (*lidrosh elohim* – a term which refers to oracular consultation). Jethro, the story continues, advised Moses to create a system of judicial delegation, and to deal himself only with the 'great matters' which the judges bring to him. According to *Exodus* 18, the newly appointed judges adjudicate on the basis of the 'ordinances and laws' which Moses teaches them. But that reflects, as the narrative itself indicates in its own way, a later stage.

In fact, we may see the introduction of adjudication on the basis of written (divinely inspired or dictated) texts as a response to a perceived problem with the earlier form of divine adjudication. It seems that the original judicial function was hereditary. However, the character traits which were conceived to be a necessary condition of a divinely inspired judge proved not to be hereditary. The problem arose already with the sons of Samuel. We read (*1 Samuel* 7: 15–8: 3):

Samuel judged Israel all the days of his life. And he went on a circuit year by year to Bethel, Gilgal, and Mizpah; and he judged Israel in all these places. Then he would come back to Ramah, for his home was there, and there also he administered justice to Israel. And he built there an altar to the LORD. When Samuel became old, he made his sons judges over Israel. The name of his first-born son was Jo'el, and the name of his second, Abijah; they were judges in Beer-sheba. Yet his sons did not walk in his ways, but turned aside after gain; they took bribes and perverted justice.

It is hardly coincidental that Samuel is the very prophet whom the people badgered, against his better judgement, for the appointment of a king; indeed, the popular demand for such a king was voiced in precisely this context. And it was Samuel who was responsible for what may well have been the first text of written law in the history of the Israelite kingdoms, namely the *mishpat hamelukhah* which (presumably) defined and restricted the powers of the king (*1 Samuel* 10: 25). Thus, in the story of Samuel we encounter a sensitivity to the problems of possible abuse of both royal (legislative?) and hereditary judicial power. If written law was seen as a remedy for the former, we may reasonably assume that it was also so viewed in relation to the latter.[24] As in the traditions of the origins of law in Greece and Rome, written law is a response to the abuse of an earlier discretion, rather than discretion being the response to the supposed rigidities of an earlier written law.

Nevertheless, the conception of the inspired judge survived for several centuries. It is reflected in the Rabbinic concept of *semikhah*, literally the 'laying on of hands', the traditional form of transmission of Rabbinic authority whose origins lie in the appointment by Moses of Joshua as his successor. The famous 'chain of authority' in *Mishnah Avot* 1: 1 commences in just the same way. It was only when the Rabbis perceived a break in this 'chain', around the fourth century CE, that *semikhah* came to acquire its present meaning: ordination as a result of qualification in the *yeshivah*. The Rabbis recognised the consequences of such a change: in a number of important jurisdictional respects, the judicial power of Rabbinical judges who lacked the original *semikhah* was reduced.

The notion that the judge was divinely inspired did not disappear with the constraints imposed by a written text. The Babylonian Talmud records approximately thirty cases where it is said that the rabbinic judge decided the case 'not in accordance with the *Halakhah*'.[25] Here are two examples:

R. Eleazar intended to allow maintenance out of movable property. Said R. Simeon b. Eliakim to him: Master, I know that in your decision you are not acting on the line of the law but on the line of mercy (*midat rahmanut*), but [the possibility] ought to be considered that the students might observe this ruling and fix it as a *halakhah* for future generations. (*Ketubot* 50b, Ben-Menahem 70)

A certain man who misappropriated a pair of oxen from his fellow went and did some ploughing with them and also sowed with them some seeds, and at last returned them to their owner. When the case came before R. Nahman he said [to the sheriffs of the court]: Go forth and appraise the increment. But Rava said to him: ... since the oxen were misappropriated they merely have to be returned intact, as we have indeed learnt: 'All robbers have to pay in accordance with [the value] at the time of robbery.' [Why then pay for any work done with them?] He [R. Nahman] replied: ... ? That man [who misappropriated the pair of oxen] is a notorious robber and I want to penalize him. (*B.K.* 96b, Ben-Menahem 112)

I believe that this is a survival of the original conception of the judicial role as based not upon written texts, but rather upon direct divine inspiration.

Such a practice of deciding 'not in accordance with the Halakhah' proved controversial: though accepted by the Babylonian Talmud, it appears to have been opposed by the Palestinian authorities, and it has never been formally incorporated into the powers of the judiciary (though that, one may argue, is precisely in line with its very nature). Nevertheless, the proceedings of the Rabbinic law court (the *Beth Din*) should not be seen as identical to its secular counterparts. The very fact that the Rabbinic court is *not* conceived as a public forum, that its proceedings are *not* reported, and traditionally there was no hierarchy of courts to sustain an appellate system, reflects the perception that the Rabbinic court is engaged in a private activity of moral/religious persuasion, and that its function is primarily to secure justice (in the sense of that which is conceived to be moral according to the tenets of the religion) in the particular situation faced by the parties.

SECULAR v. RELIGIOUS OBJECTIVES

I turn now to the objectives of the *halakhah*. Justice[26] is certainly one of them. However, a system of religious law also has specifically religious objectives, whether in terms of salvation[27] or eschatology.

The issue of justification by works or faith receives its classical expressions in the Christian tradition, though its roots are Hebraic. There is no doubt that soon after Judaism came to adopt the notion of a future life (for such a claim is doubtful through much of the Hebrew Bible), it accepted the view that the standard route[28] to such salvation was through performance of the *mitsvot* (the divine commandments). This, we may note, is simply a particular form of the central biblical association of reward or punishment with performance or neglect of the divine command. Indeed, the roots of the Pauline position – maintaining the existence of a 'new Covenant' in which performance of the law would no longer be the standard route to salvation – are to be found in *Jer.* 31: 28–34, and associated sources.[29]

The doctrine of divine reward and punishment had a 'transgenerational' element: reward and punishment of future, as well as the present, generations. Jeremiah, observing the destruction of the first temple and the enforced Babylonian captivity, despaired of the capacity of human beings to break out of this cycle of sin and punishment. If performance of the law was a voluntary matter, in the sense that observance or non-observance was a matter of free human will, history indicated that there would always be generations who would lapse, with consequent punishment of their successors. He looked, therefore, to a future age (echoing, so it seems, the position in Eden before the eating of the fruit of the tree of knowledge) when observance of the law would no longer be subject to the caprice of human will, but rather would be automatic (without, even, the need for teaching: v. 33, MT). This is the meaning of his desire for a future Covenant which would be 'written in the heart'.

I sometimes think that some of the ultra-Orthodox groups within the Jewish community are seeking to achieve precisely this, but by a different route. They try to make observance of the commandments automatic – on the one hand by ever-increasing applications of the notion of a 'fence round the Torah', through which prohibitions are extended in such a way that breach of the original prohibition becomes virtually impossible; on the other hand by creating an exclusively Jewish environment which, so far as is possible, is free even of the temptation to breach the *Halakhah*.

The aspiration of Jeremiah for a 'new covenant' was certainly eschatological. But that begs the question of the form of the *eschaton*. Was it the ultimate establishment of the Kingdom of God on this earth, the creation of a utopian form of our present material, social existence? Or was it the establishment of a purely spiritual afterlife, once heaven and earth ceased to exist? And what was the meaning and role of messianism in the context of these alternatives? These issues were clearly live already at the time of the division between Judaism and Christianity. Though speculation on the 'world to come' came to be discouraged in Judaism, we commonly find an attempt to harmonise these two conceptions into a two-stage approach: the messianic age is earthly, and characterised by perfect social justice (equated with complete observance of *Torah*); ultimately, however, this mundane *eschaton* (sometimes associated with bodily resurrection) would give way to a purely spiritual, and eternal afterlife (the *olam haba*); the ultimate objective of performance of the *mitsvot* was to gain sufficient purity of soul to merit admission to it. The status of *Torah* law once in that ultimate state is a matter of considerable obscurity and debate. I content myself by referring to the classic treatment by W.D. Davies.[30]

SECULAR v. RELIGIOUS SANCTIONS

Of course, Jewish law is concerned also with the specifically religious implications of human behaviour. A nice illustration comes from a responsum of R. Israel

b. Hayyim of Brunn,[31] who was consulted about a murder which occurred within the Jewish community of fifteenth-century Posen, in Germany. Clearly, the Jewish community did not have criminal jurisdiction over such matters. Nevertheless, the Rabbi thought it appropriate to intervene. The murder had been committed by two Jews, of whom one was said to show no remorse, and to seek no atonement. For him, R. Israel makes no provision: since the offender seeks no atonement, he will be given no penance in order to achieve it. The other murderer, on other hand, does seek atonement. For him, the Rabbi makes extensive provision: by doing penance in this world, he may achieve the salvation of his soul in the next. And so, the Rabbi requires:

> He shall journey about as an exile for a full year. Every day he shall appear at a synagogue – or at least on every Monday and Thursday. He shall make for himself three iron bands, one to be worn on each of his two hands, which were the instruments of his transgressions, and one to be worn about his body. When he enters the synagogue, he shall put them on and pray with them on. In the evening he shall go barefoot to the synagogue. The hazan shall seat him (publicly) prior to the *Vehu Rahum* prayer. He shall then receive a (symbolic [?] public) flogging and make the following declaration: 'Know ye, my masters, that I am a murderer. I wantonly killed Nissan. This is my atonement. Pray for me.' When he leaves the synagogue he is to prostrate himself across the doorsill; the worshipers are to step over him, not on him. Afterwards he is to remove the iron bands... After one year he shall continue his fasts on Mondays and Thursdays. He shall, for the rest of his days, carefully observe the anniversary month and the anniversary date of the killing. He shall fast at that time (the date) three consecutive days if he is healthy or only two days, the day of the wounding and the next day, the day of Nissan's death, if he is infirm. He shall, for the rest of his days, be active in all enterprises to free imprisoned Jews (i.e., hostages held by gentiles), charity, and the saving of lives. He shall work out an arrangement with his (Nissan's) heirs to support them properly. He shall ask their pardon and the widow's pardon. He shall return to God, and He shall have mercy on him. And since Simha has expressed remorse and seeks repentance and atonement, immediately upon his submission to the program of public degradations, he becomes our brother once again for every religious purpose (i.e., the quorum for worship, cf. *B. Makkot* 23a)...

Not only does the respondent confine himself to prescribing a penance for the one offender who does seek atonement, and who thus may be described as voluntarily submitting himself to rabbinic jurisdiction. There is no means of enforcement of the measures the Rabbi requires – other than further appeals to the conscience and to the man's standing within the religious community. But this raises no definitional issues for Jewish law.

MODALITIES AND THE INTEGRATION OF LAW AND MORALITY

There is a body of literature (the responsa literature), commencing in the Middle Ages, in which individual Rabbis and Rabbinic courts consult leading contemporary authorities as to what to do in particular situations. Sometimes, the respondents write up and publish their replies (in a form designed to educate the wider community). It is noticeable that these responsa do not always restrict themselves to the letter of the law; sometimes, they use all available means of persuasion to effect the outcome they regard as morally correct. That might involve persuasion to a higher moral standard than *halakhah* generally demands: Jewish law is familiar with the notion of supererogatory standards, termed *middat hasidut* ('the standards of the pious') or *lifnim mishurat hadin*.[32] The Sermon on the Mount is not unique in advocating such a position. The function of the Jewish judge is thus not restricted to implementing what the written law requires or permits.

This amounts not only to a denial of the positivist 'separation thesis': morality is clearly here integrated within the *halakhah*, not regarded as a system apart. It also entails a rejection of the sufficiency of the three deontic modalities so beloved of modern logicians of law. For the rabbinic structure implies that behaviour may be recommended (conversely, discouraged), as well as required, permitted or prohibited. Indeed, Islamic law explicitly adopts such a fivefold classification of modalities.[33] Jewish law does not systematise the matter in this way; nevertheless, institutions such as *middat hasidut* clearly imply the existence of such a wider range of modalities.

An interesting application of this issue exercised the Israel Supreme Court in a 1977 tort case.[34] It illustrates the tensions resulting from incorporation of a non-positivist religious system within a positivist secular system. A man employed as a watchman had lost a son in an automobile accident. He had used a lawyer to sue the driver responsible for the accident. The driver had been acquitted of the criminal charges, and the compensation paid by his insurance company fell far below the amount expected by the father. The latter was dissatisfied at the performance of his lawyer. He became mentally depressed, and began to drink heavily. In his employment as a watchman, he was in possession of a gun provided by his employer. He used the gun to shoot and kill his lawyer. The lawyer's widow then sued the employer of the watchman. The District Court awarded her damages. The employer appealed, on the grounds that there was no sufficient causal connection between the employer's allowing the watchman to keep possession of the gun, and his use of it to kill the lawyer. The Supreme Court upheld the appeal.

So far, this story has no connection with Jewish law: the case was brought in the civil courts, where secular, Israeli (here: English-based) law, rather than Jewish law, applies. However, the bench included Justice Menachem Elon, who noted that the employer had in fact offered to make a voluntary payment to the widow and her family, and observed that this type of offer corresponded to the halakhic institution of behaviour 'beyond the letter of the law' (*lifnim mishurat hadin*).

This institution was particularly relevant in cases of indirect causation in tort, where the Talmud itself used the concept of 'heavenly law' (*dine shamayyim*) in order to bridge the gap between the legal and the moral aspects responsibility. Such a moral obligation to go 'beyond the letter of the law' had, Justice Elon observed, been translated on occasion by rabbinical courts into a recommendation made to the parties to (human) litigation. He argued that the Israeli (secular) judge should similarly take an active part in seeking to persuade the litigants to follow their moral obligations and to go 'beyond the letter of the law'. Such a step would be in accordance with the spirit of Jewish law, whereby:

> there is a special reciprocal tie between law and morality... which finds
> its expression in the fact that from time to time Jewish law, functioning
> as a legal system, itself impels recourse to a moral imperative for which
> there is no court sanction, and in doing so sometimes prepares the way
> for conversion of the moral imperative into a fully sanctioned norm.

In so arguing, Justice Elon was going beyond the deontic modalities with which secular, positivist legal systems are familiar. He was advocating supererogatory action: payment of compensation which was not required by the law. The role of the judge was not simply to sit by as a neutral, and say that such a payment was permitted, but that it was a purely private matter between the parties. Rather, he saw the role of the judge as one of active persuasion to the parties to do that which the *halakhah* viewed as the 'recommended' behaviour. And this, in a case where the religious courts had no jurisdiction (unless the parties voluntarily went to them, as arbitral bodies – which had not occurred in this case).

It is hardly surprising, then, that the approach of Justice Elon was severely criticised by Justice Shamgar, who took it to represent a systematic blurring of the border between law and morality, which was totally unacceptable in a system of positive law such as that of the State of Israel. For Justice Shamgar, the Israeli legal system follows the secular, positivist model, which places great emphasis on the certainty resulting from the doctrine of the Rule of Law; for Justice Elon, on the other hand, the Israeli legal system is at heart Jewish, being the legal system of a 'Jewish State', which in his view justifies the adoption of Jewish approaches even where no positivist, Israeli source explicitly authorises them. At root, so it seems, Justice Elon would appear to regard the *halakhah* as providing the *Grundnorm* for the secular State, rather than the secular state providing the *Grundnorm* for incorporation of the *halakhah*.

CONCLUSIONS

This necessarily brief review of some of the leading characteristics of, and tensions within, the history of Jewish law suggests some answers to the problem of classification. The positivist model has certainly attracted the greatest modern support. But is it sufficient to regard the *halakhah* as a system of *ius divinum positivum*? If we were to develop the position of Justice Elon in a more systematic Kelsenian direction, we may perhaps be tempted towards an affirmative conclusion.[35] A Kelsenian hierarchy of laws does not merely command but also authorises (so that it may encompass the inspired judge as much as the revealed law); the object-ives of the law are largely irrelevant (along with other 'ideological' or 'political' factors), as is the scope of the law. More difficult, however, is the issue of modal-ities. Kelsen, despite ultimately separating the logic of norms from normative validity, does appear to endorse a version of deontic logic which has difficulty with the notion of the 'recommended' or the 'discouraged'.

In fact, such considerations address only half the issue. If we are to ask whether the *halakhah* is to be regarded as a religious legal system, we must adopt criteria not only of law but also of what makes such a system 'religious'. The answer to that question is far from self-evident. Is it 'religious law' which is applied, when the secular section of the Jewish population of Israel is required to submit to the exclusive jurisdiction of the rabbinical courts in matters of marriage and divorce? Does adherence to the law have to be from religious motives, or is it sufficient that the origins and current administration of the system are religious? A comparable question, we may recall, arises in relation to the 'rule of recognition' of Hart. He was content that it should be accepted 'from the internal point of view' by the officials, even though that point of view was not shared by the subjects. Is a comparable approach available in relation to religious law? Indeed, the application of the *halakhah* in matters of marriage and divorce of Jews in the State of Israel is itself a matter of theoretical controversy even amongst the Orthodox community. From the point of view of the (secular) State, the basis of validity of such application derives from the State itself, in the form of that legis-lation of the Knesset which confers upon the rabbinical courts their exclusive jurisdiction in such matters. This is seen by some as incompatible with the main-tenance of the religious *Grundnorm*.[36] Conversely, there are those amongst the religious community who would see the validity of the state itself as dependent upon its conformity with conditions laid down by the *Halakhah*. From this point of view, it is religion, not law, which is the major category. If so, and given the nature of the claims made by any religion which claims privileged access to the truth, comparative questions – which seek to proceed from a neutral vantage point – hardly arise.[37]

NOTES

1 René David and David Brierley, *Major Legal Systems in the World Today*, 2nd edition (London: Steven & Sons, 1978), 420.
2 id., at 27.
3 Though excluded from substantive treatment in the book on sociological grounds: 'its sphere of influence is incomparably less' than that of either Muslim law or Hindu Law, id., at 28.

4 id., at 26.

5 id., at 19.

6 id.

7 Remarkably, he speaks in this context of 'non-western societies where "rules of law" (in the western sense) remained unorganised, fragmentary and unstable, and where there is a general feeling that true law is to be found elsewhere than in legislation, custom or judicial decisions'. id., at 28.

8 See further: Bernard Jackson, 'Jewish Law or Jewish Laws', *The Jewish Law Annual* 8: 15–34 (1989); Bernard Jackson, 'Is Diversity Possible within the Halakhah?', *L'Eylah* 29: 35–38 (April, 1990).

9 M. Elon, *Jewish Law, History, Sources, Principles* (Philadelphia: Jewish Publication Society, 1994), 4 vols.; see esp. Vol. I Ch. 6: 'The Basic Norm and the Sources of Jewish Law'. My argument in the next two sections is expanded in: Bernard Jackson, 'Secular Jurisprudence and the Philosophy of Jewish Law: A Commentary on Some Recent Literature' *The Jewish Law Annual* 6: 3–6 (1987). In that piece, I also comment on O. Bondy, 'The Validity Problem in Hebrew Law' *Archiv für Rechts-und Sozialphilosophie* 54: 217–232 (1968). See also, more recently, B.S. Jackson, '*Mishpat Ivri, Halakhah* and Legal Philosophy: *Agunah* and the Theory of "Legal Sources"', *JSIJ – Jewish Studies, an Internet Journal* 1(2002), 69–107, at http://www.biu.ac.il/JS/JSIJ/1-2002/Jackson.pdf.

10 M. Elon, ed., *The Principles of Jewish Law* (Jerusalem: Keter, 1975), 10; cf. Elon, *supra* note 9, at I.232.

11 Elon, *supra* note 9, at I.232.

12 H. Kelsen, *The Pure Theory of Law,* trans. M. Knight (Berkeley: University of California Press, 1967), 200.

13 Elon, *supra* note 10, at 15; cf Elon, *supra* note 9, at I.233.

14 See also H. Kelsen, *General Theory of Law and State*, trans. Wedberg (Cambridge: Harvard University Press, 1946), 115: 'The basic norm of a religious system says that one ought to behave as God and the authorities instituted by Him command.' In Kelsen, *supra* note 12, at 193ff, Kelsen goes to some length to stress, in relation to the Decalogue, that the source of its authority is not the *fact* (real or supposed) of divine command but rather 'the tacitly presupposed norm that one ought to obey the commands of God'. This distinction is elided by Elon. On the analyses of religious law by Bentham, John Austin and Kelsen, see further B.S. Jackson, 'Structuralism and the Notion of Religious Law', *Investigaciones Semióticas* 2/3: 1–43 (1982–1983), 3–8, which passage concludes: 'For Bentham, the exclusion of religious law indicates that greater significance is being attached, for the purposes of classification, to the role of human political institutions than to either linguistic usage or the nature of the sanctions applied. Austin effected a compromise, designed in part to give greater weight to linguistic usage, while at the same time stressing (with Bentham) the role of human political institutions: religious law might be "law", but was not "positive law". Kelsen, while claiming to give weight to linguistic usage (at least as a starting point), stresses the nature of sanctions and (apparently) the perception of divine origin as the points of differentiation, while conceding that religious law may belong to the wider *genus* of normative systems. In effect, however, Kelsen is at one with Bentham and Austin in adhering to the tenet of the social sources of law. For while the political structure (that complex of relationships which we refer to as the "state") is viewed by him as synonymous with the legal system, the requirement that law involves the use of socially immanent, coercive sanctions virtually restores political institutions to their role as a significant mark of distinction'.

15 Kelsen's identification of positive law (legal norms) with the meaning of acts of will (decisions) made by authorised judges extended to a theory of the validity of legal

errata: see Kelsen, *supra* note 12, at 354; B.S Jackson, *Making Sense in Jurisprudence* (Liverpool: Deborah Charles Publications, 1996), 114–116. Similarly, in the words of Elon, *supra* note 9, at I.244: 'The *Halakhah* is thus identified with those to whom it is entrusted, to the point that even an error of the halakhic authorities is still Halakhah', quoting *Sifre Shoftim* 154 on *Deut.* 17: 11; Nahmanides, *Commentary on Deuteronomy,* ad loc.

16 Elon, *supra* note 9, at Vol. II Chs. 13–20.

17 N. Lamm and A. Kirschenbaum, 'Freedom and Constraint in the Jewish Juridical Process', *Cardozo Law Review* 1: 99–133 (1979). See also E. Dorff, 'Judaism as a Religious Legal System', *Hastings Law Journal* 29: 1331–1360 (1978), 1339.

18 Interestingly, this is denied by M. Silberg, *Talmudic Law and the Modern State*, trans. B.Z. Bokser (New York: Burning Bush Press, 1973), 51, who claims that Jewish law, being a system of religious law, 'does not define norms for deciding the law, but norms of behaviour' – thus apparently reducing Jewish law (in Hartian terms) to a system of primary rules only. He also denies (at 57) that there is any recognised competence to effect change in Jewish law.

19 Though the modern advocates of *mishpat ivri* distinguish this term from *halakhah* precisely by limiting it to topics comparable to the concerns of modern legal systems.

20 For further aspects of this, see Dorff, *supra* note 17, at 1347–1355.

21 That is the context: Moses recalls the charges he gave when he appointed judges before the people departed from the mountain of Horeb.

22 H.H. Cohn, 'Secularization of Divine Law' in his *Jewish Law in Ancient and Modern Israel* (New York: Ktav, 1971), 1–49, reprinted from *Scripta Hierosolymitana* XVI (1966). See also Dorff, *supra* note 17, at 1334–1336.

23 Chief Rabbi Jonathan Sacks, in the New Year Supplement to *The Jewish Chronicle*, 29 September, 2000, p.x, rightly stresses the basic untranslatability of such terms.

24 The dating of this change in the form of judicial adjudication is debatable. Perhaps the earliest evidence of a change in this conception occurs in *Ezekiel* 44: 24, where the Levitical priests are given jurisdiction to judge disputes, and are charged to determine them 'according to my judgments'; certainly, by the time of Ezra, some form of the 'Rule of (divine) Law' has been established – though some scholars have recently argued that this was in order to conform to Persian Imperial policy, rather than internal religious norms.

25 See Haninah Ben-Menahem, *Judicial Deviation in Talmudic Law* (Chur etc.: Harwood Academic Publishers, 1991); see also, more broadly, his 'The Judicial Process and the Nature of Jewish Law' in *An Introduction to the History and Sources of Jewish Law*, ed. N. Hecht, B.S. Jackson, D. Piattelli, S.M. Passamaneck and A.M. Rabello (Oxford: The Clarendon Press, 1996), 421–437, concluding, at 434f., that 'we are justified in doubting the sufficiency of the modern, Western concept of law for the purposes of describing the *halakhah.*'

26 Whatever that means in this context. On *tsedek*, see above, and see further: Bernard Jackson, 'A Semiotic Perspective on the Comparison of Analogical Reasoning in Secular and Religious Legal Systems', in *Pluralism in Law*, ed. A. Soeteman (Dordrecht: Kluwer Academic Publishers, 2001), 295–325.

27 See Ferrari's comments in this volume.

28 I shall not try to specify whether this had the status of necessary or sufficient conditions.

29 On this, see further my 'Historical Observations on the Relationship between Letter and Spirit' in *Law and Religion*, ed. R.D.O'Dair and A.D.E. Lewis (Oxford: Oxford University Press, 2001 = *Current Legal Issues* Vol. 4,), 101–110.

30 W.D. Davies, *Torah in the Messianic Age and/or the Age to Come* (Philadelphia: Society of Biblical Literature, 1952), Ch. IV.

31 Translated by S.M. Passamaneck in Hecht, *supra* note 25, at 346–350.

32 These concepts, of course, are already found in talmudic sources. See also the comments of Ben-Menahem, *supra* note 25, at 422, on the talmudic judgments: 'the Sages are pleased with him' and 'the Sages are displeased with him'.

33 See, e.g., Robert Brunschvig, 'Logic and Law in Classical Islam' in ed. G.E. Grunebaum *Logic in Classical Islamic Culture* (Wiesbaden: Harrassowitz, 1970), 11: 'The five *ahkam* or principal juridical types that the classical doctrine retained, according perhaps to a Stoic precedent, completing them when required with subdivisions and intermediate shadings, range from the obligatory to the forbidden by way of the recommended, the permissible, and the disapproved.' See also his remarks in 'Hermeneutique Normative dans le Judaïsme et dans l'Islam', *Accademia Nazionale dei Lincei, Rendiconti della Classe di Scienze morali, storiche e filologiche,* Ser. VIII vol. XXX, fasc 5–6, pp.1–20 (May-June 1975), at 5.

34 *Kitan* v. *Weiss,* C.A. 350/77, 33(2) P.D. 785; see D.B. Sinclair, 'Beyond the Letter of the Law', *The Jewish Law Annual* 6 (1987), 203–206.

35 Though other approaches to the philosophy of Jewish law have also been argued. See the symposium in Vols 6–7 of *The Jewish Law Annual* (1987–88).

36 I. Englard, *Religious Law in the Israel Legal System* (Jerusalem: Harry Sacher Institute for Legislative Research and Comparative Law, 1975).

37 Students seeking material for further reading might usefully begin with Dorff, *supra* note 17; Silberg, *supra* note 18; Cohn, *supra* note 22; and Englard, *supra* note 37. For the biblical period, see further B.S. Jackson, *Studies in the Semiotics of Biblical Law* (Sheffield: Sheffield Academic Press, 2000). For web sites relevant to Jewish law, see the links at http://www.mucjs.org/links.htm#8.

4

CANON LAW AS A RELIGIOUS LEGAL SYSTEM

Silvio Ferrari

CANON LAW AS A LEGAL SYSTEM

Opinions are divided on this point: some scholars deny that Canon law is a legal system at all. At the end of the nineteenth-century Rudolph Sohm underlined that Canon law provisions are not binding provisions. Membership in the Church is founded on the free will of the faithful, therefore Canon law provisions cannot be forced upon them: they lack the binding force that is a fundamental characteristic of 'real' law. A few decades later, an Italian lawyer, Francesco Carnelutti, reached a similar conclusion starting from a different point of departure. Canon law provisions, Carnelutti wrote, discipline the relationship between man and God: therefore they are not true legal provisions, as these discipline relations between man and man.[1] More recently the legal nature of Canon law has been questioned from inside the Roman Catholic Church: Eugenio Corecco, a bishop and one of the experts who prepared the 1983 Code of Canon law, stressed its theological nature. Canon law is part of theology: it is founded on divine law, which can be fully understood only through faith. Therefore a Canon law scholar must base his work primarily on faith, and only secondarily on reason.[2]

Comparative lawyers are not very interested in these subtle distinctions, but they too point to a weakness of Canon law. According to some, Canon law is not a complete legal system. René David wrote that 'le droit canon n'est pas un système de droit complet, [...] il n'a jamais été qu'un complément au droit romain ou aux autres droits 'civils', visant à régler des matières (organisation de l'Eglise, sacrements, procédure canonique) qui ne sont pas réglées par ces droits'.[3] A little later, Léontin-Jean Constantinesco supported a similar position, writing that 'le droit canonique ne constitue ni un Système ni un ordre juridique, mais seulement une branche très réduite de quelques rares ordres juridiques'.[4]

Notwithstanding these remarks, most of today's lawyers consider Canon law a legal system.[5] Sohm's theories were abandoned a long time ago, when the identification of law and State (implicit in Sohm's notion of 'binding law') declined. Carnelutti's opinion did not stand up to the criticism that a large part of Canon law regulates relations among men. Corecco's followers are very careful to point out that its theological nature does not prevent Canon law from being a legal system, although different from secular legal systems. David is right in pointing at the limited scope of Canon law (more limited, for example, than Jewish and Muslim law): but to what extent is 'completeness' a necessary characteristic of a legal system? Therefore the majority of contemporary lawyers agree that Canon law is a legal system. But is it a *religious* legal system as well?

CANON LAW AS A RELIGIOUS LEGAL SYSTEM

Most scholars take this for granted. Once it is admitted that Canon law is a legal system, they have no doubt it is a religious legal system. But what makes a legal system a religious one? The sources of law provide the first answer. Canon law is grounded on a divine law, that is on a law revealed by God to men through Jesus Christ. The supernatural character of its main source makes Canon law a religious legal system. The second answer takes into consideration the purpose of Canon law, the salvation of souls. The whole of Canon law is directed at providing men with eternal salvation. This aim gives Canon law its religious characteristic. These two answers require a more detailed examination.

Canon law and divine law

Divine law is a complex system of legal provisions whose author is God.[6] Within divine law it is possible to draw a fundamental distinction between revealed divine law on one hand and natural divine law on the other. The first has been given to men through Revelation. Its norms and principles[7] are contained in the Holy Scriptures (the Old and the New Testament) and in the Church Tradition, that is the transmission of Christ's teachings through the Apostles and later the bishops. Natural divine law is written in the hearts of men. It is given by God to men through creation: from birth every man has within himself principles and criteria which allow him to distinguish good from evil.[8] Both revealed and natural divine laws come from God, therefore they cannot contradict each other: revealed divine law completes and perfects natural divine law. Nevertheless, there are some significant differences between the two laws. First, their content is not exactly the same. Some principles – for example the respect of human life – can be found both in revealed and natural divine law; others – for example the primacy of the Roman Pontiff or the episcopal structure of the Church – are founded on the revealed divine law alone. Second, revealed divine law can be known by men only through Revelation: reason alone is not enough to grasp its content. On the contrary, natural divine law can be known through the correct use of the rational faculties every man has. Third, natural divine law is binding to every man, irrespective of his religious affiliation, while revealed divine law is primarily binding to the faithful, that is those who have been baptised.[8bis]

Divine law (both revealed and natural) is defined by four characteristics: it is a complete system of law, i.e. it contains everything necessary to attain its aims; it is superior in rank and value to human law (including laws enacted by the supreme human authority: for example, by the Pope or the ecumenical council): human laws that are conflicting with divine law are automatically void; it is universal, binding all human beings (natural divine law) or all the faithful (revealed divine law); it is eternal and cannot be changed by any human authority.[9] This last characteristic needs a few comments, as many laws which had been defined divine laws have been changed in the course of history. How can a divine law change after the conclusion of the Revelation?

There are two answers to this question. First, most Canon law scholars affirm that divine law cannot be directly operative unless it is not embedded in a human rule: as law in itself is something connected to history, divine law can be known and become binding only through a historical, human medium. This idea is connected to the theological doctrine of Christ's incarnation, which is central to Christian belief. In any case, it makes divine law more flexible, by admitting that it is possible to change the human medium through which divine law is known and becomes operative. Therefore while the rules and the principles of divine law are immutable, the legal provisions which give concrete expression to those rules and principles can change.[10] Rules and principles are divine, but legal provisions are always human. The Pope's primacy, being a rule of divine law, cannot be changed but its concrete and operative expressions can be very different, due to the fact that they are defined through human provisions.[11]

Second, it is always possible to invoke a better and fuller knowledge of divine law. Human capacity to understand divine law is limited: therefore it is always possible to improve understanding of what God really meant. The comprehension of divine law attained in a certain period can be replaced by another and better way to understand it.[12] Canon 1060 of the 1917 Code of Canon law absolutely prohibited a marriage between a Roman Catholic and a non Roman Catholic Christian when the former (and possibly his children) were in danger of losing their faith because of that marriage: this prohibition was explicitly defined as based on divine law. Canon 1124 of the 1983 Code drops any reference to divine law and does not exclude such a marriage, provided the Catholic partner will do everything possible to prevent that danger. The reason behind the dislike of 'mixed marriages' has not changed: the danger of losing the faith. But the absolute prohibition of the marriage is no longer considered the best way of attaining what divine law requires: adequate preparation of the spouses may be equally or even more effective.

These remarks lead to the first conclusion: even divine law can change or, more exactly, the ways divine law is understood by men and becomes effective can be different in time and space. Religious freedom was condemned as contrary to divine law in nineteenth century but it was warmly approved at the Vatican II Council; taking interest was forbidden *iure divino* in the Church of the Middle Ages but not now. Some of the norms *iuris divini* contained in the 1983 Code of Canon law (which is in force in the Western part of the Roman Catholic Church) have no counterpart in the 1990 Code of Canons of the Oriental Churches (which is in force in the Eastern part of the same Roman Catholic Church).[13]

It is possible such a conclusion cannot be drawn regarding Jewish or Muslim laws, since their provisions are more precise and analytical. This makes it more difficult (although not impossible, as history has abundantly shown) to change the provisions. By contrast, the New Testament contains less detailed and less numerous norms than the Old Testament or the Koran. Moreover the New Testament is not the literal word of God, but a narration of what the son of God did and said. The narration is made by men, although divinely inspired, and there are four different accounts, sometimes diverging on very important topics, for example the possibility of divorce in the case of adultery. In conclusion, the legal structure of the New Testament allows considerably more room for interpretation and evolution, than does the Old Testament or the Koran. In any case, as far as Canon law is concerned, the divine origin of law does not prevent change even in the parts of Canon law which are more directly connected to divine Revelation. Therefore the statements which affirm or at least imply that the central nucleus of Canon law (i.e. divine law) is immutable[14] should be reformulated: divine law is immutable in itself but it is apprehended by men through instruments which are subject to change. From man's point of view the distance between secular laws[15] and Canon law is less than usually expected. Secular laws and Canon law are not different because the first can change and the second cannot: both change. What can be said is that some parts of Canon law are grounded on immutable norms and principles, so that the change of the provisions which apply these norms and principles is slow and difficult, probably slower and more difficult than in any secular law. But it is not a fundamental difference as some parts of secular law presents a similar resistance to change.

The purpose of Canon law

Canon 1752 of the 1983 Code of Canon law says that 'the salvation of souls must always be the supreme law of the Church'. According to some scholars, this purpose makes Canon law a religious legal system and makes it different from any secular legal system. Are these statements correct? It is quite evident that secular legal systems do not have the salvation of souls among their aims. In the past it was not so, but now these systems tend to believe that salvation of the soul is a private affair which has little or nothing to do with law. On the contrary, Canon law and some other religious laws have a great deal of interest in the salvation of souls. But what are the consequences of this supernatural orientation of Canon law? Does it have an impact on the way Canon law works?

The Canonical discipline of marriage can provide an initial answer. According to the Roman Catholic doctrine, marriage is at the same time a contract and a sacrament. As a sacrament it confers on the spouses the grace, that is a divine help to sanctify their married life. Therefore performing the sacrament of marriage has spiritual effects which are relevant to the eternal salvation of the spouses: but these effects depend on the fact that the marriage they have concluded is a sacramental marriage. It may happen that a spouse celebrates a marriage by declaring his consent in front of the other spouse and the religious minister but, in his heart, he firmly excludes a fundamental element or property of the Canonical marriage, for example its indissolubility. This marriage is not a sacrament and can be declared void at any time. Nullity can be declared even when the exclusion of indissolubility was kept secret to everybody and in particular to the other spouse, who was *bona fide* convinced he had concluded a valid Canonical marriage: 'If one or both partners positively exclude marriage itself or some essential element or property of marriage, they contract invalidly.'[16] It is so even if the spouse declares his consent to the marriage without showing any reservation or limitation and the intention to exclude an essential element or property of marriage is confined to his inner sphere. Canon law gives the effective intention priority over the intention manifested by words at the celebration of the marriage. Of course that exclusion must be proved by the partner who asks the ecclesiastical court to declare he contracted invalidly and that is possible only if he expressed in some way his intention to exclude an essential element or property of the marriage. But the proof can be based on indirect indications and in any case the exclusion does not need to have been known by the other partner.

This is not the way secular legal systems work. If a spouse excludes some central characteristic of the civil marriage (for example monogamy), that does not invalidate the marriage: the more so when the exclusion is not declared and the other spouse has no chance of knowing it. The legal system protects the *bona fide* spouse, who is legitimately convinced he had concluded a valid marriage. The *mala fide* spouse cannot take advantage of his own 'secret' exclusion and have the marriage declared void. Declared intention prevails over the effective (but not declared) intention. Why do Canon law and secular laws assume such strikingly different positions on this issue? Because, according to Canon law, nobody can be kept bound to a marriage which is not a sacrament: that would prevent him from receiving divine grace by concluding another, sacramentally valid, marriage. This outcome would amount to imperilling his eternal salvation.

From this example it is possible to draw two conclusions. First, the eternal salvation of the spouses is paramount in Canon law. The legitimate expectations of the innocent spouse, who was convinced he had celebrated a valid marriage, are disregarded because something more important is at stake. Second, Canon law takes great interest in what happens in the conscience of every man, much more interest than secular legal systems do. A decision taken in *foro interno*, even if it is not known by anybody, has important effects in *foro externo*, determining the nullity of a marriage. What happens inside human conscience is not completely irrelevant to secular laws either: but it seldom gains so much importance. This is not surprising: supernatural salvation is directly affected by intentions, even if they are not translated into facts;[17] the welfare of society (which is the main purpose of secular legal systems) is much more dependant on facts than on intentions.

'In interiore homine habitat veritas': in Canon law St. Augustin's statement still has the force of a legal principle.

Criminal Canon law could provide other illustrations of these statements. But what has been said is enough to affirm that the supernatural orientation of Canon law and the consequent importance given to what happens in *foro interno* makes Canon law different from most secular laws. It is likely that the specific feature of Canon law as a religious legal system can be found here.

CANON LAW AND OTHER RELIGIOUS LEGAL SYSTEMS

It is possible to look at Canon law as a religious legal system from a different point of view, asking the question: what are the common elements on one hand and the different elements on the other between Canon law and other religious legal systems? This question cannot be answered by taking into consideration all religious legal systems: they are too many and too different. Therefore it is necessary to narrow the examination down to some of them, namely the Jewish and Islamic ones. Even so, this paragraph will contain only a few introductory remarks. The question is too broad and complicated to be discussed exhaustively in a few lines.

It is quite clear there are some common elements. Divine law is one of them. Jewish and Islamic law share with Canon law the idea that God revealed to men binding principles and norms which cannot be changed by any human authority, are superior to any human law, and constitute a complete and universal system of law.[18] Also the supernatural orientation is not exclusive to Canon law: *Shari'a* and *Halakhah* too promise to help men not only to live a righteous life in this world but also to attain eternal life in the other one.

But, as soon as the examination is pushed a little further, some differences take shape. The distinction between revealed and natural divine law, typical of Canon law, has no counterpart in Islamic law. 'Successive generations of legal philosophers in all systems have been groping after the "higher law" or the "ideal law" or the "natural law", which stands above all legal systems and to which all legal systems should conform. All students of jurisprudence will know how important is that a set of principles should exist which no ruler is at liberty to ignore ...Islam's solution to this problem is to offer the principles of this higher law in the word of the Qur'an.'[19] Therefore, as Anderson writes referring to Ash'arī's doctrine, 'all rest, firmly and unequivocally on the divine will; there is no scope for any doctrine of natural law, or for human positive law in any significant sense: instead the whole Shari'a is basically and essentially divine'.[20] Of course, this is not to say the debate on the relationship between revealed divine law and another law, divine in its origin but understandable by reason, is unknown in the long history of Islamic philosophy and theology: but it has had a limited impact on the elaboration of Islamic law.

In Jewish law it is possible to point to the distinction between the law given by God to Moses and to Noah: the first is binding for the Jewish people only, the second for all humankind.[21] There is an analogy here with Canon law and the idea that revealed divine law binds the faithful only, while natural divine law binds every man. But it is debated whether the Nohaide law could have been understood by reason only, without the help of divine Revelation. Therefore the idea that Noahide law is a kind of natural law is far from being the majority opinion among Jewish law scholars.[22]

It is likely that the prominence that the distinction revealed/natural divine law has acquired in Canon law is due to the influence of the Greek and Roman philosophical and legal culture, much stronger in this legal system than in Jewish and Islamic law. During the Middle Ages, St. Thomas and other theologians incorporated a large part of the Greek philosophical legacy into Christian theology and a similar task was performed by Gratianus, who transferred a large number of Roman legal categories to the field of Canon law. Through these channels, the notion of natural law elaborated by Cicero and the Stoics found its way into Christian theology and law. The same did not happen in the Islamic and Jewish world, or at least it did not happen on the same scale.

This difference among the three legal systems is not without consequences. According to the Roman Catholic doctrine, human beings can reach eternal salvation even if they do not know the Christian revelation or reject it 'bona fide'. It is enough that they sincerely seek God and try to live according to God's will as understood by their own conscience, that is according to natural divine law.[23] This principle has been repeatedly affirmed in the documents of the Vatican II Council and more recently reiterated by John Paul II.[24] This position is not shared without reservations by Jewish law. Can a righteous gentile, who lives according the Nohaide law, reach the eternal life? The Tosefta answers in the affirmative[25] and this is the position of most contemporary Jewish law scholars.[26] But Maimonides writes it is not enough to respect the Noahide precepts because they are rational, it is necessary to respect them as the revealed law of God, that is by faith:[27] only in this case will a gentile have a share in the world to come. And can a 'righteous' polytheist (supposing that a polytheist can live a righteous life) attain salvation according to Islamic law? The answer is doubtful at the very least.[28] The lack of the notion of natural divine law makes it difficult to accept there is salvation outside the revealed divine law.

The interplay between revealed and natural divine law has other consequences. It affects for example the place religious legal systems give to secular laws (i.e. laws enacted by States, international organisations, etc.). According to Canon law, secular laws are legitimate and binding as long as they do not conflict with natural law: revealed divine law stays out of the picture. Where such an interplay is not possible (as in Jewish and Islamic law), the legitimacy of secular laws tends to be judged according to the revealed divine law. It would be interesting to examine whether these different approaches to natural law have had an impact on the Western 'Etat laïc' on the one hand and the Eastern 'millet' system on the other. Has the presence of a natural law theory influenced the development of a State which aims to include people of different faiths on an equal footing? And has the absence of such a theory had anything to do with the development of a State based on the co-existence of different and separate civil and religious societies?

It would take up too much space to answer this question. It is better to conclude this comparison between Canon, Jewish and Islamic law by referring to another difference, which depends on the centralised organisation of the Roman Catholic Church and the decentralised structure of Jewish and Islamic communities. In the Roman Catholic Church the task of adapting divine law to change has been taken up mainly by authorities which act through legislation, as opposed to interpretation. Virtually since the beginning of Christianity, there has always been an authority (the ecumenical council and later the Pope) empowered to promulgate binding provisions on the whole of Christianity and later on the whole of the Roman Catholic Church.[29] Therefore it is not surprising that the law is the first and paramount in the hierarchy of the sources of human Canon law[30] and that in the last century codification attained a particular importance, greater than in the Jewish and Islamic legal systems.

On the contrary, in these latter systems, interpretation is the main source of law and plays a more important role than legislation. In the Jewish as well in the Islamic legal tradition 'works of scholarship have often fulfilled the functions of both legislature and judiciary':[31] the system depends on the legal expert rather than on the man or the legal body empowered to promulgate a law. Analogy and custom have larger room in this legal framework. Lacking a central authority empowered to solve a problem through a binding provision, different and even contradictory solutions coexist as long as the consensus (of the community or the scholars) is reached on one of them.

According to Ze'ev W. Falk, relying on interpretation rather than legislation places the focus of a legal system 'in the past rather than in the future, in *lege lata* rather than in *lege ferenda*'.[32] Interpretation is limited by the content and the context of the norm that is interpreted, while legislation can produce something new, that cannot be found in the pre-existing norms: that is why the *fictio iuris* is a device more common in Jewish and Islamic law than in Canon law.[33] The existence of a centralised legislative authority makes Canon law more rapid in adjusting to historical changes but, on the other hand, less flexible and less capable of tolerating internal differences than systems based on interpretation.

CONCLUSION

In the first part of this contribution the religious nature of the legal system 'Canon law' has been discussed. Two elements have been taken into consideration, the divine foundation and the supernatural orientation of Canon law. The question has been asked whether they really differentiate Canon law from the secular legal systems. Of course these latter systems are not grounded in divine law, but it is questionable whether the divine foundation really gives Canon law a peculiar structure and way of operating. Even if the central nucleus of divine law cannot change, this law is understood by men through historical (and therefore changeable) instruments. This brings Canon law close to the secular laws, although the former changes at a slower pace. The supernatural orientation of Canon law and the attention it devotes to what happens in the conscience of men is more significant. It provides a distinctive structure to some parts of Canon law and therefore it might be a distinguishing element between Canon law and secular legal systems. Further research, particularly in the field of criminal Canon law, is likely to substantiate this statement.

In the second part of the article a few characteristics of the Canonical legal system have been compared with the characteristics of other religious legal systems, Jewish law and Islamic law. Some common ground has been identified but, as soon as one probes a little deeper, differences emerge. A real comparison of the various religious legal systems is yet to come. The few comparative remarks contained in the previous paragraph show how interesting and fruitful it could be.

NOTES

1 In this chapter the noun 'man', the pronouns 'he' and 'him', and the adjective 'his' are meant to include also the noun 'woman', the pronouns 'she' and 'her', and the adjective 'her'.

For a general overview of the theories affirming that Canon law lacks one or more essential characteristics of law see Iván C. Ibán, *Derecho canonico y ciencia jurídica* (Madrid: Universidad Complutense, 1984), 82–242; Carlos J. Errázuriz M., 'Sull' antigiuridismo canonico classico: visione d'insieme', 799–832 of *Studi in onore di Francesco Finocchiaro* Vol. I (Padova: Cedam, 2000).

2 Corecco's positions are shared by other scholars like Antonio Maria Rouco Varela and Remigiusz Sobanski; previously similar theories had been sustained by Klaus Mörsdorf. See: Carlo R.M. Redaelli, *Il concetto di diritto nella Chiesa* (Milano: Glossa, 1991), 53–161. One of the most important works written by Corecco has been translated into English as *The Theology of Canon Law. A Methodological Question* (Pittsburgh: Duquesne University Press, 1992).

3 René David, *Les grand systèmes de droit contemporain* (Paris: Dalloz, 1982), 473.

4 Léontin-Jean Constantinesco, *Traité de droit comparé* Vol. III, *La science des droits comparés* (Paris: Economica, 1983), 110. It is possible that Constantinesco confuses Canon law as the law of the Roman Catholic Church and the parts of Canon law that are in force in some State legal systems (as happens for example in Italy and Spain).

5 Among many others, Canon law is taken into consideration by Adolf F. Schnitzer, *Vergleichende Rechtslehre* (Basel: Verlag für Recht und Gesellschaft, 1961), 325–348; Felipe de Sola Cañizares, *Iniciación al derecho comparado* (Barcelona: Inst. De Derecho comparado, 1954), 169–181; John Gilissen, *Introduction historique au droit* (Bruxelles: Bruylant, 1979), 128.

6 About the notion of divine law see Chester James Antieau, *The Higher Laws: Origins of Modern Constitutional Law* (Hein: Buffalo, 1994), 1–48. Interesting remarks are contained in Haim H. Cohn, 'The Secularization of Divine Law' in H. Cohn, *Jewish Law in Ancient and Modern Israel* (New York: Ktav, 1971), 1–49.

7 It is debated whether there are norms of divine law: some scholars deny divine law contains norms and affirm there are only principles and values of divine law. See: Helmuth Pree, 'The Divine and the Human of the *Ius Divinum*' in Katholieke Universiteit Leuven, *In diversitate unitas*. Monsignor W. Onclin Chair 1997 (Leuven: Peeter, 1997), 35–36. Most canonists affirm that divine law includes both principles and norms (see Pedro Juan Viladrich, 'El derecho canónico' in Catedráticos de derecho canónico de Universidades españolas, *Derecho canónico*, I, (Pamplona: Eunsa, 1974), 52.

8 See Giorgio Feliciani, *Le basi del diritto canonico* (Bologna: Mulino, 1984), 65–66; *Catechism of the Catholic Church* (London: Chapman, 1994), n.1960.

(8bis) See Pierre Andrieu-Guitrancourt, Introduction sommaire à l' étude du droit en général et du droit canonique contemporain en particulier (Paris: Sirey, 1963), 212; Raoul Naz, Infidèles, in Dictionnaire de droit canonique, V, (Paris: Letouzey et Ané, 1953), 1360.

9 About these characteristics see Pree, *supra* note 7, at 24; Salvatore Berlingò, *Diritto canonico* (Torino: Giappichelli, 1995), 38–39.

10 See Remigiusz Sobanski, 'Immutabilità e storicità del diritto della Chiesa: diritto divino e diritto umano' in *Ius Ecclesiae*, 9:38 (1997); Gaetano Lo Castro, 'La dimensione "umana" del diritto divino' in A. Filipponio – R. Coppola (a cura di), *Diritto umano e legislazione divina* (Torino: Giappichelli, 1998), 40.

11 See Lo Castro, *supra* note 10, at 36 and 39; Salvatore Berlingò, 'Diritto divino e diritto umano nella Chiesa' in *Il diritto ecclesiastico*, 1995, I 50; Pree, *supra* note 7, at 39.

12 See Sobanski, *supra* note 10, at 27–28

13 See Pree, *supra* note 7, at 25.

14 See, for example, Gilissen, *supra* note 5, at 69: 'le droit [hébraïque] est donné par Dieu à son peuple . . . Le droit est dès lors immuable, seul Dieu peut le modifier, idée qu'on retrouve dans le droit canonique et dans le droit musulman.'; James A. Coriden, *An Introduction to Canon Law* (New York: Paulist Press, 1991), 33: 'Canons are said to embody divine law if they are drawn directly from God's revelation or from natural law, God's creation. The vast majority of canons are human law ("merely ecclesiastical law", c. 11) that is, enactments of the church's own authority and, consequently, alterable.' It is easy to infer from this statement that divine law is not alterable.

15 In this contribution the expressions 'secular law' and 'secular legal system' refer to the State laws and State legal systems in the West today.

16 Canon 1101 §2 of the 1983 *Code of Canon law*.

17 It is easy to recall here the passage of Matthew's Gospel 'he who lusts after a woman has already committed adultery in heart'.

18 See Richard Puza, 'Die Religionen und das Recht. Grundlagen, Prinzipien und Strukturen des religiösen Rechts im Judentum, Islam und Christentum' in ed. Ulrich Nembach, Heinrich Rusterholz and Paul M. Zulehner *Informationes Theologiae Europae* (Frankfurt: Lang, 2000), 280. The universal characteristic of divine law means it is binding on every person who is member of a general group (i.e. the Islamic or Jewish community).

19 C.G. Weeramantry, *Islamic Jurisprudence. An International Perspective* (London: McMillan Press, 1988), 65. See also Majid Khadduri, 'Nature and Sources of Islamic Law' in ed. Ian Edge *Islamic Law and Legal Theory* (Aldershot: Dartmouth, 1996), 90–92.

20 J.N.D. Anderson, 'Law as a social force in Islamic culture and history' *Bulletin of the School of Oriental and African Studies* 20: 14–15 (1957). See also Mohammad Kashim Kamali, 'Methodological Issues in Islamic Jurisprudence' *Arab Law Quarterly* 11: 3–33 (1996), 15; N.J. Coulson, *A History of Islamic Law* (Edinburgh: Edinburgh University Press, 1964), 85; Bernard Weiss, 'Interpretation in Islamic Law: the Theory of *Ijtihād*' *The American Journal of Comparative Law* 26: 194–212 (1978), 204; Nabil Saleh, 'Origins of the Sanctity of Contracts in Islamic Law' *Arab Law Quarterly* 13: 260–261 (1998); Chafik Chehata, 'Logique juridique et droit musulman' *Studia*

islamica 23: 7–11 (1965); Nabil Saleh, 'L' "equité" en tant que source de droit hanafite' *Studia islamica* 25:23 and 137 (1966).

21 Suzanne Last Stone, 'Sinaitic and Nohaide Law: Legal Pluralism in Jewish Law' *Cardozo Law Review* 12: 1157–1214 (1991), 1158. More generally on Noahide Law see David Novak, *The Image of the Non-Jew in Judaism. An Historical and Constructive Study of the Noahide Laws* (New York: Edwin Mellen Press, 1983); Nahum Rakover, 'Jewish Law and the Noahide Obligation to Preserve the Social Order' *Cardozo Law Review* 12: 1073–1136 (1991).

22 For a general overview of this debate see David Novak, *Natural Law in Judaism* (Cambridge: Cambridge University Press, 1998). According to Novak 'Noahide law is the Jewish way of thinking natural law', at 191. Jacob I. Dienstag, 'Natural Law in Maimonidean Thought and Scholarship' *The Jewish Law Annual* VI: 64–77 (1987). Novak's opinion is shared by Rakover, *supra* note 21, at 172; Norman Lamm and Aaron Kirschenbaum 'Freedom and Constraint in the Jewish Judicial Process' *Cardozo Law Review* 1: 105–120 (1979); Aaron Lichtenstein, 'Does Jewish Tradition Recognize an Ethic Independent of Halakha?', 62–65 of ed. Martin Fox *Modern Jewish Ethics* (Columbus: Ohio State University Press, 1975), 62–65; *contra* Marvin Fox, 'Maimonides and Aquinas on Natural Law' *Diné Israel*, V: V–XXXVI (1972); José Faur, 'Understanding the Covenant' *Tradition*, Spring 1968, 41. J. David Bleich advocates a very limited notion of natural law: 'Judaism and Natural Law' *The Jewish Law Annual* VII: 5–42 (1988), 5ff.

23 For an overview of the Roman Catholic doctrine see Mikka Ruokannen, *The Catholic Doctrine of Non-Christian Religions According to the Second Vatican Council* (Leiden: Brill, 1992). The salvation of non-Christians had already been considered possible in the encyclical *Quanto conficiamus moerore* of 1863 (n. 288).

24 See the Vatican II Dogmatic Constitution *Lumen Gentium* (n. 14). The Vatican II Decree *Ad Gentes* (n. 7) says that salvation is denied only to those who know the Church has been divinely instituted to bring men to eternal salvation and, in spite of this knowledge, refuse to be members of it. See also John Paul's II encyclical *Redemptionis missio* of 1990 (par. 10). Even texts that are principally devoted to fighting the mentality of indifferentism, which leads to believe that one religion is as good as another, have kept firm this principle. 'For those who are not formally and visibly members of the Church, salvation in Christ is accessible by virtue of a grace which, while having a mysterious relationship to the Church, does not make them formally part of the Church but enlightens them in a way which is accommodated to their spiritual and material situation'. Therefore 'individual non-Christians' can receive 'the salvific grace of God' in ways known to God himself (Congregation for the doctrine of the faith, Declaration *Dominus Iesus*, 6 August, 2000, n. 20–21). The Declaration adds that 'if it is true that the followers of other religions can receive divine grace, it is also certain that objectively speaking they are in a gravely deficient situation in comparison with those who, in the Church, have the fullness of the means of salvation.' (ibid., n. 22)

25 See Tosefta Sanhedrin 13: 2.

26 See for example Rakover, *supra* note 21, at 1087–1089; George Horowitz, *The Spirit of Jewish Law* (New York, Central Book Company, 1953), 233–234; 'Right and Righteousness' *The Jewish Encyclopedia*, Vol. 10 (1925), 424.

27 See *The Code of Maimonides*, Book Fourteen, The Book of Judges (New Haven: Yale University Press, 1949), 230.

28 Against this possibility see Umar Sulaiman Al-Ashqar, 'The Final Day. Paradise and Hell' *Light of the Qur'an and Sunnah* (Riyadh: International Islamic Publishing House, 1999), 62; Md. Alauddin Al-Azhari, *The Theory and Sources of Islamic Law for Non-Muslims* (Dacca: Asiatic Press, 1962), 26–30; Abdur Rahmān Doi, *Non Muslims*

under Shari'ah [Islamic Law] (Brentwood: International Graphics, 1981), 121; Muhammad Abul Quasem, *Salvation of the Soul and Islamic Devotions* (London: Kegan Paul, 1983), 30–34. In favour of the salvation of non-believers are Ismail Raji al-Faruqi, *Islam and Other Faiths* (Leicester: The Islamic Foundation, 1998), 141 and, at least as far as Jewish and Christians are concerned, Farooq Hassan, *The Concept of State and Law in Islam* (Washington: University Press of America, 1981), 152.

29 On the development of the legislative powers of the Pope see Carlo Fantappiè, *Introduzione storica al diritto canonico* (Bologna: Mulino, 1999), 165ff.; Constant Van de Wiel, *History of Canon Law* (Louvain: Peeters, 1991), 76ff.

30 See can. 7ff. of the 1983 *Code of Canon law*.

31 Ze'ev W. Falk 'Jewish Law' 15–40 of ed. J. Duncan M. Derrett, *An Introduction to Legal Systems* (London: Sweet & Maxwell, 1968), 30. About Islamic law see Weiss, *supra* note 20, at 201; Noel Coulson, *Conflicts and Tensions in Islamic Jurisprudence* (Chicago: The University of Chicago Press, 1969), 9.

32 Ze'ev W. Falk, 'Jewish Law and Medieval Canon Law' 78–96 of ed. Bernard S. Jackson *Jewish Law in Legal History and the Modern World* (Leiden: Brill, 1985), 85.

33 In the Jewish legal system, change 'often took the form of a legal device or fiction, rather than of legislation': Falk, *supra* note 31, at 40. This statement would also apply to Islamic law, though not so well to Canon law.

5

ISLAMIC LAW: STUCK WITH THE STATE?

Lynn Welchman[1]

In his inaugural lecture, 'An Islamic Triangle: Changing Relationships between *Shari'a*, State Law, and Local Customs', Professor Léon Buskens insists that 'a comparative perspective is vital in order to understand the peculiarities of the different legal systems of the Islamic world' and calls for research on the diversity and development of these systems.[2] The three domains in Buskens' 'Islamic triangle' correspond broadly to those employed by Menski to identify sources of legal norms: religion, the state, and society – except, possibly, that Menski's use of 'society' embraces not only 'social norms' (Buskens' 'local customs') but also the activities of 'social reform movements of any kind [making] their claims of or against the state'.[3] Similarly, 'religion' might more expansively include establishment (or 'orthodox') interpreters of the religion – or the 'religious law' – who pronounce upon the legitimacy of action by society (social norms and the aspirations of social reform movements) and by state (hence, state actions including legislative acts).[4] As for state, in relation specifically to Islamic law, Buskens remarks that:

> Study of the process of state formation, in which a central government claims the monopoly on the imposition of uniform and generally valid legal norms, offers a key to understanding the constantly changing relationships between the three domains.

I propose, in this paper, to respond to Buskens' invitation with a snap-shot view of the positioning of actors in the three domains around the place of 'Islamic law' and the *shari'a* court system in the emerging legal system of the Palestinian state-to-be. I therefore confine my focus, in this paper, to those elements of *shari'a* implemented by the state – 'formal' *shari'a*, in the terms of Maurits Berger, as compared to 'informal' *shari'a*, which covers a far wider field of conduct.

In the West Bank and Gaza Strip, efforts are apace to forge a unified legal system out of the differing post-1948 legal histories of the two areas as well as the older remnants of British colonial and Ottoman imperial legislation. These include examining the models offered by neighbouring Arab states which themselves incorporate elements of transplanted laws, as well as Islamic law and other indigenous legal responses. Donor agencies have been funding different parts of this process, including law-focussed civil society efforts; experts trained in different legal traditions contribute in various ways. As Bernard Botiveau notes, 'jurists make no bones about the fact that acculturation to models imposed from outside is part of the Palestinian legal experience'.[5] The particular status of *shari'a* as a 'religious law' would suggest its exemption from most if not all of such developments and influences. In fact, as this paper will show, the operative form of state-issued codifications of *shari'a*-based law has opened it up to just such jostlings and accommodations.

In both substance and operation, Islamic law in Palestine[6] has features recognisable from the earliest days of Muslim governance[7] and Islamic jurisprudence, more directly passed on from the heritage of centuries of Ottoman rule. With the defeat of the Ottomans towards the end of the First World War, Palestine passed under British colonial rule through the Mandate arrangements formalised in 1920, which were succeeded, after 1948 and the establishment of the Israeli state in most of Mandatory Palestine, by Jordanian rule over the West Bank and Egyptian administration in the Gaza Strip. In 1967, Israel occupied the West Bank, including East Jerusalem, and the Gaza Strip. Israeli military occupation began to be removed in parts of the West Bank and Gaza Strip (but not yet East Jerusalem) as of 1994, as a result of the Israel–Palestine Liberation Organisation agreements concluded within the framework of the Oslo peace process.[8] The Palestine National Authority now has limited jurisdiction in parts of Gaza and the West Bank, as part of the arrangements for the transitional (or 'interim') period intended to precede full resolution of the conflict.

Among the implications of this chronology are, first, the above-mentioned resonance through the centuries of certain elements of the substance and operation of Islamic law. Second, now is the first time that there is a Palestinian executive and a legislature elected by those Palestinians entitled by the Oslo framework to participate. Both have been the objects of advocacy efforts by different sectors of their constituency focussed on the content of that part of Islamic law to be implemented in a future Palestinian state. However painful and drawn out the progress towards statehood is proving to be, even at this late stage, for the Palestinian people, during this transitional stage participants premised their advocacy efforts on the imminent establishment of a sovereign state, necessarily forcing into focus the relationship of *shari'a* with political authority, and the relationship of both with society.

SHARI'A, STATE AND SOCIETY: ILLUSTRATIONS FROM THE TRIANGLE

'Islamic law' is the inadequate translation of *ash-shari'a al-islamiyya*, literally 'the Islamic way', short-handed in English as *shari'a*. The terms or rules (*ahkam*) of the *shari'a* are to be sought from the Qur'an as the word of God revealed incrementally and intermittently to the Prophet Muhammad in the Hijaz in the early seventh century;[9] and the *hadith*, the reports of the *sunna* (normative practice in words and deeds) of the Prophet.[10] To these primary, textual sources Sunni jurisprudence adds *ijma'*, consensus, which Wael Hallaq explains as 'a sanctioning instrument whereby the creative jurists, the *mujtahids*, representing the community at large, are considered to have reached an agreement, known retrospectively, on a technical legal ruling';[11] and *qiyas*, reasoning by analogy. Those most immediately responsible for the articulation of the rules of the *shari'a* – or, in the first place, the articulation of opinions as to the content of those rules in the cases where evidence from the texts was held not to be definitive – were the 'scholar-jurists'[12] of the centuries following the death of the Prophet. Through application of jurisprudential technique to the texts and to social reality, the scholars (*'ulama*), acting in private capacity (i.e. not as part of the political authority) developed their 'understanding' (*fiqh*) of *shari'a* into substantial collections of divergent opinions over the course of the centuries, largely unaffected, at least in private law, by the changing identities of political regimes that followed the Prophet. This relationship has been held to be a determining characteristic of Islamic law, referred to by Frank Vogel as 'the profound tension or dialectic, apparently endemic in the Islamic legal venture, between the *ulema* and the ruler':

> While the former are the bearers and advocates of *fiqh*, the latter is the inheritor of another principle – namely power – which is as indispensable to the fulfillment of the Islamic legal ideal as is *fiqh* itself. [. . .] The structure of an Islamic legal system arises most essentially from the complex interaction of these two legitimacies and institutions – *siyasah* [political power] and the ruler on the one hand, and *fiqh* and the *ulema* on the other – as they enter into relations of cooperation and competition.[13]

In today's world, this dynamic can arguably be examined in all of the fifty-six state members of the Organisation of Islamic Conference, and possibly beyond. The question of whether and how Islamic law can and should 'fit' into the pattern of territorial states in today's world is asked against the background of the abolition of the Caliphate by Turkey in 1924. Current debates on the feasibility and/or desirability of restoration of the (a?) Caliphate and the requirements of Islamic constitutional law take place against the background of untold variations in political, legal and social systems, along with the development of what Buskens refers to as 'post-modern' Islamic legal thinking.[14]

If theories of Islamic law (ancient and modern) show discussion of the ruler/state-*'ulama/fiqh* dynamic in the *shari'a* as God's law, the third 'domain' of society/custom formed the context for God's revelation to the Prophet, and for the interpretative efforts of the jurists, not only in the 'formative period' of Islamic law but in the succeeding centuries. John Esposito has written that classical Islamic law 'as finally formulated was the product of Quranic reform and customary practice',[15] and the emphasis on the 'reforming' nature of the revelation (particularly in regard to women's status) is a reference to its corrections to existing practice among the pre-Islamic Arab communities. While 'Arab customary laws' are neither monolithic nor unchanging, certain themes in custom and *shari'a* recur in the history of Islamic law as applied in Arab Palestine. Thus, one of the 'reforms' to customary law revealed in the Qur'an and considered as part of the empowerment (in context) of women was the rule that a married woman was entitled to sole rights over the dower paid by her husband, who under customary law would have paid it to her father or brother.[16] Evidence from different periods including the twentieth century in Palestine indicates circumstances in which the older custom prevails, to the disapproval of the *'ulama* who had occasion to invoke the *shari'a* position by way of rebuke and correction.[17] By contrast, Haim Gerber deduces from his examination of Turkish court records in more central Ottoman areas in the seventeenth and eighteenth centuries that local custom there was more closely in harmony with the *shari'a* rule protecting the wife's absolute entitlement.[18]

Another example of a recurring focus of the jurists showing the interface of local practice with the rules articulated by the jurists is the capacity of an adult woman to contract her own marriage; or, conversely, her need for a marriage guardian (in the person of a male family member or absent him the judge) to either contract the marriage for her or at least to give his permission. The dissent among the jurists on this issue indicates the lack of agreement on a definitive position in the source texts of the Qur'an and the *hadith*, by contrast to the clarity they found in the Quranic text on a woman's right to her dower.[19] Noel Coulson considered the contrasting opinions of two early groups of scholars (in Iraq and the Hijaz) on this question as illustrative of the effect of the different socioeconomic environments in which the scholars lived and worked.[20] In time, the majority of jurists of the four Sunni schools of law that survived into the mediaeval period[21] held for the necessity of a marriage guardian. A minority of jurists from the Hanafi school held that a sane adult woman could legally contract herself in marriage, granting the guardian the right to seek dissolution of such a marriage after the fact if it were unsuitable.[22] This was one of the very few areas of family law in which the sixteenth-century Ottoman Sultan Sulayman intervened, forbidding the marriage of women without the permission of their guardians. *Fatwa*s (legal opinions) from his chief legal officer, the *Mufti* (jurisconsult) of Istanbul, Ebu's-su'ud, insisting that judges in the Empire (which generally gave the Hanafi school preference) did not have the licence to act on alternative Hanafi opinions indicate that some were minded to apply the apparently earlier view attributed to the eponymous founder of the school, Abu Hanifa.[23] In succeeding centuries in Palestine, Judith Tucker's reading of *fatwa* collections establishes that non-establishment *mufti*s (private scholars not appointed by Ottoman authorities) consistently affirmed Abu Hanifa's view, to the effect that a sane, adult woman could choose her own husband and make her own marriage arrangements, without having to establish the consent of her guardian and, conversely, that she could not be married off without her freely given consent. Tucker notes that many of these *fatwas*:

> pitted the jurists against irregular social practices, especially those whereby a family attempted to arrange a marriage without taking proper account of legal procedure and a young woman's rights.[24]

In the contemporary West Bank, the law on marriage guardianship is somewhat unclear, but does contain an explicit provision to the effect that previously married women aged over eighteen are entitled to marry on their own authority and have no need to register the consent of a male guardian. Records of the *shari'a* courts however show that this is almost entirely ignored in practice, with the courts recording a guardian's consent in practically all cases, including where there is unequivocally no legal requirement to do so. A wide-ranging social survey carried out in the West Bank, Gaza Strip and East Jerusalem and published in 1993 found that 80 per cent of men and 76 per cent of women surveyed felt that the choice of a girl's husband should be 'mainly the daughter's choice' – thus weighting the woman's opinion while maintaining participation of the family as represented by the marriage guardian.[25] It may be this social attitude rather than the letter of the law that is reflected in the court records, and indeed the obscurity of the legal text may be an attempt to provide – albeit indirectly – for that balance. In the transitional period, guardianship in marriage proved again to be one of the most controversial of the issues raised in proposals for changes to Muslim family law.

Besides such directives to the judges on particular matters, the Ottoman rulers did not centralise control over the range of *shar'i* rules applied in the courts. A substantial amount of ruler's law, *qanun*, was issued on matters to do with the running of the Empire: Colin Imber refers to 'two distinct bodies of law, one sacred, the other imperial'.[26] But it was only at the beginning of the twentieth century that the Ottomans – at the end of Empire – issued state codifications of *shar'i* rules for implementation by the *shari'a* courts in their territory.

THE STATE GETS STRONGER

Over the course of the nineteenth century, the *shari'a* courts had been stripped of much of their jurisdiction with the transfer of large areas of law (in the *Tanzimat* reforms) to the newly-constituted regular or 'statute' (*nizhamiyya*) courts which applied codifications modelled on European (largely French) imports. Remaining in the *shari'a* courts were matters of *waqf* (pious endowments) and personal status issues and *diya* (financial compensation for physical harm) where the parties were Muslim or where the parties were mixed but the non-Muslim party agreed to *shar'i* jurisdiction; they were ruled on by judges trained in the classical schools of *fiqh* and having recourse to the traditional texts. The *shari'a* courts also retained residual jurisdiction from other courts being created in the far-reaching reforms, reflecting their original, wider role in the Empire's judicial system, and the 'reach' of state-issued law remained less, for the moment, in the *shari'a* courts than in the statute courts.

In civil law, the Ottomans stopped short of importing a civil code from foreign sources, and had a committee draw up the Majalla, a compilation of Hanafi rules and guidelines, complete with examples, as a reference text for the state court judges untrained in 'finding' the law in the traditional Hanafi texts.[27] Certain sections of the Majalla, completed at the end of the nineteenth century, remain part of the law applied in the Palestinian *shari'a* courts today. This was followed in 1917 by the Ottoman Law of Family Rights, in which the legislators drew on *fiqh* opinions beyond the Hanafi jurists to produce a law of marriage and divorce which bound the judges in the *shari'a* courts.[28] In the event that a subject was not covered in the law, the judges were directed to the traditional Hanafi texts. These texts marked a significant shift in the state–*'ulama* relationship to *shari'a*. While the state still did not seek to articulate the substance of *shari'a*, it did take broader and fuller control of which rules could be enforced, and how. As Brinkley Messick puts it:

> the production of an entire corpus of *shari'a* law was taken out of the hands of the jurists and allocated to a new breed of public officials constituted as a drafting committee, with their work to be passed before the sultan for approval and promulgation.[29]

As the ambit of succeeding codifications in independent Arab states increased, the areas of personal status law left uncodified were further reduced, and the selection (*takhayyur*) of rules[30] utilised more eclectic juristic sources; on occasion, the political authority asserted the right of exercising *ijtihad* – i.e. the right to re-interpret the source texts rather than work from the existing juristic interpretations, but this has remained very much the exception.[31] The debates on the future of personal status law in Palestine are an illustration of this dialectic working itself through in the complex dynamics of a political transition. The *'ulama*-state relationship here plays out between established and mostly establishment *'ulama*, notably those holding prominent positions in the *shari'a* court system, teachers of *fiqh,* imams and others. An examination of the debates suggests that on some level, these *'ulama* seek to maintain the status of a kind of preliminary 'drafting committee' in the preparation of *shari'a*-based codifications, living now in a time and a place where such state-promulgated codifications have become the norm.

As for the Ottoman codifications, they were carried over by the non-Muslim British Mandate authorities, backed up in some cases by penal sanctions for non-compliance. Colonial administration and the influence of English legal principles thus had far less impact on the rules applied by the *shari'a* courts during the Mandate than on the law applied in the regular court system. On the other hand, the OLFR had included provisions for Jewish and Christian subjects as well as for the Muslim population, but these were not implemented by the British; rather, in a departure from the Ottoman intentions towards the state relationship with family law, the non-Muslim communities were expected to apply their own traditional laws without centralised codification.[32]

Furthermore, under the British colonial authorities, the *shari'a* courts lost their remaining residual jurisdiction. The restriction of *shar'i* jurisdiction to matters (broadly) of Muslim family law, along with the specific institutions of *waqf* and *diya*, has been seen by some commentators as resulting from colonial assumptions about the centrality of this area of 'religious' law, matched by a lack of direct political or financial interest in such matters on the part of the colonial administrator – although the process of restricting *shar'i* jurisdiction had been initiated by the Ottomans, the Tanzimat reforms were undertaken under direct pressure from imperial European powers. In considering processes of acculturation and importation of laws, family law is considered among the areas least vulnerable to penetration; and a further assumption is that this area of law, worked out in enormous detail by the jurists on the basis of substantial Quranic material, was historically the 'part of the sacred law that has always been most meticulously applied'.[33] Messick challenges these assertions one by one, commenting that

> An implicit contrast was made with the 'heart' of Western law, located in forms associated with the market...Descriptions of the *shari'a* as being viable only with respect to its ritual and *statut personnel* sections diverted attention from the existence of deeper and broader family resemblances to Western law.[34]

The picture of family law as the 'last stronghold' of the *shari'a* is also a little simplified when applied to the Palestinian and wider Arab context. Notably, not only was the Majalla comprised entirely of rules drawn from Hanafi *fiqh*, but a series of civil codes of independent Arab states from 1949 onwards have drawn increasingly on principles of Islamic law in organising civil capacity, contract and tort. The Jordanian Civil Code of 1976, for example, designed for application in the regular court system, has as its residual reference 'the principles of Islamic *fiqh* most suited to the terms of this Code'. These days, in the public pronouncements of *shar'i* officials in Palestine, the perceived centrality of the substantive area of family law is connected to the system that applies it – the *shari'a* courts – as much as to the substance of law in regulating the Muslim family and through it Muslim society, and protecting against the depredations of immorality and dissipation identified with the West. Thus the first Palestinian Chief Islamic Justice, the *Qadi al-Quda*, upon being asked his opinion of a draft constitutional document for the Palestinian National Authority (PNA) during the transitional period, insisted upon its revision to include 'the three agencies of an Islamic character': *shar'i* adjudication, the institutionalisation of *ifta* (the function of pronouncing – in the form of *fatwa*s – upon the legitimacy or otherwise of acts or objects according to Islamic law), and the regulation of *waqf*s.[35]

SHARI'A COURTS IN STATE SYSTEMS

The *Qadi al-Quda*'s vigorous efforts in support of all three agencies, and particularly the *shari'a* court system for which he was directly responsible, gives an interesting perspective on 'institution-building' in the political transition. Shaykh Muhammad Abu Sardane was appointed initially by Yasser Arafat to direct affairs of the *shari'a* courts from within the Department of Justice, which governs the regular court system; within months, after Jordan announced that it was turning over to the PNA the running of the West Bank *shari'a* courts, he petitioned, with the support of the body of *shari'a* court judges, for the creation of the ministerial post of *Qadi al-Quda*, and duly took over this Office as a separate department from the Ministry of Justice, reproducing the structural features of the Jordanian system in this regard.[36]

The *Qadi al-Quda*'s alacrity in these matters might have been anticipated in light of the fate of the *shari'a* courts elsewhere in the region. Arab states had followed different paths in their treatment of the *shari'a* courts upon independence from various forms of colonial rule. Nathan Brown identifies as bureaucratisation, codification and amalgamation the 'three sorts of measures taken by centralising governments to exert greater control over the *shari'a* courts'.[37] Codification in this sense meant controlling more closely the substance of the law applied in the courts, and the 1950s saw a series of personal status laws issued by the legislatures of newly independent post-colonial states, of which Jordan was the first, issuing the Jordanian Law of Family Rights of 1951. The law applied only to Muslims, including West Bankers as a result of Jordan's 'unification' of the two banks of the Jordan.

The Jordanian Constitution (1952) showed also its 'bureaucratisation' of the *shari'a* court system, identifying three types of courts: regular (*nizhamiyya*), religious courts, and special tribunals.[38] The regular courts were now clearly the 'national' system: they hold jurisdiction over all persons in all civil and criminal matters except those specifically under the jurisdiction of the religious courts or special tribunals. The *shari'a* courts regained none of the former residuary jurisdiction of Ottoman times, which now fell to the regular court system. The Jordanian Constitution specifies as exclusive *shari'a* court jurisdiction over questions of personal status where the parties are Muslims, issues of *diya* where the parties are Muslim, or one is a non-Muslim but both agree to *shari'a* court jurisdiction, and matters relating to Islamic *waqf*.[39] The *shari'a* courts compromise first instance courts (including those in the Palestinian West Bank, until 1994, as well as those in Jordan itself) and a *Shari'a* Court of Appeal sitting in Amman;[40] the courts are under the direction of the Jordanian *Qadi al-Quda*, and are distinct from the regular court system in their professional appointments, their body of employees, and the rules of procedure that apply.[41] The explicitly plural legal system separating out matters identified as within the jurisdiction of the 'religious courts' was thus maintained in Jordan, but subjected to increasingly bureaucratic and centralised state control; similarly plural legal systems are maintained in the neighbouring Mashreq states of Syria and Lebanon.

In Egypt, where independence had come much earlier, a number of laws had been passed affecting specific areas of personal status law in the 1920s and 1940s, but there had been no promulgation of a more extensive codification as attempted elsewhere in the 1950s. Egypt followed, in Brown's words, the path of 'amalgamation' of the *shari'a* court system, folding it gradually into the general civil court system, replacing *shari'a* trained judges, on retirement, with judges trained in statute law, and ending finally with the abolition of the *shari'a* court system. Personal status matters are dealt with by the 'family chambers' of the national court system.[42] Egypt has however maintained the separate laws for different communities, unlike, for example, the Maghreb states of Algeria, Tunisia and Morocco, which have to varying extents issued territorial codes of personal status law applying to all their citizens. Left in military control of the Gaza Strip after the war of 1948, Egypt maintained the status of an administrator, appointing a Governor General to the Gaza Strip and issuing legislation specific to the Gaza Strip.[43] Unlike the courts in the West Bank, the Gaza courts were not integrated into the Egyptian national system, and the *shari'a* courts in the Gaza Strip thus retained their jurisdiction over Muslim personal status matters when in 1956 the *shari'a* and other communal courts in Egypt were abolished and had their jurisdiction transferred to the national courts.

Today, the *shari'a* courts in the West Bank apply the Jordanian Law of Personal Status (JLPS) of 1976 which replaced the 1951 Jordanian Law of Family Rights (JLFR).[44] This is an anomaly, since in all other areas Jordanian law was 'frozen' in its pre-occupation state.[45] However, from the start of the occupation, insisting on their Jordanian (critically, Muslim) institutional affiliation, the *shar'i* establishment put an Acting *Qadi al-Quda* at the head of an Islamic Board they established to administer Muslim affairs in the West Bank, particularly in East Jerusalem, in the absence of a Muslim sovereign. The Acting *Qadi al-Quda* directly supervised the work of the *shari'a* courts, providing the link between the *shar'i* systems in Jordan and the West Bank; the *shar'i* system maintained a position of non-recognition of the occupation authorities throughout the years 1967–1994.[46]

By contrast, the *shari'a* courts in the Gaza Strip were administered during the direct Israeli occupation by the Military Governor of the Strip through the Officer for Religious Affairs.[47] They apply the Law of Family Rights (LFR) of 1954, issued by the then Egyptian Governor of the Strip.[48] The *shari'a* courts in Gaza do not apply post-1967 Egyptian law, so more recent (and more precedent-setting) Egyptian law has not been applied; nor did the 1954 Law of Family Rights constitute a codification of the then existing Egyptian personal status legislation. The LFR bears a much closer resemblance to the Ottoman Law of Family Rights which was applied in Palestine but not in Egypt, with some Egyptian additions from laws issued in the 1920s. The JLPS includes these and other Egyptian-inspired provisions, as well as others of Syrian provenance and some Jordanian responses. Both the JLPS and the LFR retain a residual reference to the dominant opinion of the Hanafi school in the event of the lack of an explicit reference in the text.[49] In turning their attention to these texts during the transitional period, concerns articulated across the range of non-state actors who got involved included the generally recognised need to unify the rules applicable in the West Bank and in the Gaza Strip; the fact that as well as being outdated, neither codification was Palestinian; and the implications of the substance of such a code and the manner of its application for the vision of the future state aspired to by the Palestinian people as expressed by their political authorities.

PALESTINE: TRANSITIONAL TALK ON STATE AND *SHARI'A*

Despite the poor level of protection of rights, livelihoods and national identity afforded to the Palestinians during the course of the twentieth century by law in the hands of their various rulers, a remarkable amount of effort and attention has been focussed since the beginning of the transitional period on the drafting and discussion of legal texts presented as the first 'national' Palestinian legislation. Examining the implications of 'internal pluralism' for the emerging Palestinian state (including the territorial division between the West Bank and Gaza Strip), Botiveau seeks to explain the dynamics behind the 'quest for legal homogenization' discernible in different sectors of society as well as at the level of the governing authorities, as a process involving shared central values expressed as 'the quest for the formulation of a Palestinian identity'.[50] This law-focussed quest inevitably interrogates the place of *shari'a* in such formulation. The *'ulama*-political authority dynamic may be discerned in the vigour with which the *Qadi al-Quda* pressed ahead in developing the infrastructure of the three 'Islamic agencies' in governance, most particularly the *shari'a* courts, which he describes as 'a basic pillar of governance in Islam',[51] as well as the engagement with the arguments around Islamic law as a source of Palestinian legislation in general and the substance of personal status law in particular. Here, the fact that the *shari'a* courts are perceived as something of a legal and cultural constant despite the vicissitudes of political authority in the last century is emphasised in an association of the *shar'i* system with an explicitly articulated national Palestinian identity and cultural heritage as a feature of the claims for its place in the future Palestinian state. In these claims, the 'rootedness' of the *shar'i* system both in terms of time and in terms of its presentation as 'indigenous' is held up for comparison, at least, with the statute court system and laws 'imported' from the West as of the nineteenth century.

On the other hand, more recent Palestinian history has occasioned participation by a range of non-state actors in what Botiveau calls 'regulatory activities' in the 'non-state legal field'.[52] During the direct Israeli occupation, Palestinian non-governmental organisations played highly significant roles in this regard, and in the transitional period they mobilised major efforts around the dissemination and discussion of various pieces of proposed Palestinian legislation and mounted campaign and advocacy efforts in support of particular goals. In the case of the draft Basic Law, which brought up the issue of the place of *shari'a* as a source of Palestinian legislation, a broad range of NGOs from diverse sectors participated in the public debate, with human rights organisations getting involved in drafting alternatives. In the case of personal status law, the main NGO actors have been women's rights groups. These groups brought different arguments to bear in their claims for the ear of both society and the political authority in articulating the 'national identity' and the shape of the future state. These included norms drawn from international human rights law, the non-discrimination undertaking in the 1988 Palestinian Declaration of Independence, and, in the case of an individual text discussed below, the demonstration of 'national unity' through the unification of the court system and the end of separate communal laws.

On the specific subject of personal status law, although no 'legislation' marked the transitional period, a heated public debate that began in 1998 took the discussion beyond the *shar'i* judiciary, where the *Qadi al-Quda* had announced his intention to unify the laws in the West Bank and Gaza, and beyond the women's movement where a series of activities in the NGO sector had led up to the final debating sessions convened by the Model Parliament: Women and Legislation project. Although this project had been preceded by a number of meetings and conferences at which personal status law had been discussed, none had provoked the responses that were directed at the Model Parliament, or had the same impact in focussing public debate on the issues at stake. Questions that were posed in the context of the debate included not only particular positions to be adopted in the text of a future Palestinian law of personal status, but whether the law should not only be unified geographically but should also apply to all citizens (i.e. of whatever religion), what should be the sources from which it should be drawn and the principles by which it should be bounded.

By that time, however, the *Qadi al-Quda* and subsequently his Deputy had paid sustained attention to 'institution-building' within the putative Palestinian state, including the level and staffing of senior appointments and the expansion and upgrading of the *shar'i* judiciary and staff of the *shari'a* courts. These efforts met with a positive response from the executive and clearly presumed the continuation of the separate communal jurisdiction of the *shari'a* courts in a future state. Further commitments in this direction were elicited during the transitional period from the executive and from the Palestinian Legislative Council (PLC) in the form of draft 'constitutional' texts which, although not passed yet into 'law', must be seen both as indicative of a consensus in the current legislature, with the accord of the executive, and as setting the broad framework for the constitution of the Palestinian State.[53]

'CONSTITUTIONAL' TEXTS

The draft Basic Law, a sort of draft interim constitution, attracted wide-ranging discussions in Palestinian civil society as of 1994, particularly on the guarantee of human rights and the rule of law, and the structuring of relations between the executive, legislative and judicial authorities. It was widely seen as not only vital for the transitional period but as indicative of things to come in a future Palestinian state, and it proved highly contentious for the executive: despite passing its third reading in the PLC it had still not received ratification by President Arafat by the formal end of the interim period in 1999.

Commenting on the extensive public debates on the suggested text that he had originally presented in 1994, the main drafter noted that women's organisations had raised questions to do with personal status issues, but that 'it was explained and accepted that a basic law was not the place for such subjects and that that had to be attended to in special legislation'. In similar vein he explained the absence, in his draft texts, of any reference to the place of *shari'a* in the Palestinian legislative process:

> It has been the regular practice in the Arab states to declare that Islam is the religion of the state and *shari'a* the main source or a source of its legislation. Within the Palestinian community, there are various trends on the subject: the secular, the modernist and the fundamentalist. It was thought that such an issue should be decided upon in an atmosphere of freedom when the time comes for the preparation of a permanent constitution.[54]

However, right at the beginning of this process, in June 1994, the man subsequently appointed *Qadi al-Quda*, Shaykh Abu Sardane, presented to Yasser Arafat and other senior PLO members a memorandum, emphasising, as noted above, the need for explicit mention of the three 'Islamic agencies' (*shar'i* adjudication, *ifta* and a Ministry of *Awqaf*). He reports that a decision was taken to implement his recommendations, and indeed by the end of that year the separate administration of the *shari'a* courts had been established under his direction, a 'state' *Mufti* ('of Jerusalem and the Palestinian lands') had been appointed to head a Council of *Ifta*, and a Minister of *Awqaf* had taken up office.[55]

Predictably, when the PLC published its own draft version of the Basic Law in the summer of 1996, and began discussions of it in plenary, the place of *shari'a* gave rise to impassioned interventions.[56] The published discussions revolved around the role of Islam and whether the *shari'a* – or 'the principles of *shari'a*' – were to be 'a source', 'a principal source' or 'the principal source' of legislation. Al-Qasem's cautious position regarding the timing of legislating on such issues was overturned, and by the time of its third reading the draft Basic Law included the provision that 'the principles of the Islamic *shari'a* are a principal source of legislation'.

In addition, Article 92(1) of the draft Basic law provided that 'matters of personal status are to be dealt with by the *shari'a* and religious courts in accordance with the law'. The following year this article was relied upon by the *shar'i* judiciary in a further argument over legal drafting. In 1997 Shaykh Abu Sardane had left for Amman, and his deputy Shaykh Taysir Tamimi[57] has led efforts to assert the role of the *shar'i* system in debates over draft legislation, including a memorandum to the PLC's Legal Committee objecting to the omission, in the text of a draft Law Regulating the Judicial Authority, of any mention of the *shar'i* judiciary.[58] In an ensuing meeting between members of the *shar'i* judiciary and members of the Legal Committee, the press reported that it was agreed that 'not mentioning the *shar'i* judiciary was an oversight'. For his part, Tamimi reportedly declared that the draft Judicial Authority Law was unconstitutional as a result of the omission, and himself presented to the Committee a draft Law of Establishment of *Shari'a* Courts in Palestine. He described 'the attempt to wipe out the *shari'a* courts' as 'aimed at dealing a blow to our national struggle and our historical battle with those who deny our rights'. He also called on the PLC to 'rely on the Islamic *shari'a* as the sole source of legislation'. Although the PLC had already declined to take that particular wording on the source of legislation in Palestine, members of the *shar'i* judiciary thus worked in the transitional period to set out and as far as possible secure their position both on *shari'a* input into substantive law and the continuation of the *shari'a* court system to apply it.

THE 'MODEL PARLIAMENT'

For its part, against a background of advocacy efforts from the beginning of the transitional period, the women's movement organised a series of high-profile and wide-ranging activities in the West Bank and Gaza in the spring of 1998 in the framework of the Model Parliament, including the dissemination of texts associated with the project. The Model Parliament was organised by a non-governmental women's organisation, the Women's Centre for Legal Aid and Counselling (WCLAC), with support and participation from a number of other groups. The project ran for a period of two years in an effort to identify in all areas of existing law those provisions discriminatory to women's rights and to draft, debate and build consensus on proposed amendments to those provisions, to be forwarded for the attention of the PLC. A independent study by lawyer and human rights activist Asma Khadr published by WCLAC in the lead-up to the final sessions of the Model Parliament in the West Bank and Gaza, and a set of draft proposals for modifications to personal status law drawn up by Karem Nashwan for discussion in the Gaza final session, received particular attention in the press and in meeting halls.[59] The two different texts nod towards the rifts noted by Glenn Robinson between the West Bank and Gaza legal communities over matters of legal unification; although there is not, in matters *shar'i*, such considerable differences as exist between the common law tradition in Gaza and the 'continental' system of Jordan in the West Bank, suggestions that Palestinian personal status law should more or less follow the Jordanian model[60] might feed into the resentment he notes on the part of Gazans at 'the traditional focus on the West Bank at their expense'.[61]

Khadr's study reviewed a range of legislative texts with a view to identifying provisions and positions discriminatory towards women and proposing alternative texts, in some cases giving more than one option for amendment. As her optimal system, Khadr argued for reliance on human rights principles, including gender equality (and the incorporation of these principles in domestic law), with an explicit constitutional text on the plurality of sources of legislation. She then set out the case for a unified civil law system, including the principle of 'the rule of legal and judicial uniformity' apparent in all other spheres of the law, and the need for 'legislative harmony'. She held that the current system of communal jurisdictions 'violates the principle of legitimacy' since, if continued in a Palestinian state, non-elected authorities with no constitutional status would be setting laws for part of the population – i.e. the personal status laws for non-Muslims. Although she acknowledged the Islamic *shari'a* – along with international law – as among the 'authoritative frameworks/sources' (*marja'iyyat*) for Palestinian legislation, she took on the religious court system directly, by arguing that optimally a unified civil code embodying the principle of gender equality should regulate family affairs for all Palestinians regardless of religion, and that the religious authorities should maintain a guiding and counselling role but no longer have a legislative or judicial role in personal status matters. Her specific proposal was that the civil authorities should be responsible for the registration of marriage contracts and other such transactions, and that disputes on family law should be heard in the regular court system 'which could annex a specialised family law chamber, which in its turn could hear judges from the religious courts appointed in accordance with the law' – here she gave Egypt as an example. Khadr conceded that this would need time and effort and would necessarily affect the powers and functions of the religious authorities, but insisted on the principle of gender equality as the basic authoritative principle in reformulating family law, and offered certain suggestions in regard to personal status law until such time as her preferred goal might be realised.[62]

Khadr prefaced her specific proposals on personal status law with the requirement that if the present system were to continue, the legislature must rely on the range of *fiqh* schools and opinions, must 'open the gate of *ijtihad*' and that at least one third of any committees working on drafting family or personal status law should be women. Her proposed amendments addressed *inter alia* raising the age of marriage, and increasing the criminal penalties for breaking the rules on conclusion and registration of the contract.[63] More controversially, she proposed that documentation and registration of the contract be a 'condition of conclusion of the marriage',[64] thus suggesting the invalidation of unregistered marriages, and added a complicated suggestion on guardianship in marriage that recognised the concerns of parents, seeking to make that 'space' for their view in law that is generally recognised in Palestinian society, but without conceding the principle of legal capacity of the individual or accommodating gender discrimination.[65] In the areas of maintenance and divorce,[66] her proposals took on core issues in the 'traditional' *fiqh* rules still reflected in the law applying in the West Bank and in

Gaza: the validity of extra-judicial *talaq*, non-recognition of an assumption of injury in the event of a polygynous marriage, and the 'maintenance-obedience' equation regulating the spousal relationship. All these issues have of course been debated elsewhere in the region; with variations, they have been targets of the women's movements in other countries, and in some cases they have been approached in legislation, but Jordan currently has no legislation in place substantially amending the traditional positions, and the rather complicated rules in place in Egypt – from early legislation in regard to marriage, and more recently in regard to *talaq* – do not apply in the Gaza Strip.

In terms of both framework and of specific provisions, Khadr's work found a certain amount of resonance in Nashwan's document, which dealt only with personal status law. A similar emphasis was laid on the fact that the personal status laws being criticised are 'inherited laws' – i.e. not issued by Palestinians for Palestinians – and that a Palestinian law must conform to the spirit of the 1988 Declaration of Independence and to the guarantee of gender equality made in the draft Basic Law, as well as having regard for international human rights law. At the same time, the document proposed development of Muslim family law within its own framework, stating that the *shari'a* is a principal source of personal status law and claiming the space for interpretations of the sources beyond the classical rules to give substance to the principles of equality and justice: this, possibly, a suggestion of a 'postmodern', if very much textually focused, approach. The document did not propose a civil law, nor did it question the role of the *shari'a* (or other religious) courts.

The Model Parliament provoked a reaction far beyond that expected by those involved in the activities, ranging from denunciations of particular proposals to criticisms of the discussions taking place at all. Some of the reactions from individuals and groups identified broadly as 'Islamist' translated into personal attacks on women involved with the project – on their morals and their loyalty to the Palestinian national cause and their religious beliefs. The exercise was portrayed by some as a 'conspiracy' of hostile forces linking the UN, the EU and Israel; women leading the debates were portrayed as Westernised and removed from 'authentic' Palestinian society and values.[67] This response in turn provoked a counter-mobilisation of those defending the legitimacy of holding the debate; human rights organisations, the wider women's movement, political parties and members of the PLC lent their support, and the Ramallah final session in the West Bank was opened by the governor of Ramallah with a message from President Arafat.[68] It was clear to observers that many aspects of this battle in the press and other public fora owed as much to strictly political maneuvering as to strong reactions on issues of personal status. Hammami and Johnson, for example, note a 'strong sense that the parliament had posed a challenge to the Islamic social vision, which Palestinian nationalist factions had failed to mount', accounting at least in part both for the reaction from 'Islamist' groups and individuals and the counter-reaction from others, including the Palestinian Authority.[69]

For its part, the *shar'i* judiciary as an institution cannot be identified with the more political attacks on the Model Parliament and its organisers. Hammami and Johnson consider an intervention by a judge from the *Shari'a* Court of Appeal in the Parliament's Nablus meeting on personal status as 'the spark that touched off the larger Islamist attack on the model parliament and the women's movement'.[70] A memorandum to the Speaker and Members of the PLC signed by eleven *shari'a* court judges and about seventy other *'ulama* associated with the *shar'i* establishment objected to a number of specific proposals under discussion as well as to Khadr's suggestion that the *shari'a* courts – as the memorandum paraphrased it – be abolished. As the political debate heated up, however, leading figures in the *shar'i* judiciary distanced themselves.[71] The *Mufti* of Jerusalem, agreeing with the need to amend the existing personal status law, declared that there was 'nothing wrong if the Model Parliament presents its suggestions to the Department of the *Qadi al-Quda*' on the basis that the Department would be drafting a proposed law and sending it to the PLC: the concern of the *shar'i* judiciary, according to the *Mufti*, was that non-specialists (i.e. in the *shari'a*) would pass a 'raw' text to the legislature for approval.[72]

This insistence on the adequate qualification of anyone involved in drafting a personal status law for consideration by the legislature was a constant theme from members of the *shar'i* establishment as it responded to these non-state actors: in effect it might be read as a defence of the territory so far preserved by the *'ulama* in relation to both state and society. One interview with Shaykh Tamimi was headed with the summary: 'Humans may not try to prohibit what Allah has permitted: the scholars of *shari'a* and the PLC members are the only parties empowered to set the law of personal status.'[73] In the interview, he conceded concerns on some of the matters being discussed while insisting that other suggestions were 'not *ijtihadi* matters' – i.e. not matters on which the established *fiqh* rules might be revisited or revised. The *shari'a* courts, he said, frequently found fathers trying to marry their daughters off below the minimum age of marriage, and while this was wrong, marriage after the age of puberty brought 'no injury' to males or females. He agreed with the need for some sort of legal mechanism to ensure that women did in fact receive their *shari'a*-assigned inheritance entitlement, while rejecting any idea of changing the rules on succession. Among the suggestions he dismissed as 'not *ijtihadi* matters' was marriage guardianship for females: he cited a *hadith* purporting to establish the need for the guardian, as well as concern for the vulnerability of women as prey to impious men. At the final West Bank session of the Model Parliament, the issue of guardianship was reported to have provoked an uproar, with Shaykh Tamimi, who attended the session, threatening to withdraw from the session *inter alia* on the grounds that a vote could not be taken on a matter covered by a *hadith*.

For the *shar'i* judiciary, the Model Parliament forced a clarification on the kind of personal status law they would envisage in Palestine, and gave direct impetus to a drafting process confined to the circle of *shar'i* scholars but by no means uninformed of the concerns articulated during this turbulent process. For those who were or became involved in the Model Parliament and/or other sectors of the women's movement, the reaction to the Parliament's activities forced a reflection on strategies and provoked a discussion on, among other things, the appropriate approach to *shari'a* in seeking a more egalitarian personal status conforming more closely to the principle of gender equality.

THE AFTERMATH

In direct response to the discussions at the Model Parliament, Shaykh Tamimi announced the establishment of a preparatory committee to work towards the drafting of a personal status law. The committee was to be made up of 'the elite, men of law and *ifta*, teachers and deans in religious studies and lawyers in the West Bank and Gaza Strip' and there were to be a number of sub-committees, 'among the most important of which is a woman's committee of those qualified to participate'. Tamimi described the motivation as a need to unify the West Bank/Gaza laws 'as a basic step in establishing the state and the principle of unified and inalienable Palestinian sovereignty'. The draft would be drawn from 'the Qur'an, the Sunna, and the recognised schools of *fiqh*' and all those with suggestions were invited to contact the Office of the *Qadi al-Quda*. It was announced that the committee would study other Arab and Islamic personal status laws, and would in time present a draft to the PLC's Legal Committee for discussions before presenting it to the PLC.[74]

A number of key phrases in the public statements by leading members of the *shar'i* judiciary are repeated in these announcements. First it might be noted that Shaykh Tamimi continues to assert the right (or interest) of the *shar'i* establishment (in the form of his committee) to draft and present a personal status law for the attention of the legislature, retaining in this projection a measure of *'ulama* control over the content of the law. Second is the linkage between matters *shar'i* and the process of state-building and the principle of national unity: here, the appeal is to pre-occupation and pre-European colonial history and the sense of continuity represented by the *shari'a* courts – a suggestion of 'authenticity' which is expressed directly in arguments about the nature of personal status law. Third, there is the insistence that persons working on drafting a personal status law are to be 'qualified'. The clear implication is that they should be qualified in *fiqh* and 'religious studies'. The status of the *shari'a* as the sole source of legislation for personal status issues is not open to discussion, any more than the future of the *shari'a* courts and the whole system built around them. Firm indications in the draft constitutional 'texts' for the Palestinian state, that communal jurisdiction over personal status matters is set to continue for the foreseeable future, put Palestinian personal status law solidly within the pattern of neighbouring Arab states.

Palestine also fits a pattern, however, in having an active and articulate women's movement seeking change and alternatives. In the Palestinian women's movement, differences in evaluation of the events of 1998 and the 'phenomenon' of the Model Parliament have led to a number of different strategies towards family law being proposed and pursued. These strategies range from in-depth work on reinterpretation of the *fiqh* sources to produce a radically new 'Muslim family law' (by persons outside the ranks of the established *'ulama*) to proposals for a unified personal status law that would include the *shari'a* as a principal source but would also draw on international human rights principles.

A further proposal that has been discussed in this forum is the promulgation of an optional civil code under which those who chose to do so could marry and regulate their family affairs outside the religious court system. The early indications – from before the Model Parliament – are that such a proposal would be vigorously opposed by the *shar'i* establishment. In the meantime, Deputy *Qadi al-Quda* Shaykh Tamimi responded to certain practical concerns articulated in the 'texts' associated with the Model Parliament and with the surrounding discussions through a series of administrative directives to the *qadi*s and other officials in the *shari'a* courts. These have included an attempt to tighten up registration procedures for marriage and for the division by the *shari'a* courts of inheritance portions between the various heirs to an estate (implicitly with a view to protecting the rights of female heirs).[75] Although such moves are piecemeal, they do respond to real and practical concerns identified by lawyers working in the *shari'a* court system as well as by sectors of the women's movement, and thus illustrate a certain give and take between these sectors of civil society and the *shar'i* establishment. Responding to such concerns poses no perceived risks to the integrity of the *shar'i* system, nor does it implicate the substantive law it applies; rather, it serves to demonstrate the extent of flexibility that the *shar'i* system retains during this transitional period.

CONCLUDING COMMENT

Muslim Palestinian society would seem at the moment to be relatively supportive of the *shari'a* court system (in general) and the continued regulation of family relationships by *fiqh*-based law (again, in general). A 1999 survey found a vast majority of women in support of *shari'a*-based personal status law; a broader based one the following year found 76 per cent of men and women respondents opposed to an optional civil law, while a majority supported the principle of unification and reform of the existing personal status laws in light of changes and needs in Palestinian society. This latter survey also demonstrates changes in attitudes since the beginning of the transitional period, possibly as a result of heightened awareness of these issues after the events described in this paper.[76] The lobbying activities of the women's movement and associated civil society actors, and on the other hand of the *shar'i* judiciary, as well as of interested political parties (particularly the 'Islamist' tendencies) and the wider public response to further debate on the issues as mapped by such surveys are all likely to have an impact on the conduct of both the executive and the legislature in considering a future Palestinian law of personal status, as much as on the substance of such law.

In this transitional period, the field is more active and diverse than it has ever been. The current dynamics of the state-religion-society triangle illustrate vividly the interplays of appeals to different authorities, and different expectations of the role that is to be played by state-issued law in Palestine. The dynamics include the establishment *'ulama*, who perceive themselves as in some ways the guardians of the sacred law; thus for example the PA-established *Fatwa* Supreme Council has issued opinions on critical issues of personal status law, with reference to the traditional *fiqh* sources rather than to existing codifications of personal status law, as well as on areas of conduct not covered by state-implemented *shari'a*, such as the drinking of alcohol-free beer. The voice of the establishment *'ulama* on 'formal *shari'a*' does not go unchallenged, and their own appeals to the putative state authorities reflect a solid recognition of the latter's significance in the reformulation, for application by the courts, of some of the term of the *shari'a*. Explicitly comparative efforts are made to seek models appropriate for Palestine in the laws of Arab and other states, including the cooption of lawyers from those states to explain the process, pitfalls and legal challenges of their own efforts at legislative reform: the Model Parliament, for example, sought the expertise of scholars from Morocco and Tunisia. Add to this the West Bank/Gaza debate, and the fact that it was the British Mandate power that declined to include non-Muslims in the original Ottoman-issued family law, and the picture opens even further. As a state-to-be preparing its legal system, Palestine clearly warrants the attention of scholars of comparative law. As for the *shari'a* within that system, not only do the factors indicated in this overview fully justify Buskens' exhortation to a comparative perspective with other manifestations of the relationship of Islamic law and the state, but, arguably, they merit the inclusion of 'Islamic law' as a mainstream site of comparative law, rather than its exemption as the 'other' system of 'religious law'. The boundaries between state-implemented *shari'a* and *shari'a* that falls outside the formal legal system are an important crux of the state-*'ulama*-society relationship. In the meantime, the field of *shari'a* not implemented by the formal legal system provides another source of normative authority for those who seek to understand and comply with its terms.

NOTES

1 My thanks to Andrew Harding, Andrew Huxley and Leila Othman Asser for their comments.

2 Léon Buskens, 'An Islamic Triangle: Changing Relationships between *Shari'a*, State Law, and Local Customs' extracted in *International Institute for the Study of Islam in the Modern World Newsletter* 5: 8 (June 2000).

3 Werner Menski, *Comparative law in a global context: The legal systems of Asia and Africa* (London: Platinium Publishing, 2000), 287.

4 Non-establishment interpreters might in this pattern be better classified among social reform movements.

5 B. Botiveau, 'Palestinian Law: Social Segmentation Versus Centralization' 73–88 of
   ed. Dupret *et al. Legal Pluralism in the Arab World* (The Hague: Kluwer, 1999), 77.
6 Here to be taken as referring to the Palestinian West Bank, including East Jerusalem,
   and Gaza Strip; where reference is made to Mandatory Palestine this includes the
   entire original territory of Palestine before the creation of the Israeli state in 1948.
7 Jerusalem was conquered by the Muslim Arab forces in 638 under the leadership of
   'Umar Ibn al-Khattab, the second successor (Caliph) to the Prophet Muhammad's
   political authority for the Sunni community.
8 For a rigorous examination of the legal content of these agreements, see Raja Shehadeh,
   From Occupation to Interim Accords: Israel and the Palestinian Territories (The
   Hague: Kluwer Law International, 1997).
9 The year of the emigration (*hijra*) from Mecca to Medina and the establishment in the
   latter of the first Muslim polity in 622 CE is the first year of the Muslim calendar.
10 A 'vulgate' of the Qur'an had been collected by 656 CE; the authoritative bodies of
   Sunni *hadith* are contained in collections dating from the late ninth century CE.
11 W. Hallaq, *A History of Islamic Legal Theories: An Introduction to Sunni usul al-fiqh*
   (Cambridge: Cambridge University Press, 1997), 1.
12 This is the preferred term of Noel Coulson in his classic, if now somewhat dated,
   History of Islamic Law (Edinburgh: Edinburgh University Press, 1964). Marshall G.S.
   Hodgson uses 'piety-minded' as well as the more general *'ulama* (the learned, the scholar
   class) in *The Venture of Islam* Vol. I (Chicago: University of Chicago Press, 1974).
13 F. Vogel, 'The Closing of the Door of *Ijtihad* and the Application of the Law' *American
   Journal of Islamic Social Sciences* 10: 396–401 (1993), 397.
14 Buskens uses this in reference to certain Indonesian intellectuals. One might apply the
   same term to thinkers such as Abdullahi An-Na'im who used the expression in the title
   of this current piece (to effect that in thinking about Islamic law at present, we are all
   'stuck with the state') in his presentation 'The *Shari'a* and Positive Legislation: Is An
   Islamic State Possible or Viable?' originally given as the 1998 Noel Coulson memorial
   Lecture at SOAS and subsequently published in *Yearbook of Islamic and Middle Eastern
   Law*, 5: 29–41 (1998–1999).
15 His comment was specifically referring to family law: J. Esposito, *Women in Muslim
   Family Law* (Syracuse: Syracuse University Press, 1982), 15.
16 See for example Esposito, *supra* note 15, at 24–25.
17 L. Welchman, *Beyond the Code: Muslim Family Law and the Shar'i Judiciary in the
   Palestinian West Bank* (The Hague: Kluwer Law International, 2000), 137–139. See
   also A. Moors, *Women, Property and Islam: Palestinian Experiences, 1920–1990*
   (Cambridge: Cambridge University Press, 1995), 96–99.
18 H. Gerber, *State, Society and Law in Islam: Ottoman Law in Comparative Perspective*
   (Albany: State University of New York Press, 1994), 31, examining court records from
   Burqa and Istanbul.
19 The textual evidence of all four Sunni schools for their positions on the various aspects
   of female capacity and marriage guardianship is set out in the twelfth century text of
   Ibn Rushd ('Averroes'), translated into English as: *The Distinguished Jurist's Primer*
   Vol. II, trans. I.A.K. Nyazee and M. Abdul Rauf (Reading: Garnet Publishing, 1996),
   1–15.
20 Coulson, *supra* note 12, at 30.
21 The Hanafi and Maliki schools, respectively successors to the tradition of the early
   scholars in Iraq and Medina; and the later Shafi'i and Hanbali schools.
22 Suitability of the groom in this sense was to be assessed by a set of social, economic
   and religious criteria defined relative to the bride and her male family members. See:
   F. Ziadeh, 'Equality (*Kafa'ah*) in the Muslim Law of Marriage,' *American Journal of
   Comparative Law* 6: 503–517 (1957); and M. Siddiqui, 'Law and the Desire for Social

Control: An Insight into the Hanafi Concept of *Kafa'a*' 49–68 of ed. M. Yamani *Feminism and Islam* (London: Ithaca Press, 1996).

23 C. Imber, *Ebu's-su'ud: The Islamic Legal Tradition* (Edinburgh: Edinburgh University Press, 1997), 167–169.

24 J. Tucker, *In the House of the Law: Gender and Islamic Law in Syria and Palestine, 17–18th Centuries* (Berkeley: University of California Press, 1998), 50–51.

25 R. Hammami, 'Women in Palestinian Society', 283–311 of ed. M. Heiberg and G. Ovensen *Palestinian Society in Gaza, West Bank and Arab Jerusalem: A Survey of Living Conditions* OSLO FAFO REPORT 151 (1993), 293, table 10.6. See Welchman, *supra* note 17, at 121–133.

26 Imber, *supra* note 23, at 24.

27 See B. Messick, *The Calligraphic State: Textual Domination and History in a Muslim Society* (Berkeley: California University Press, 1993), 55–66, on the 'newly-discovered obscurity of the *fiqh* texts'.

28 It was accompanied by a Law of *Shar'i* Procedure.

29 Messick, *supra* note 27, at 57.

30 On *takhayyur* as a method of legal reform, see J.N.D. Anderson, *Law Reform in the Muslim World* (London: The Athlone Press, 1976), 47–58. Hallaq criticises this method for its lack of 'any type of cohesive legal methodology': Hallaq, *supra* note 11, at 211.

31 Coulson, *supra* note 12, at 202, refers to this as 'neo-*ijtihad*'; Hallaq, *supra* note 11, at 211 uses the term 'quasi-*ijtihad*'.

32 In practice some of the Christian sects had been applying *shari'a* law, particularly in succession: F.M. Goadby, *International and Inter-Religious Private Law in Palestine* (Jerusalem: Hamadpis Press, 1926), 119, notes the practical difficulties faced some of the smaller communities who 'either do not possess any traditional law of succession or guardianship, or, if such law did exist, it has fallen into oblivion in Palestine.'

33 J.N.D. Anderson and N. Coulson, 'Islamic Law in Contemporary Cultural Change', *Saeculum* 18: 13–92 (1967), 39.

34 Messick, *supra* note 27, at 62.

35 M.H. Abu Sardane, *Al-qada' ash-shar'i fi 'ahd as-sulta al-wataniyya al-filastiniyya* (The *shar'i* judiciary under the Palestinian National Authority) (Gaza, n.d.), 45.

36 Abu Sardane, *supra* note 35, at 52, 93.

37 N. Brown, '*Shari'a* and State in the Modern Muslim Middle East' *International Journal of Middle East Studies* 29: 359–376 (1997), 370.

38 In the section entitled 'The Judiciary', Article 99.

39 Articles 103(2) and 105 of the Constitution.

40 The *Shari'a* Appeal Court was convened in East Jerusalem after the Israeli occupation, since the Amman court was no long accessible from the West Bank. See further: Welchman, *supra* note 17, at 51–76.

41 Law of *Shar'i* Procedure no.31/1959.

42 Brown, *supra* note 37, at 370; and see N. Safran, 'The Abolition of the *shari'a* Courts in Egypt' *Muslim World* 48: 20–28 and 125–135 (1958).

43 From 1962 this legislation was passed by a Legislative Council and approved by the Governor General, in accordance with a Basic Law issued for the Gaza Strip by the Egyptian Prime Minister. Shehadeh, *supra* note 8, at 77.

44 For a comparison of the JLFR provisions with those of the 1976 Jordanian Law of Personal Status see Welchman, 'The Development of Islamic Family Law in the Legal System of Jordan', *International and Comparative Law Quarterly* 37: 868–886 (1988).

45 See Shehadeh, *Occupier's Law: Israel and the West Bank* (Washington: Institute for Palestine Studies, 1988) for an account of the legal changes enacted by the Israeli occupation authorities through military orders after the 1967 occupation.

46 See further Welchman, *supra* note 17, at 51–75.
47 Abu Sardane, *supra* note 35, at 247; M. Dumper, *Islam and Israel: Muslim Religious Endowments and the Jewish State* (Washington: Institute for Palestine Studies, 1994), 92.
48 Published in the *Palestine Official Gazette (Al-waqa'i' al-filastiniyya)* no. 35 6/15/54 as Order no. 303 of 1954.
49 See Welchman, *supra* note 17, at 10–15.
50 Botiveau, *supra* note 5, at 84.
51 Abu Sardane, *supra* note 35, at 46.
52 Botiveau, *supra* note 5, at 79–86.
53 A draft of a Temporary Constitution for promulgation by the Palestine National Council (as compared to the Basic Law passed by the Palestinian Legislative Council, see below) had been drawn up by the summer of 2000.
54 A. Al-Qasem, 'Commentary on the Draft Basic Law for the Palestinian National Authority in the Transitional Period,' *Palestine Yearbook of International Law* IV: 187–211 (1992–1994), 198.
55 Abu Sardane, *supra* note 35, at 42–51.
56 *Al-Quds*, 9 June, 1996, reported 'heated discussions' on this topic in the PLC during the first reading of the draft Basic Law.
57 A. Bakri, *'Al-ab'ad al-qanuniyya wa'l-idariyya wa'l-taghyirat 'ala al-mahakim ash-shar'iyya fi filastin 1995–2000* (legal and administrative measures and changes to the *shari'a* courts in Palestine 1995–2000), Working Paper for the Comparative Islamic Law Project at Birzeit University's Women's Studies Centre, 2000, 17.
58 The original draft is published by the Palestinian Independent Commission for Citizens' Rights *in Mashru' qanun as-sulta al-qada'iyya – dirasat wa mulahizhat naqdiyya* (Ramallah: PICCR) 1998, 53–74. Reports of the intervention in *al-Quds*, 9 and 10 June, 1998.
59 A. Khadr, *Al-qanun wa mustaqbil al-mar'a al-filastiniyya* (Law and the future of Palestinian women), (Jerusalem: Women's Centre for Legal Aid and Counselling, 1998); K. Nashwan, *Muswada maqtadayat li-qanun al-ahwal ash-shakhsiyya al-muwahad* (Draft requirements for a unified law of personal status) (Gaza: discussion paper for the Palestinian Model Parliament: Women and Legislation, 1998).
60 As implied by Abu Sardane, *supra* note 35, at 49; and interviewed in *al-Quds* 14 July, 1994 and *al-Hayat al-Jadida* 26 January, 1996.
61 G.E. Robinson, 'The Politics of Legal Reform in Palestine,' *Journal of Palestine Studies* XXVII: 51–60 (1997), at 54–57.
62 Khadr, *supra* note 59, at 119–124.
63 Khadr, *supra* note 59, at 201; she proposed the same in regard to registration of *talaq*.
64 id., at 133.
65 id., at 134–135.
66 id., at 141–143.
67 *Al-Masar*, 25 May, 1998; *al-Ayyam*, 30 March, 1998; *Al-Ahram Weekly*, 2–8 April, 1998; *Palestine Report*, 20 March, 1998.
68 *Al-Quds*, 30 March, 1998; R. Hammami and P. Johnson, 'Equality with a Difference: Gender and Citizenship in Transitional Palestine' *Social Politics*, Fall 1999, 315–343, 334.
69 id., at 335. N.I. Sa'id in *al-Ayyam*, 15 March, 1998.
70 Hammami and Johnson, *supra* note 68, at 332. Report of his intervention in *ar-Risala*, 5 March, 1998 and *al-H.ayat al-Jadida*, 14 March, 1998.
71 Including the said judge: Hammami and Johnson, *supra* note 68, at 336.
72 *Al-Ayyam*, 14 March, 1998.
73 *Al-Quds*, 8 March, 1998.
74 *Al-Quds*, 2, 5 and 14 April, 1998; *al-Hayat al-Jadida*, 1 May, 1998; *al-Ayyam*, 4 April, 1998.

75 Administrative directives 15/481 15 April, 2000; 15/1358 11 November, 2000; 15/1366 12 September, 2000; texts annexed to Bakri, *supra* note 57.

76 These are, necessarily, simplifications of the detailed breakdowns and analyses presented in the two surveys. The 1999 survey was the work of the Palestinian Working Women's Society and the Jerusalem Media and Communications Centre; the 2000 survey was carried out under the auspices of the Comparative Islamic Law project at the Women's Studies Centre of Birzeit University in the West Bank and is broken down by region and gender of respondents: Rema Hammami, 'Attitudes Towards Reform of Personal Status Law in Palestine', forthcoming.

6

LAW AND RELIGION IN EARLY CHINA

Randall Peerenboom

The Prevailing Majority View is that religion exerted only a minimal influence on law in China. Representative of the majority position, Bodde asserts that whereas in many civilizations laws were attributed to divine origin, in striking contrast 'no one at any time has ever hinted that any kind of written law – even the best written law – could have divine origin' in China.[1] By the time law appeared, the gods and demigods of religious myths and stories had been historicized into the 'denatured sage-kings, heroes, or rebels of pseudo-history.'[2] Accordingly, 'when we turn to the legal sphere . . . the atmosphere is entirely secular.'[3] Law, moreover, was not used to uphold traditional religious values: 'Rather, its primary purpose was political: that of imposing tighter political controls upon a society which was then losing its old cultural values and being drawn by inexorable new forces along the long road leading eventually to universal empire.'[4]

Similarly, Joseph Needham argues that the development of law and science in China was inhibited in part by the lack of a transcendent religious source for laws and in particular an autochthonous supreme being. In many Western traditions, such as Islam and Judaism, natural law and the laws of nature often flow from the same source: a divine lawmaker who made laws for all things to obey. It was not permissible for human law to run contrary to divine law, including the God-given laws of nature. Needham denies, however, that 'the ideas of natural law (in the juristic sense) and of the laws of nature (in the sense of the natural sciences) go back to a common root' in China.[5] Reading Confucianism as a kind of natural law, Needham asserts that:

> In so far . . . as natural law came to be overwhelmingly dominant in China, and positive law reduced to a minimum, one would expect that so different a balance might have had important effects on the development of the formulation of the regularities of Nature in the natural sciences. . . . The stronger the role of natural law, the greater facility there might have been in conceiving of the Laws of Nature as a kind of inescapable natural *li*[6] in which the whole non-human world concurred.[7]

Unfortunately, claims Needham, early Chinese never developed an interest in the laws of nature. As a result, they failed to develop a theory of natural law based on the natural order and to develop scientifically.

In traditions where law is the product of a divine lawmaker or grounded in a transcendent religious order, law is (allegedly) sacrosanct. Lacking a divine origin, law in China was held in low esteem as a means of achieving social order, especially by Confucians. Confucius maintained that to rely solely or even predominantly on law to achieve social order was folly. Laws, backed up by punishments, may induce compliance in the external behavior of individuals, but they are powerless to transform the inner character of the members of society. Confucius' goal was not simply a stable political order in which everyone coexists in relative harmony and isolation from each other, with each afraid to interfere with the other for fear of legal punishment. Rather, Confucius set his sights considerably higher. He sought to achieve a harmonious social order in which each person is able to realize his or her full potential as a human being through mutually beneficial relations with others. Thus Confucius declares, 'Lead the people with government regulations and organize them with penal law (*xing*), and they will avoid punishments but will be without shame. Lead them with virtue and organize them through the *li*, and the people will have a sense of shame and moreover will become humane people of good character.'[8]

To be sure, Legalists among others believed that laws were necessary for effective governance. But while advocating the impartial application of publicly codified laws, law for the Legalists was simply a pragmatic tool for obtaining and maintaining political control and social order. According to the Legalists, people are self-interested. To avoid interpersonal conflict and achieve social order, people must be manipulated through a reliable and impartial system of rewards and punishments. Clear, codified, public law lets every person know what is expected and what the consequences will be of one's actions. In short, Legalist law was positive law, not natural law.

The amoral character of Legalism's positive law contributed to law's lowly status among many Chinese, who saw law as a necessary evil at best. Unable to forego law entirely, the imperial legal system beginning in the Han tempered the harsh positivism of Legalism through the infusion of Confucian values – a process suitably described as the Confucianization of law.[9] At the same time, Confucianism was 'legalized.' The imperial legal system, therefore, was primarily a synthesis of amoral, positivist Legalism and secular Confucianism. Thus, argues Needham, in the Han, 'law again became...firmly embedded in ethics, and successive emperors...justified their mandates by invoking natural law, i.e. norms of behavior universally considered moral – in fact – *li* – and not positive law.'[10] Bodde adds, 'The *li* derive their universal validity from the fact that they were created by the intelligent sages of antiquity in conformity with nature and with the cosmic order. [Positive] law has no moral validity because it is merely the ad hoc creation of modern men who wish by means of it to generate political power'.[11]

THE MINORITY DISSENT

In contrast to the standard view, some commentators suggest that religion exerted more influence on law than normally suggested. While agreeing that law was not derived from some divine lawmaker, Dennis Twitchett takes exception to the received account of China as a purely secular state:

> Law was a function of the state, and the state was believed to rule thanks to its possession of the mandate of Heaven, which in effect meant that a regime's legitimacy depended on its acceptance of a system of common ideals.... The exercise of power in China took place in a setting of complex symbols, rituals, and observances suffused with awe, all of which were prescribed by codified legislation and in the context of deeply held religious beliefs.[12]

Even the Legalist ruler ruled by virtue of Heaven's mandate. At some fundamental level, therefore, law remained tethered to moral and religious beliefs.

In a similar vein, Chang Wejen observes that *fa* or law was only one of many social norms in China.[13] Other norms included *dao* (conventionally translated as the Way), *de* (virtues), *li* (rites) and *xisu* (customs). While Daoist leaned heavily on *dao* and Legalists on *fa*, most early Chinese thinkers maintained that all of these various types of norms are necessary for social order. Moreover, adds Chang:

> most Chinese accepted the basically Confucian view that the various norms form a hierarchy, with the Way at the top, the law at the bottom, and others in between. When a lower norm was unclear or inadequate, it was to be interpreted or supplemented in accordance with the higher norms, and when a conflict existed between a higher and a lower norm, the higher one prevailed.[14]

In this view, *tian, dao* and even the Confucian *li* provided a general normative constraint on, and basis for, the legal system. Not only was the legitimacy of the legal system as a whole grounded in *tian, dao* and *li*, specific legal rules and decisions derived their legitimacy from them. To the extent that legal rules were inconsistent with these higher norms, legal rules gave way.

The intimate relation of law to a seemingly transcendent moral cum religious order was also reflected in the notion of cosmic harmony. A central and persisting tenet of much Chinese thinking is that the human world and natural world are interrelated and form an organic whole. Thus, the standard account holds that because 'the spheres of man and nature were inextricably interwoven to form an unbroken continuum,' violations of law in the Chinese world represented not just transgressions of the human social order but disruptions of 'the total cosmic order'.[15] The standard account's endorsement of the theory of cosmic harmony is, however, doubly paradoxical. On the one hand, it would seem to call into question the characterization of the legal system as wholly secular and the claim that religious beliefs had little impact on the legal system. On the other hand, the origins of the doctrine of the cosmic harmony are difficult to explain given the standard account's view that the legal system was primarily a synthesis of Legalism and Confucianism. As Bodde himself notes, such a concept could not have arisen from early Confucians because 'law to them was itself a violation of the social order. Nor could it have started with the Legalists, since these men used law quite consciously to destroy and remake the old social order.'[16] The classical Daoists – Lao Zi and Zhuang Zi – rejected codified law as a means of effecting social order. Who, then, was responsible for the naturalization of law? And how could such a theory develop if early Chinese were not interested in the laws of nature, as Needham claims?

When one turns from the origins of laws and regulations to their implementation, the line between law and morality becomes even fainter, raising further problems for the standard account. Indeed, according to Weber's criteria, Chinese law was hardly law at all. For Weber, the hallmark of a modern legal system is formal rationality.[17] In such a system, autonomous legal professionals decide cases according to distinctively legal criteria and methods, applying general legal principles to the facts in particular cases. In contrast, substantive rationality refers to a system in which particular cases are decided on the basis of general ethical, political or religious principles rather than legal principles and specific provisions of the legal codes. Given that the magistrates appeared to decide cases based on such general non-legal principles, China's imperial legal system seemed to be substantively rational at best.[18] Indeed, the standard account questions whether the system even merited the label of substantively rational. Confucius rejected heavy reliance on laws in part because they were too gross to allow for a more particularized justice. Thus, according to the standard view, magistrates and even more so the literati responsible for the informal mediation of disputes – trained as they were in the Confucian classics – allegedly determined what was best in a given situation based on their own judgment and interpretation of the *li* rather than by appeal to fixed standards or principles of general applicability, whether legal or nonlegal.[19] In Weber's terminology, such a system is nothing more than a kind of arbitrary or irrational kadi justice.[20]

In response to such arguments in support of the claim that there was a more intimate relation between religion and law than normally assumed, proponents of the standard account offer several counterarguments. They reconcile their claim that religion had little impact with the acknowledged Confucianization of law and the Confucian emphasis on particular and context-specific decision-making based on general nonlegal principles by arguing that Confucianism is not a religion. It is, however, somewhat more difficult to reconcile the notion of cosmic harmony and the role of *tian/dao/*the natural order in providing the normative basis for the legitimacy of the system. Some, such as Needham, simply deny that China developed a natural law system grounded in the laws of nature. Others, such as Bodde, who claim *pace* Needham that early Chinese did conceive of the laws of nature as determining both the cosmic and social order, nevertheless deny that *tian*/*dao*/the natural order are religious concepts. Still others claim that to the extent that they are religious or quasi-religious ideas or precepts, they did not have much impact on the actual operation of the legal system in that they were not reflected in significant measure in legal institutions, laws or the implementation of laws.[21]

ADOPTING A MIDDLE POSITION

I would like to take issue with certain aspects of both the standard portrait and the revisionist minority position. First, however, I will need to clarify some of the key terms. Whether it is appropriate to describe early Chinese law as religious law, and even if it is not, what the relationship between religion and law has been, depends on what one means by religious law, religion and law. Having clarified the terminology, I then take up specific ways in which religion may have influenced law, focusing on the issue of whether religion was a source of law in the sense that law was ultimately grounded in a religious order or sensibility. In particular, I consider the influence of *tian* and Confucian *li* on the legal system, and whether they are religious in nature.

I then turn to Huang-Lao, a late Warring States to Han school of thought that promotes a natural law in which the way of humans (*ren dao*) is predicated on and implicate in the normatively prior way of the natural order (*tian dao*). One of the problems with the majority position is that it is based on what was known about Chinese law before the recent discoveries of early legal texts, most notably the Huang-Lao Boshu (Silk Manuscripts of Huang-Lao), which was excavated from the tomb of a prince in Mawangdui in 1973. Some aspects of the standard account, such as Needham's assertion that early Chinese never developed a natural law theory based on the laws of nature, are no longer tenable in light of the recently discovered Huang-Lao Boshu. Yet whether the natural law of the Huang-Lao Boshu should be considered religious in nature is subject to debate, and will turn on one's definition of religion.

Finally, I consider the lasting impact of these various ideas on the legal system. How were Huang-Lao ideas about the relationship between the cosmic order and the human order reflected in the day to day operation of the legal system? To what extent did judges actually decide cases based on general moral and/or religious principles? Here, my view merges with the standard account in arguing that the enduring practical impact, particularly of Huang-Lao natural law ideas, was minimal. Moreover, while Confucian *li*/rites were incorporated into law, allegations of rampant discretionary reliance by magistrates on extra-legal moral or religious principles appear to be somewhat overstated based on recent empirical studies of legal imperial era archives.

Terminology

The term 'religious law' conjures up images of a tradition where the formal legal system is based on a sacred text attributed to god or his disciples. In such a tradition, the sacred text would be directly justiciable in court. Parties would cite specific provisions of the text when making their arguments, and judges would rely on such provisions in deciding cases and justifying their decisions.

Of course, this view of a paradigmatic religious legal system is very narrow. First, the account of law is limited. The focus is primarily on the formal legal system, with an emphasis on rules, courts, the judicial decisionmaking process, and the legal effect of particular texts and provisions in specific cases. The interpretation of religion is equally restricted: a transcendent, anthropomorphic deity directly or indirectly lays down the law as set forth in sacred texts.

Both law and religion, however, are essentially contested concepts, and have been interpreted in myriad ways, many much broader than just stated. At minimum, law includes institutions, rules, practices, values and outcomes. On a broad reading, law may encompass informal institutions and methods for avoiding and resolving disputes as well as formal court-centered dispute resolution. Religion could play a different role in the informal and formal systems: the informal system could be religious in the sense that priests, rabbis or other religious leaders resolve disputes by appealing to a sacred text while the formal legal system is entirely positivist in nature, with references to a sacred text considered out of bounds. Moreover, law serves many purposes other than dispute resolution. Part of its value lies in the creation of norms, standards and practices that will reduce disputes in the first place. Many of the norms of the formal legal system may be derived directly or indirectly from religious values. Religious values may also complement the formal legal system by creating an additional set of norms above and beyond what is required by law. If so, religion may play an important role in guiding people's behavior even though litigants may not rely on religious texts or precepts in court.

Religion is equally open-ended. The legal scholar Harold Berman, who has spent much of his career writing about the interaction of law and religion, characterizes religion as 'people manifesting a collective concern for the ultimate meaning and purpose of life – it is a shared intuition of and commitment to transcendent values'.[22] In his view, law is 'a living process of allocating rights and duties and thereby resolving conflicts and creating channels of cooperation.'[23] As for the relation between them, the legal system is connected to religion and the ultimate transcendent reality via rituals, traditions, authority and universality. Although at times in tension,[24] law and religion are on the whole complementary and interdependent; law gives religion its social dimension and prevents it from degenerating into religiosity, while religion gives law its spirit and normative direction 'as well as the sanctity it needs to command respect.'[25] Accordingly, says Berman, religious elements play an indispensable role in the effective working of law even in modern, technologically advanced countries such as the United States.

Although religion for Berman does not require an anthropomorphic deity, it does entail some form of transcendence. Yet not all religions are other worldly or have a transcendent dimension. Ultimate meaning and value may lie in an immanent and holistic natural order or be derived from self-generated social practices.[26] In either case, an individual is able to achieve self-realization and fulfillment through integration with the whole. Religion binds members of the faith or society together through their common beliefs, rituals and practices, leading – ideally – to social and cosmic harmony. Thus, religion may be defined in various ways, including in terms of transcendence, ultimate meaning or the binding function or character of beliefs and practices.

In light of these broader understandings of law and religion, we can distinguish at least four ways in which law and religion interact. First, religion could be the source of law in the narrow sense that all laws are derived from religious texts handed down directly or indirectly from god and directly justiciable in state courts.

Second, and more nebulously, religion may provide a general normative foundation for legal institutions, rules, practices and outcomes, as suggested by Berman. Thus, the legitimacy of the legal system as a whole and particular institutions, rules and practices may require that the system or institutions, rules and practices be seen as complying with god's will, the social practices of a particular religion (e.g., the Confucian *li*, assuming there is a religious dimension to them) or a spontaneous, atheistic natural order (*tian*, *dao*, *tiandao*).

Third, specific legal rules, principles, practices or even institutions may incorporate or reflect religious ideals, values, practices and norms, though litigants may not appeal directly to religion. Thus, for instance, the law of the state may punish adultery or eating meat on Fridays because these acts are at odds with analogous religious tenets. In comparison to legal rules, legal principles exhibit a higher degree of abstraction. Thus, for example, the legal system in a Buddhist state might seek to uphold the principle of protecting all forms of life because Buddhism assigns great importance to the taking of life, even nonhuman life. As for practices and institutions, a legal system might give great powers to the ruler to decree law, decide cases and issue amnesties because the ruler is conceived of as the son of heaven and thought to rule by virtue of heaven's mandate. In contrast to the first category, however, religious texts are not directly justiciable; religious ideas, beliefs and tenets must be transformed into positive law by statute or practice before they have legal effect, at least in formal court proceedings. Thus, someone accusing another of adultery would base his or her claim on the law against adultery rather than the religious principle prohibiting it. Moreover, although there will be some overlap between religious tenets and positivist law, many legal institutions, laws and practices will not be traceable to any specific religious source.

Fourth, the legal system may contain provisions relating to religion. For instance, there may be laws protecting, prohibiting or limiting certain religious practices.

The term religious law clearly applies to the first category. Arguably, it could also apply to the second and third category as well, though if religion is interpreted very broadly, most legal systems would then be considered religious legal systems, depriving the term of any explanatory value. For instance, an expansive interpretation of religion in terms of ultimate meaning, or one that collapses the distinction between religion and morality, would result in all legal systems being considered religious legal systems as long as the legitimacy of the system or particular institutions, rules or practices turns on their compliance with such broadly defined religious beliefs. Similarly, most if not all legal systems will have some rules that may be traced back to religious concerns. Put differently, if it is true, as Berman suggests, that religious elements play an indispensable role in every legal system, and any legal system with religious elements is considered a religious legal system, then all legal systems are religious legal systems. Ironically, even a socialist legal system that prohibited or limited religious practices would still be a religious legal system, because the metanarrative of Marxism-Leninism would provide ultimate meaning for the true believers and lend legitimacy to the legal system. Rather than becoming preoccupied with whether the early Chinese legal system may be characterized as a religious legal system, it may be more informative to focus on the particular ways in which certain ideas, beliefs and practices that might be considered religious in nature affected the legal system.

What, then, was the relationship between religion and early Chinese law through the Han period? The standard account is clearly correct in asserting that early Chinese law was not religious law in the sense that religious texts handed down from an anthropomorphic deity were directly justiciable in formal court proceedings. Just as clearly, religion had an impact in the third sense of legal rules and practices incorporating or reflecting religious ideals, values, practices and norms.[27] For instance, pre-Han and Han reliance on sworn oaths, animal slayings and the drinking of wine to create legal obligations had a religious origin.[28] Similarly, the influence of correlative cosmology and in particular yin yang five phases thinking is evident in laws limiting punishment to certain seasons and rules regarding amnesties.[29] To be sure, there may also have been secular justifications for some of the practices. For instance, covenants and oaths serve an evidentiary function and remind the parties that they are assuming obligations with potentially serious consequences. Over time, the secular dimensions may have assumed primary importance.[30] Moreover, in some cases rulers may have honored the religious cum legal principles in the breach or simply out of a pragmatic sense of expediency rather than a sincere belief in them.[31]

Apart from the incorporation of specific rules and practices reflecting religious ideas and beliefs, imperial Chinese legal codes contained laws relating to religion. In some cases, state laws conferred special privileges on religious sects or their individual members. For instance, a crime against a monk was punished more severely than the same crime against a lay person; conversely, monks who committed certain crimes were punished more heavily.[32] Indeed, the imperial legal system developed a special body of law for Buddhist and Daoist clergy.[33]

For the most part, however, the state sought to control religion by limiting the formation of religious sects, the spread of religious ideas and particular religious practices. There were rules, for example, against magical practices, prophecies and predictions; there were limits on heterodoxy; and private persons were prohibited from performing state religious rituals. The Chinese state's distrust of religion is still evident today in rules requiring that all religious organizations register with the state and that individuals carry out their religious practices at the registered sites of the state-recognized religions.

Such distrust is not without cause. Buddhism's introduction into China in the first century A.D. challenged directly the authority of the state. The *dharma* – with various meanings ranging from truth to law, virtue, righteousness or duty – represented an absolute authority other than the state or ruler.[34] Worse yet, Buddhists established monastic institutions, the *samgha*, governed by their own rules (*vinaya*) that took precedence over the laws of the state and even the Confucian concern for filial piety. Monks were expected to cut off ties with their family and the state.[35] Further, religious sects have been the source of social chaos from the Han uprisings by the popular Daoist Five Pecks of Rice and Yellow Turban groups to the White Lotus, Boxer and Taiping rebellions in the Qing.

Given the state's hostile attitude toward religious sects, it might seem unlikely that religion in China would play the more fundamental role suggested by Berman and some commentators; that is, that it would provide the normative ground for, and thus sanctify, the law. To what extent then was law grounded in and limited by *tian, dao* and the Confucian *li*?

Confucianism

Whether Confucianism is a religion has been endlessly debated. Some claim that Confucianism is not a religion because it lacks a deity, there is no accepted doctrine of salvation and it does not rely on sacred stories to aid propagation.[36] On the other hand, Confucius himself expressed a somewhat ambivalent view about the spirits, suggesting we should 'keep a distance from the gods and spirits while showing them due reverence.'[37] Moreover, though Confucius at times naturalized *tian*, treating it as the regular pattern of the cosmos, he also referred to *tian* in anthropomorphic terms, treating it as a personal god:[38]

> When Confucius was surrounded in K'uang, he said: 'Since King Wen has already passed away, does not culture thus reside here? If [*tian*] is going to destroy this culture, those who follow us will not be able to participate in it.' If [*tian*] is not going to destroy this culture, what can the people of K'uang do to me!'[39]

Furthermore, whether *tian* is anthropomorphized or treated as a natural force, some find in *tian* a transcendent dimension.[40] As Mou Tsung-san states,[41]

> the concept of [*tianming*, conventionally translated as the mandate of heaven] as expressed in its transcendent aspect has imperceptibly within

it an immutable, unchangeable standard which causes us to feel that under its sanction we must nor err or transgress at all in our conduct. To have a sense of [*tianming*], one must first have a sense of transcendence, a possibility only when one accepts the 'existence' of the transcendent.

Mou goes so far as to describe *tian* as 'a moral order which corresponds to "justice" in Greek philosophy'.[42] *Tian*, therefore, provides the normative foundation for the human order. Accordingly, the legitimacy of the political regime as a whole and, presumably, the legitimacy of the legal system, are judged against the standards of this transcendent moral order.

In contrast, Hall and Ames deny that *tian* is transcendent in a strict sense: that is, A is transcendent with respect to B if the meaning or import of B cannot be fully analyzed and explained without recourse to A but the reverse is not true.[43] *Tian*, however, is not some predetermined moral order that unilaterally dictates legal rules or other features of the human order. Rather, the relationship between *tian* and humans is much more interactive, as captured in the Han expression of *tianren heyi* – or the interaction of unity of *tian* and human beings. This unity is nicely captured by Tu Weiming, notwithstanding his attribution of transcendence to *tian:*

> The relationship between Heaven and man is not an antinomic biunity but an indivisibly single oneness. In this sense, the sage as the utmost authentic manifestation of humanity does not coexist with Heaven.... Despite the possibility of a conceptual separation between Heaven and man, inwardly, in their deepest reality, they form an unbreakable organismic continuum.[44]

In the Confucian world view, human beings become a source of normative order through a process of moral cultivation and self-realization. The Confucian sage-ruler rules by virtue of his moral vision. His authority to lead is a function of his ability to know the heavenly way (*tian, dao, tian dao*). Dao refers to the patterns in the world, the ways in which things are related and the possible ways in which they might be related. To know *tian* or *dao* is to perceive these patterns and relations. As a moral achievement, knowing the way requires that one overcome the limited perspective of one's narrow self-interest to see oneself in relation to others. The more truly cultivated one is, the more relations and possible relations one sees. Thus, one who wants to lead the country must begin by first cultivating oneself and putting one's own affairs in order. Only then will he be able to bring order to the family, state and world.[45]

In the process, individual human beings become the co-creator of the universe with *tian*/heaven. They become the counterpart of *tian*. In assisting in the transformation of the social and natural orders, they form a trinity with heaven and earth.[46] In so doing, they become, in a sense, god-like (or, more accurately, *tian*-like): as Mencius states, to be a sage is to be divine.[47]

Just as *tian* cannot be conceived of as a transcendent predetermined source of social order, neither can *dao*. Notwithstanding the common interpretation of *dao* as a single, correct, all-encompassing way,[48] Confucius states: 'It is human beings who are capable of broadening the way. It is not the way that is capable of broadening human beings.'[49] *Dao*, then, emerges out of the particular context in the process of creating a harmonious social and natural order. As a normative concept, harmony is at odds with the notion of a single, objective, predetermined universal order. Rather, harmony requires the efficacious combining of the diverse elements of a particular social and natural orders at a particular time into a single cohesive whole. Individuals must exercise their moral cum aesthetic judgment (*yi*) as to what is most appropriate in the particular circumstances.

According to Hall and Ames, in a tradition in which law is handed down by a transcendent deity or grounded in a transcendent order, individuals must defer to law. All that is required is their compliance. In contrast, the structure of Confucian religiousness is fundamentally different:

> Religion does not impose the demand of obedience or dependence. Rather, it requires that a person constitute himself as an authoritative model. That is, meaning, value, and purpose do not exist as a given standard in the person of God, but are created in interaction between the human being and his context, between [humans] and [*tian*].[50]

Hall and Ames arguably overstate the creative role of human beings in the Confucian process and downplay the extent to which meaning and value lies elsewhere, particularly for later Confucians such as Mencius, Xun Zi and Neo-Confucians.[51] Conversely, they underestimate the role of humans in a system in which laws are the product of a transcendent deity.[52] Even where there is a divine lawmaker, laws need to be interpreted and implemented. In the process, there is ample room for human input. Indeed, without the possibility of such input, religious legal systems would ossify and become obsolete. In that sense, Hall and Ames' definition of transcendence is unduly restrictive, and would apply to few religions or religious legal systems.[53]

But at any rate, not all religions have a transcendent dimension. Thus there is a religiousness to Confucianism for Hall and Ames, even if Confucianism differs in important ways from religions in which an ontologically distinct and temporally prior anthropomorphic deity creates human beings and the natural world and dictates the laws that govern both the natural and human realms. What unites Confucian religiousness with such a religion is that they both facilitate the achievement of individual self-realization and fulfillment through integration with the whole. Both serve the religious function of binding members of the faith or society together through common beliefs, rituals and practices, leading at least for Confucius to social and cosmic harmony.

For Confucians, the *li* provide the means of integration. The *li* link the present to past, family members to ancestors and humans to nature. In binding people to each other and to the cosmos, the *li* structure the worldview of individuals, providing the common normative ground on which to base social solidarity and ultimate meaning to members of that society. As Herbett Fingarette states in his aptly titled work *Confucius: The Secular as Sacred*, there is a sacredness, an ultimate solemnity, to the *li*, which are capable of evoking in men's souls a deep, archaic response.[54] Arguably, then, the *li* constitute religious norms or precepts.

If Confucianism is considered a religion, then the Confucianism of law in the Han would seem to support the view that the religion played a greater role in the legal system than the received wisdom suggests. But before turning to the influence of such notions as *tianming* and the *li* on the actual operation of the legal system, it may clarify matters to contrast Confucianism with the foundational natural law theory of Huang-Lao.

Huang-Lao: transcendent natural law

While there may be doubt about the transcendence of *tian* and *dao* for Confucius, there can be no such doubts that Huang-Lao attempted to ground the legitimacy of the law in a transcendent normative order.[55] In contrast to the interactive, open-ended cosmos of Confucius, the normative universe of Huang-Lao is meta-physically predetermined. Unlike Confucius, who urges humans to extend the way, the author of the Huang-Lao Boshu time and again exhorts one just to hold fast to the Way. Instead of creatively determining a novel way to fit one's particular circumstance, one merely instantiates a preconfigured pattern. Neither the Way nor the laws, principles or rules which constitute the underlying structure of the Way are open for negotiation. They are simply taken as given, something to be discovered rather than created.

In this respect, *dao* is transcendent in the narrow sense stipulated previously: A (the normatively correct Way) is transcendent with respect to B (human society, the legal order) if the meaning or import of B cannot be fully analyzed and explained without recourse to A but the reverse is not true. In the Boshu, the normatively correct Way exists independently of the actual order created by humans, and is therefore transcendent. Ideally, of course, the social/legal order would instantiate the Way.

For Huang-Lao, laws are implicate in the natural order; they arise from and are a manifestation of the Way. Thus the very first sentence of the text declares: 'The Way generates the laws.'[56] As guideposts of the Way, laws constitute an object-ive standard of right and wrong: 'There is a distinction between right and wrong: use the law to adjudicate between them. Being empty, tranquil and listening attentively, take the law as the tally.'[57] The human social order, delimited by laws, is one half of the tally. The normatively correct order, reality, the Way, is the other half. The two halves must fit: laws must correspond to reality, to the Way. Correct laws are foolproof indicators of the right Way, which, if relied on, ensure success: 'Having instruments and using them properly, one will not err.

Relying on the gauge and checking it, one will not be confused. Governing according to the law, one will not be disordered.'[58]

The author of the Boshu believes that it is possible to directly apprehend and understand (*jian zhi*) objective reality. To do so, one must overcome all subjective biases. One must become empty (*xu*) and tranquil (*jing*). This will enable one to be impartial, without personal biases (*wu si*). One will then achieve an intuitive or spiritual clarity (*sheng ming*), which allows one to 'apprehend and understand without confusion' (*jian zhi bu huo*) the natural order variously articulated as the Way, principles (*li*),[59] laws (*fa*) and the forms and names (*xing ming*) of all things. As a result, one is able to distinguish right from wrong, reality from pretense. One is able to comply with the natural order (*wu wei*), know the origins of fortune and misfortune, ensure that names correspond to reality, promulgate the right laws and correctly apply them, and make punishments match the benchmark of heaven. One will, in short, be able to govern, to rule over a properly regulated empire. Having discovered the Way, one will be able to carry it out.

The Huang-Lao sage is distinguished by his ability to go beyond the confines of subjective biases to penetrate the mysteries of the Way itself. In emptying oneself of prejudice, one becomes tranquil, at ease. Not blinded by one's own interests, one is able to observe with detachment, with a level-headed equanimity that for the author ensures a spiritual-like intuitive clarity or spiritual enlightenment (*shen* or *shenming*). Benjamin Schwartz's characterization of Huang-Lao epistemology as synoptic or gnostic intuition is particularly apt: that it is a kind of intuition captures the directness of the discovery of Huang-Lao knowledge and the inner certainty that accompanies it; that it is synoptic intuition marks the breadth of scope of the sage's understanding; that it is gnostic intuition affirms the sage's ability to fathom the unfathomable.[60]

> Only the sage is able to scrutinize the formless,
> to hear the soundless.
> Having discovered the repleteness of emptiness,
> one is able to realize great emptiness.
> One will then penetrate the essence of heaven and earth,
> and thoroughly identify with the seamless sameness . . .
> One of clarity will surely be able to
> > scrutinize the extremities,
> > discover what others cannot discover
> > and follow what others cannot obtain.
> This is called scrutinizing the model and knowing the limits.[61]

Intuitive clarity is grounded in the Way. One who attains it is able to go beyond the standards, to fathom the Way. Knowledge within the boundaries is everyday, fallible, perspectival knowledge – or as Plato would call it, doxa: opinion. When one becomes empty, one overcomes the limits of one's own perspective and gains a synoptic, gnostic awareness of reality itself, of the Way that is beyond the boundaries of the everyday limited awareness. One discovers an objective, common ground available to all such that no one need be of two minds.

Yet the author of the Boshu is not advocating a mystical experience within the confines of one's own room or mind. His sage is not the sage of Lao Zi who 'without going beyond his doors knows the world, without looking out the window apprehends the heavenly Way.'[62] Rather, his epistemology is intended for the ruler who oversees the empire and must make practical decisions about concrete affairs of state. The sage-ruler begins with empirical observation and ends by applying his insights to the world. It is simply that one's empirical observation will be accurate only if one is able to be clear-headed and free from subjective bias.

Whether or not one wants to classify Huang-Lao as a religion and Huang-Lao law as religious law, Huang-Lao clearly advocates a natural law system in which the legitimacy of the legal system as a whole as well as the legitimacy of specific institutions, laws and practices are grounded in a transcendent normative natural order. Moreover, not only does Huang-Lao share a transcendent dimension with other religions, the experience of the Huang-Lao sage in the meditative process of overcoming bias is similar to that of the Christian mystic who as a result of an apophatic process comes face to face with the deity.[63] However, in the absence of a deity, the process is arguably more comparable to the natural mystic experience of the type described by William Blake.

On the other hand, Huang-Lao is a very practical philosophy. Power is concentrated in the hands of a single ruler (even allowing that the purpose of grounding the law in a transcendent order was to provide normative limits on the power of the ruler). It is the sage-ruler in particular that is supposed to know the Way, and on the basis of the direct apprehension of the Way, put the state in order by promulgating and ensuring the correct application of laws. The result will be a properly ordered state, which will redound to the benefit of all. Andrew Huxley summarized Huang-Lao as 'Blake meets Bentham'. This captures some of the paradoxical character of Huang-Lao as part starry-eyed mysticism, part no-nonsense realpolitik.

FROM THEORY TO PRACTICE: RECONSIDERING THE IMPACT OF RELIGION ON THE LEGAL SYSTEM

Even assuming a religious dimension to Confucianism and Huang-Lao and to *dao, tian* and *li*, the impact of religion on the legal system is limited and more difficult to discern when one turns from theory to practice. From the collapse of the Qin in 206 BC to the enthronement of Han Wudi in 140 BC, Huang-Lao was arguably the dominant court ideology. During this period, various specific Huang-Lao policies were implemented, including a relaxation of the harsh laws of the Qin, lighter punishments, a reduction of taxes and so on.[64] But by the end of the reign of Han Wu Di, the fortunes of the Huang-Lao school had reversed. Its fate was sealed when Emperor Wu, following Dong Zhongshu's advice, banned non-Confucian schools of thought and established the imperial university and examination system with the Confucian classics as the core curriculum.

There are many reasons for Huang-Lao's demise, including that Han rulers grew tired of Huang-Lao economic policies mandating low taxes, minimal government expenditures and frugality on the part of rulers.[65] More fundamentally, Huang-Lao's transcendent normative order is at odds with a more interactive cosmology that assigns a greater role to humans, and in particular to the ruler, in determining the proper order. As such, its replacement by the more interactive ying yang five phases correlative cosmology of Dong Zhongshu is not surprising as the latter is both more consistent with the dominant Chinese world view and the desire of rulers to be free of the strictures of a predetermined moral cum natural order.

Significantly for our purposes, Huang-Lao failed to have a lasting impact with respect to its central purpose: to provide a normative foundation for law that could support legal and institutional limits on the ruler, thereby overcoming the key weakness shared by Confucianism and Legalism. In that sense, Huang-Lao rose largely as a response to the failures of Confucianism and Legalism, and fell because it too failed to provide an effective remedy. Confucianism, in emphasizing context-specific solutions to problems that fully attended to the uniqueness of the individuals involved and the circumstances, ceded considerable discretion to allegedly morally-cultivated decisionmakers, who were generally members of the elite class. In practice, such wide latitude combined with inevitable shortcomings in the wisdom of the decisionmakers, their class biases and legitimate differences over what was appropriate, resulted in abuses of discretion, disgruntled parties and social tensions. In response, the Legalists advocated clearly codified, publicly promulgated laws applicable to commoner and noble alike as a means of under-mining the dual class system in which 'the *li* do not reach down to the common people; penal law does not reach up to the great official.'[66] Yet, as we have seen, Legalism failed to provide a normative basis to law. Moreover, neither Confucianism nor Legalism imposed effective restraints on the power of the ruler, particularly institutional and legal restraints.

Huang-Lao attempted to limit the power of the ruler and provide a theoretical and moral foundation for a law-based rule by grounding the sociopolitical order in a normatively predetermined natural order. Whereas the Legalist ruler was the ultimate authority as to what the law is and how it should be interpreted and thus above the law, in the Huang-Lao universe the Way is the ultimate authority, and thus the ruler, like all others, must abide by the law. Accordingly, law for Huang-Lao is not merely a political tool to be used by the ruler to further his own ends. The ruler cannot change the law at will. Nor can he circumvent it by issuing pardons. However, while there may have been limits on the ruler in theory, there were no such limits in practice. Given that there is no way to verify the ruler's claim to have discovered the Way and hence the correct laws, the ruler's power remains as unchecked in practice as that of either the Confucian or Legalist ruler. Nor did Huang-Lao propose effective institutions for controlling the ruler or government officials.

Although it may be true as a theoretical matter that the legitimacy of the legal system was grounded in the normative order of *tian* and *dao*, as a practical matter such religious cum normative concepts played a limited role with respect to particular institutions, rules or practices. On the whole, the transcendent dimension received short shrift. The formal legal system was heavily penal and positivist in nature. The purpose of the legal system was to serve the state. There was, for instance, no notion of individual rights. To be sure, the concept of *tianming* or heaven's mandate did confer on the people as a group the right to rebel, and provided support for the idea that rulers had a moral if not legal obligation to ensure the material and spiritual wellbeing of the people.[67] But in reality *tianming* rarely if ever served as the rallying cry for the disgruntled, oppressed masses. Rather, it simply served to legitimate whatever warlord or faction was able to vanquish its rivals and rise to power.

One area where Huang-Lao ideas had an impact is with respect to the doctrine of cosmic harmony. As noted previously, the standard account was at a loss to explain the 'naturalization' of law. Building on the linkages between the human and natural world established by the Daoists and the causal correlative yin yang five phase cosmology of Zou Yan, Huang-Lao grounded law and the legal system in a natural order. However, in the foundational naturalism of Huang-Lao, humans simply conform to the normatively given natural order. In contrast, among late Han correlative cosmologists, humans are able to interact with and effect change in the natural order. The process is bidirectional rather than unidirectional. As a result, violations of law and other disruptions of the social order are understood literally as disrupting the natural cosmic order.

The notions of cosmic harmony and correlative cosmology did affect legal institutions and particular laws. For instance, executions were to be carried out during the fall and winter, during the seasons of death and decay; and they were to be avoided during the spring and summer, the seasons of new life and growth. Similarly, amnesties were often granted in response to natural disasters. On the other hand, while such rules were at times observed, they were ignored at other times. Moreover, even when they were observed, it is not clear that they were followed out of a genuine sense of religious commitment. In some cases, rulers may simply have followed the practices out of a sense of convention or political expediency.[68] Indeed, Brian McKnight demonstrates that amnesties were driven in part by short term political considerations and the desire on the part of the emperor to reinforce his legitimacy by appearing benevolent while simultaneously reconfirming his power and control over life and death.[69]

As part of the Confucianization of law during the Han and imperial periods, Confucian *li* and ethical concerns were also incorporated into law. For instance, the legal system paid particular attention to familial relations and filial piety. One of the unpardonable 'ten offenses' was unfilial behavior. Another was the murder of one's parents. In keeping with the deference owed to parents, a son could be punished for simply accusing his father of a crime. Conversely, sons were allowed to conceal the crimes of the parent, except in the case of treason, where the interests of the state prevailed over moral niceties. Children also had a legal duty to support one's parents – as is still true today. The legal codes even allowed for a reprieve for those sentenced to death if they were an only child so that they could look after their parents.

In addition, the influence of Confucianism and the *li* is reflected in the hierarchical nature of the legal system. Punishments were meted out in accordance with one's status and the status of the victim. Officials were treated more favorably than commoners. They could not be arrested, investigated or sentenced without permission of the emperor. Some were exempt from torture for certain crimes. All benefited from sentence reductions, and could redeem certain punishments either by paying a fine or accepting a demotion. Status was also important for the official *qua* victim.[70] Generally speaking, the higher the status of the victim and the lower the status of the offender, the more severe the punishment. In addition, the legal codes took into consideration gender, age and moral character in determining sentences.

Even allowing, however, that Confucianism may be considered a religion in a broad sense, and that the *li* may be considered religious principles to the extent that they serve to bind members of the community to each other and the cosmos, the *li* seem to lose most if not all of their religious character when they are selectively incorporated into the positive law. The state appears to have incorporated moral norms that it found useful in maintaining order. The emphasis on filial piety ensured that the family would be responsible for inculcating norms of obedience and deference to authority. The incorporation of status concerns allowed the state to purchase the allegiance of the elite, who were the main beneficiaries, in exchange for their political support. Not surprisingly, the local elite were more than willing to shoulder much of the responsibility for upholding the hierarchical social order through their role in the informal resolutions of disputes.

More generally, the influence of Confucian ideals may underlie the tendency of the imperial legal system to pursue a particularized substantive justice at the cost of procedural justice and formal equality, as indicated in the emphasis on fact-finding, the use of torture to extract the truth, the importance of confessions and the ready availability of appeal and, arguably, in the reliance on discretion-based moral judgments in deciding cases. Indeed, according to Chang Wejen and even the standard account of Bodde, Needham *et al.*, magistrates in imperial China regularly decided cases based on general moral and religious principles. In support of this position, Chu T'ung-tsu notes that magistrates generally did not cite the legal authority for their decisions even though they were required to do so by law.[71] Further, magistrates enjoyed considerable discretion because of the general nature of many laws and the practice of relying on case-specific substatutes to create new precedents. In addition, magistrates were able to take advantage of broad catch-all laws such as 'conduct that ought not be done' and provisions authorizing them to find crimes by analogy to tailor a decision to the circumstances based on their own sense as to what was appropriate.[72]

Recently, however, Philip Huang has challenged many of the assumptions about the traditional legal system, including that magistrates decided non-penal cases based on general Confucian principles and in so doing tended to split the loaf between the plaintiff and defendant. In a survey of some 600 Qing civil cases, he found that over three-fourths of the cases that made it all the way to judgment ended up with one party a clear winner.[73] Moreover, he claims that in deciding cases, judges tended to rely on legal codes, not custom or general moral principles. In support, he notes that one could find a tenable basis for most decisions in the code or substatutes.[74]

On the other hand, in many cases the code and substatutes are very vague, and thus consistent with a variety of outcomes in particular cases, or they call for penal sanctions, which the judges routinely ignored. Indeed, Mark Allee, reviewing some of the same cases, reached a quite different conclusion.[75] He found that magistrates decided cases based on three factors – the code, broad cultural norms and local customs – and tried to harmonize them. Magistrates appealed to morality in part because moral norms often supported state objectives in maintaining social order. In addition, parties presumably would be more likely to accept the judgment if they felt the judgment was based on moral principles with which they agreed. Satisfied parties would be less likely to appeal, which could result in the judgment being overturned and adverse consequences for the magistrate. Accordingly, magistrates for their own reasons would be expected to appeal to general moral principles to justify decisions to the parties.

Moreover, Allee notes that magistrates seldom cited the code – only four times in 77 cases, and even among those four, only two of the citations were on point, and in one case the magistrate proceeded to ignore the prescribed punishments. Huang attributes this tendency not to cite the code to the fact that the magistrate's judgment is directed to the parties, who generally are lay people of inferior social status that are not likely to know much about law anyway.[76] Nevertheless, presumably the magistrate has an interest in persuading the parties that the decision is legally justified, if for no other reason than to decrease the possibilities of appeal, and so there would still be value in citing the code.

To sort out this issue requires test cases where the code is at odds with general moral principles and local customs. In most cases, the general legal principles cited by Huang are indistinguishable from widely accepted religious precepts, moral norms and local customs – for example, legitimate market transactions should be upheld and parties should repay their debts. Moreover, in all systems, judges try to reconcile the law with religious precepts, moral principles and local practices, and in some cases – such as runaway juries or civil disobedience – religion, morality and custom trump the law. At present, the empirical basis for broad conclusions, particularly about how the decisionmaking process compares to that in other systems, is lacking. However, it does seem safe to say that positive law played a somewhat greater role in the magistrate's decisionmaking than often suggested.

Of course, the formal legal system was complemented by a large informal system. Disputes were frequently mediated by the clan elders, guild leaders or village heads in accordance with clan or guild regulations and communal practices and norms. Arguably, the influence of the Confucian *li* and other religious norms and practices, including folk religion, may be greater in informal fora than in formal legal proceedings. On the other hand, while the heavy reliance on informal or semi-formal means to settle disputes is in part a product of the Confucian tradition, it is also a product of the harshness of the formal legal system and the economic constraints of the state. State resources were limited. The magistrate received a budget to cover all expenses, including the costs of administering justice. The funds fell far short of the amount required to meet all of the costs of governing. By relying heavily on informal mechanisms to resolve many disputes, magistrates were able to put the available funds to other arguably more productive uses.

CONCLUSION

The influence of religion on law in China depends in large part on what one means by religion and law. Broadly interpreted, religious ideas and practices were reflected in particular laws. More generally, religious ideals and norms may have provided a normative dimension to the legal system and tempered the harsh, amoral positivism of Legalism. Nevertheless, the impact on the day to day operations of the legal system was minimal. Whole areas of positive law had little if anything to do with religious beliefs, even broadly construed.[77]

To be sure, the ultimate role of religious and ethical ideals in most legal systems is difficult to measure, and this is true of early Chinese law as well. Typically, the legal system as a whole and specific legal rules and decisions accord with some general prevailing, even if contested, ethical or religious norms. In the absence of test cases, where specific laws violate some clearly defined ethical or religious norm, whether magistrates in China decided cases based on positive law or nonlegal principles (or both) cannot be determined.

To claim that the day to day impact was minimal does not mean that the role of religion was unimportant. That the early Chinese legal system operated within the particular religious cum normative context that it did may explain in part the different paths of development of the Chinese and foreign legal systems, though surely the trajectory of any legal system is the product of a multitude of factors, of which religion is only one.

NOTES

1 Derke Bodde, 'Basic Concepts of Chinese Law: The Genesis and Evolution of Legal Thought in Traditional China', *Proceedings of the American Philosophical Society* 107: 375–398 (1963), 378. For the claim that even in its early days Chinese law was not

significantly influenced by religion, see also Yongping Liu, *Origins of Chinese Law* (Hong Kong: Oxford University Press, 1998), 13; Joseph Needham, *Science and Civilisation in China* Vol. 2 (Cambridge: Cambridge University Press, 1962), *passim*.

2 Bodde, *supra* note 1, at 380.

3 Id.

4 Id., at 379.

5 Needham, *supra* note 1, at 518. Like Needham, Roberto Unger attributes the different paths of development of the Chinese and European legal systems in large measure to the lack of a transcendent deity. *See* Roberto Unger, *Law in Modern Society* (London: Macmillan, 1976), 99. Yet there were no doubt many factors contributing to the different paths. Moreover, as noted below, Huang-Lao clearly attempted to ground law in a transcendent normative order. For a critical account of Unger's account of traditional Chinese law, see William Alford, 'The Inscrutable Occidental? Implications of Roberto Unger's Uses and Abuses of the Chinese Past' *Texas Law Review* 64: 915–972 (1986).

6 *Li* is often translated as rites but has a much broader meaning that includes religious rituals, conventional etiquette, social customs, norms, mores and institutions.

7 Needham, *supra* note 1, at 214–215. I have argued elsewhere against the interpretation of Confucianism as natural law, at least in a foundational sense that construes the *li* as universal principles. *See* Randall Peerenboom, *Law and Morality in Ancient China: The Silk Manuscripts of Huang-Lao* (Albany: State University of New York Press, 1993), 81–84.

8 Analects, 2:3. Citations to Confucius' Analects follow the numbering in D.C. Lau, *Confucius: The Analects* (Harmondsworth: Penguin Books, 1979).

9 Chu T'ung-tsu, *Law and Society in Traditional China* (Paris: Mouton, 1961).

10 Needham, *supra* note 1, at 214.

11 Bodde, *supra* note 1, at 383.

12 Dennis Twitchett, 'Law and Religion in East Asia' 8: 469–472 of ed. Mircea Eliade *Encyclopedia of Religion* (New York: Macmillan, 1987), 470.

13 Chang Wejen, 'Forward' to ed. Karen Turner et al. *The Limits of the Rule of Law in China* (Seattle: University of Washington Press, 1999), viii.

14 Id.

15 Bodde, *supra* note 1, at 375.

16 Id., at 394.

17 Max Weber, *Economy and Society* ed. Guenther Roth and Claus Wittich (Berkeley: University of California Press, 1968), 656–657, 844–845.

18 Information regarding the implementation of early legal codes is extremely limited. However, one would assume legal reasoning in the pre-imperial legal system was, if anything, less technical (or formally rational) than during the imperial legal system, given the less developed nature of the legal system and the codes. Accordingly, decisionmakers would have been even more likely to appeal to general normative and religious principles in resolving disputes. For a discussion of imperial law as substantively rational, see Philip Huang, *Civil Justice in China: Representation and Practice in the Qing* (Palo Alto: Stanford University Press, 1996), 224–229.

19 Benjamin Schwartz, 'On Attitudes Toward Law in China' ed. Milton Katz *Government Under the Law and Individual* (Washington: American Council of Learned Societies, 1957); Chang Wejen, *supra* note 13, at viii.

20 Weber's sharp distinction between formal rationality and substantive rationality – between a peculiar type of legal reasoning and reasoning in legal cases that relies to one extent or another on general moral principles, social values and political philosophy – is difficult to maintain today. Legal Realists made easy sport of legal formalism, which assumed a mechanical model of law and that a legal system is based on clear rules that

can be applied in a mechanical, syllogistic way to a set of facts to produce a legal conclusion or judgment. Critical Legal Scholars have demonstrated that any such formalistic understanding of the legal system is misguided at best and pernicious at worst in that it reifies the existing legal order, masking the contingency of the law and the way in rule of law serves as an ideology. In so doing, CRITs have challenged the determinacy of law and argued that formalism draws too clear a line between law and politics. Ronald Dworkin has argued for a greater role for moral philosophy in legal reasoning in that his ideal judge Hercules is required to make the legal system the best it can be by reflecting on fundamental moral principles. Nevertheless, Weber's categories may still be useful as end points on a continuum and helpful in sorting out extreme cases. Thus, even allowing that magistrates did have a more specific form of legal reasoning that was much more constrained by legal texts and principles of interpretation than normally suggested, it would still appear that legal reasoning in the imperial era was much less differentiated from general moral reasoning and problem solving than in other legal systems, as discussed below.

21 *See, e.g.*, Liu, *supra* note 1.

22 Harold Berman, *Faith and Order, The Reconciliation of Law and Religion* (Atlanta: Scholar's Press, 1993), 3.

23 Id.

24 While religion may buttress the legitimacy of a legal system that incorporates its basic principles, it may also undermine its legitimacy by serving as an alternative source of normative order. A religion founded on the inherent dignity and equality of all before god is at odds, for instance, with a legal system that sanctions apartheid. Similarly, religious principles that support nonviolence may be at odds with legal rules mandating military service. In some cases, religious principles may require citizens to reject the state's authority and engage in civil disobedience.

25 Berman, *supra* note 22, at 4.

26 Influenced by the views of Paul Tillich, the U.S. Supreme Court in *United States v. Seeger*, 380 U.S. 163 (1965) and in *Welsh v. United States*, 398 U.S. 333 (1970) defined religion in terms of 'ultimate concern', which need not entail a belief in god and may consist of purely ethical and moral considerations. Needless to say, this definition hardly solved all of the interpretative questions concerning the meaning of religion. See Kent Greenawalt, 'Religion as a Concept in Constitutional Law' *California Law Review* 72: 753–816 (1984), 752.

27 Dennis Twichett, *supra* note 12, at 470.

28 For a discussion of the religious dimension of contractual agreements, including the abundance of references to supernatural spirits: Hugh Scogin, 'Between Heaven and Man: Contract and the State in Han Dynasty China' *Southern California Law Review* 63: 1326–1404 (1990), 1325, 1382–1384. W.A.C.H. Dobson, 'Some legal instruments in ancient China: the ming and the meng' 269–282 of ed. Chow Tse-tung *Wen-lin; studies in the Chinese humanities* (Madison: University of Wisconsin Press, 1968), 271–272.

29 Geoffrey MacCormack, 'Natural Law and Cosmic Harmony in Traditional Chinese Thought' *Ratio Juris* 2: 254–273 (1989), 254. Brian McKnight, *The Quality of Mercy: Amnesties and Traditional Chinese Justice* (Honolulu: University Press of Hawaii, 1981).

30 Liu argues that Dobson and others make too much of the religious aspects of oaths and the invocation of spirits. Oaths were followed more out of a sense of faithfulness and obligation than fear that spirits would bring about calamities. Over time, oaths and covenants were replaced by more formal and rigorous legal instruments. Liu, *supra* note 1, at 164–168. *See also* Scogin, *supra* note 28, at 1382 (noting that Hulsewe and Niida also deemphasize the religious component).

31 See the discussion of cosmic harmony below.

32 R.P. Peerenboom, 'The Victim in Chinese Criminal Theory and Practice: A Historical Survey' *Journal of Chinese Law* 7: 63–109 (1993), 63, 84.

33 Twitchett, *supra* note 12, at 470; Luke Lee and Whalen Lai, 'The Chinese Concept of Law: Confucian, Legalist, and Buddhist' *Hastings Law Journal* 29: 1307–1329 (1978), 1322–1325.

34 Lee and Lai, *supra* note 33, at 1312.

35 Twitchett, *supra* note 12, at 470.

36 Frederick Tse-Shyang Chen, 'The Confucian View of World Order' 31–45 of ed. Mark Janis *The Influence of Religion on the Development of International Law* (Dordrecht: Nijhoff, 1991), 31.

37 Analects, 6:22.

38 In addition, as Hall and Ames point out, Confucius described *tian* as the maker of sages and the determiner of social status and wealth. David Hall and Roger Ames, *Thinking Through Confucius* (Albany: State University of New York Press, 1987), 206.

39 Analects, 9:5.

40 Tu Weiming, *Centrality and Commonality: An Essay on Chun-Yung* (Honolulu: University Press of Hawaii, 1976), 104, 116, 127 (1976).

41 Mou Tsung-san, *Zhongguo zhexue de tezhi [The Special Character of Chinese Philosophy]* (Taibei: Student Book Store, 1963), 16.

42 Id.

43 Hall and Ames, *supra* note 38, at 13.

44 Tu, *supra* note 40, at 129.

45 This image of the moral influence of the sage ruler growing and spreading out in increasingly larger concentric circles or waves as the ruler grows as a moral being is most succinctly stated in the *Daxue* (Great Learning), one of the four great Confucian classics. James Legge, *The Chinese Classics* Vol. 1 (London: Trübner & Co., 1985), 355, 358–359.

46 Zhong Yong (Doctrine of the Mean), in Wing-tsit Chan, *A Source Book in Chinese Philosophy* (Princeton: Princeton University Press, 1963), 107–108.

47 Mencius, 7B/25. *See* D.C. Lau, Mencius 199 (1970).

48 *See, e.g.*, Arthur Waley, *The Analects of Confucius* (1938), 30. Lau, *supra* note 8, at ix.

49 Analects, 15: 29.

50 Hall and Ames, *supra* note 38, at 244.

51 This is not to claim that the human creative dimension is not important for other Confucians – it is. See R.P. Peerenboom 'Confucian Jurisprudence: Beyond Natural Law' *Asian Culture Quarterly* 36: 12–39 (1990), 12. Nor is to claim that Hall and Ames ignore entirely natural conditions and other contingent constraints on creativity. In the end, it is a question of degree.

52 Alan Watson and Khaled Abou El Fadl discuss at length the similarities between Jewish rabbinic law, Islamic law and Roman law, particularly with respect to the role of interpretation in reaching decisions. Although they note there were differences between secular Roman law and the other two forms of "religious law", what is striking is the similarities. See Watson and Abou El Fadl, 'Fox Hunting, Pheasant Shooting, and Comparative Law' *American Journal of Comparative Law* 48: 1–38 (2000).

53 For a similar point, see: Robert Neville, *Boston Confucianism* (Albany: State University of New York Press, 2000), 147–151. Neville also argues that *tian* and *dao* are transcendent in the strict sense proposed by Hall and Ames. His main concern, however, is to suggest several other senses of transcendence that are applicable to Confucianism. Ironically, in an otherwise sympathetic foreword to Neville's book, even Tu Weiming feels the need to question Neville's 'strong thesis that the creation

myth and, by implication, the transcendent God are necessary conditions for Confucian spirituality.'

54 Herbert Fingarette, *Confucius: The Secular as Sacred* (New York: Harper & Row, 1972), 63.

55 I distinguish between Huang-Lao and Judeo-Christian transcendence by drawing a distinction between strong (*chaojue*) and weak transcendence (*chaoyue*) in *supra* note 7 at 83. The latter is consistent with an immanent organismic cosmology, with vitiates Needham's claim that the organismic world view of early Chinese prevented them from conceiving of laws of nature in the natural science sense, as is clearly the case for Huang-Lao.

56 Huang-Lao Boshu, 43: 1a. Citations of the Mawangdui silk manuscripts of Huang-Lao are to *Mawangdui Hanmu Boshu* Vol. 1 (Beijing: Wen Wu Press, 1980).

57 Huang-Lao Boshu, 58: 74b.

58 Id., at 81:144a.

59 This *li*, meaning principles, is a homophone – i.e. the same sound but different Chinese character – of the Confucian *li*, meaning rites.

60 Benjamin Schwartz, *The World of Thought in Ancient China* (Cambridge: Belknap Press, 1985), 249.

61 Huang-Lao Boshu, 87: 171a.

62 D.C. Lau, *Lao Tzu: Tao Te Ching* (Harmondsworth: Penguin Books, 1963), 108.

63 The process is apophatic as opposed to kataphatic in that it involves clearing or emptying the mind of all images rather than concentration on or filling the mind with images.

64 Peerenboom, *supra* note 7, at 242–248.

65 As is true of all systems, it is difficult to translate abstract religious or ethical norms into concrete institutions and rules. Does *tian* require high taxes or low taxes? It strains credulity to presume that *tian* favors libertarians over social welfare liberals.

66 Li Ji [Book of Rites], 1: 35a.

67 Alford, *supra* note 5, at 955 (arguing that the Mandate of Heaven imposed a fiduciary-like set of obligations on those in power, though noting that the constraints of the Mandate of Heaven and the *li* were not always observed in practice).

68 For a critical account of the theoretical and practical influence of cosmic harmony reasoning, see MacCormack *supra* note 29 (arguing that some rulers did not take seriously the view of the interaction between man and nature and that the doctrine of cosmic harmony could be manipulated to achieve a politically desired result). Ocko, on the other hand, argues that cosmic harmony was an explicit concern in the day to day administration of justice. *See* Jonathan Ocko, 'A Review of Geoffrey MacCormack, The Spirit of Traditional Chinese Law', *McGill Law Journal* 42: 733–750 (1997), 748.

69 MacKnight, *supra* note 29, at 113.

70 Peerenboom, *supra* note 32.

71 Chu, *supra* note 9.

72 MacCormack argues that this catch-all clause was invoked during the Qing primarily to punish those who had contributed in some ancillary way to someone else committing a crime. Ocko, however, argues that the clause was used to enforce general ethical obligations. *See* Ocko, *supra* note 68, at 739.

73 To be sure, the vast majority of cases were resolved through mediation, either informally or through the intervention of the magistrate. Cases that went forward were arguably more likely to result in winner take all judgments because if a compromise had been possible, the parties would already have settled, particularly given that the magistrate often would oversee mediation and push the parties toward settlement. As Huang notes, mediation occurred against the backdrop of the formal legal system. Indeed, parties frequently filed cases and then settled through mediation once the

magistrate had reviewed the petition and expressed a preliminary opinion. Huang, *supra* note 18.

74 Id. McKnight and Liu argue that it would be a 'serious misreading of the record' to claim that Sung judges could decide matters on the basis of their inner conviction. In support, they note that even though judges often fail to cite particular provisions, they frequently state that 'the law says …' when making their judgment. They also suggest that while judges had a certain amount of discretion to adjust sentences to accord with the circumstances, their discretion was limited. Brian McKnight and James Liu, transl., *The Enlightened Judgments, Ch'ing Ming Chi* (Albany: State University of New York, 1999), 15.

75 Mark Allee, 'Code, Culture, and Custom' 122–137 of ed. Kathryn Bernhardt & Philip Huang *Civil Law in Qing and Republican China* (Palo Alto: Stanford University Press, 1994), 124.

76 Philip Huang, 'Codified Law and Magisterial Adjudication', in ed. Bernhardt & Huang, *supra*, note 75, at 142, 154–155.

77 Furthermore, religious legal systems and secular legal systems, despite certain differences, share many features. *See, e.g.*, Watson & Abou El Fadl, *supra* note 52.

7

HINDU LAW AS A 'RELIGIOUS' SYSTEM

Werner Menski

Having agreed to take part in this important workshop on comparative law and religion, I originally proposed a title that sought to express the difficulties surrounding the topics of 'religion', 'law', and 'comparative law' from internal Hindu and external legal perspectives. I offered a paper called 'Once religious, always religious? Debates about the nature of Hindu law.' However, the programme dictated the uniformising heading used above, which I took as legitimate intellectual guidance in a conference on comparative law. But to what extent does one need to read such a title as a significant reflection of our continuing inability to work on methods of comparative law? Or did the conference organisers simply want to channel all thoughts in a particular direction? Either way, a feeling of *déjà vu* arose. Was I expected, as the Hindu law specialist, to repeat common stereotypes about Hinduism and Hindu law for the purposes of a so-called comparative legal discussion? To what extent would the panel be ready for the provocations which ancient, unqualified pluralism and limitless Hindu diversity offer to the menu of comparative legal theories? Some of my colleagues at SOAS would expect this kind of comment from their in-house 'Hinduist', but in a wider forum the same points need to be emphasised. The topic as set is either deceptively simple, or impossibly large. Feeling like a cat sitting on the edge of an ocean of milk, which cannot be lapped up in any allotted amount of time, I conquered fears of indigestion and apprehensions of *déjà vu* and proceeded to give this topic a try for the sake of comparative legal analysis, only to find that, as a regional specialist, one is not even treated as a comparative lawyer. So much for pluralist perspectives!

In view of the briefings from the conference organisers, I endeavour to skirt around the originally given three questions by not providing a clear answer about the usefulness of delineating legal families, their potential labelling as 'religious systems', and the issue of whether Hindu law should be included under the label of the religious systems family. This is so for a variety of reasons. First of all, perhaps one should admit that we, as a collectivity of legal scholars of various orientations and specialisations, are unlikely to know the answers to these three 'big questions' because they all concern issues of religion. Since we do not even see eye to eye on what we mean by 'law', how can we expect to come to agreed conclusions on 'religion' or 'religious law'? Anyway, I shall try to add some thoughts to the debate by providing a focus on perceptions arising from classical Hindu legal philosophy, which is at the same time religious and secular, and hence makes the stipulated basic distinction seem impractical, if not outrightly nonsensical. If this stance is not accepted, I am thrown back to my initial assertion that 'once religious, always religious' would be a better title, since there can be no doubt that Hinduism is a major religious system and that Hindu law, arising from it, is based to some extent on such religious foundations, which may well be as much social as religious, but which we somehow perceive as traditional and as religious. If Western-style, Christian legal systems have been able to shake off the flakes of their religious membranes, why should the same process not have been possible for Hindu law? Are we dealing with different shades of deliberate obfuscations about 'religion' rather than legal debates? Does it suit us to call 'the other' religious, to buttress our own insincere assertions of secularity? Is it possible to speak of a positivist, secular Hindu legal tradition? Too many questions arise at once, so I shall make a beginning from the periphery instead of diving straight into the ocean.

DROWNING IN COMPLEXITIES: THE DEARTH AND DANGERS OF HINDU LEGAL SCHOLARSHIP

Less than a handful of Western scholars today could claim to be experts in 'Hindu law', and there is also only one major Japanese scholar working in the field, Professor N. Watase from Tokai University. As a member of such a dying breed, one is out on a limb in many ways talking about Hinduism and Hindu law to comparative lawyers, and even to regional South Asia specialists from other academic disciplines. Hindu law expertise is not dying out because there is nothing to say about the field, but because it remains so vast, complex and difficult that nobody dares go into it any more. In addition, there are manifest ideological reasons for modernist scholars of any background not to venture beyond certain boundaries of 'tradition'. The voices and messages of ancient Hindu law and religion are widely treated as a dangerous call from a past which modernity claims to have left behind, declares irrelevant and seeks to proscribe for further study.[1] Since it seems to make a huge difference whether one's starting point is the internal positioning of the classical Sanskrit-based scholar or the comparatist's more or less explicitly 'detached' outsider perspective, potential participants in necessary debates, which could of course be most fascinating, not only do not meet, but appear to display much unspoken contempt for 'the other'.

It is by no means a fact that 'othering' takes place only in a West-East direction. If one approaches Hindu law through Western-style legal scholarship rather than classical indological training, the resulting perceptions may differ so considerably and radically that the Western analyst is not recognised as a partner in debate but a dabbling outsider, whose presence and views pollute the learned insider's sphere and environment. On the other hand, listening to classically trained pandits in a symposium on comparative law in the twenty-first century would be made harder by the fact that we simply do not speak the same language when it comes to legal and religious comparisons. Rearing its many heads all the time, the frightful snake of continuing doubt over what actually is 'Hindu law', let alone questions over the links of law and religion within South Asian cultural traditions, cannot be ignored and require rather careful approaches. In a climate of religious fundamentalism and competition, it has become positively dangerous to be an expert in Hindu law, since shots are fired from all kinds of directions to silence assertions of difference and claims to universal truth.

It is partly for such reasons that comparative law books like those written by David and Brierley[2] or Zweigert and Kötz[3] cannot really make full sense of systems like Hindu law (not to speak of African laws and some others) and have consequently lumped them into some kind of 'other' category, which also happens to be the non-European ragbag, rather than just a bin for outdated rubbish marked 'religious systems of law'. Unfortunately, this goes even more so for the most recent comparative endeavour in Glenn.[4] This malaise points to Eurocentrism as a major culprit for creating obfuscating legal scholarship, whose designs may be more focused on strengthening Western supremacy than analysing legal theories in truly and globally comparative fashion.[5] In the 'other' category of legal families suggested by David and Brierley,[6] religious content is certainly one element, but it cannot be the main distinguishing ingredient, since one could certainly argue with Allott[7] and others that all legal systems are culture-specific and hence comparable on that ground alone. I would go further and suggest that, therefore, by implication, all legal systems have certain religious elements in them which may be invisible, but which are present and should be brought out by comparative legal analysis. This is a preferable methodology compared to the somewhat desperate, ideologically contaminated argument of many Chinese legal experts, for example, to the effect that certain legal systems have no religious connection whatsoever, while others (mainly Hindu law in this case of comparison) are deeply embedded in religion.[8] This is why Masaji Chiba[9] in his 'three-level structure of law', presents such a useful and sensible model of comparative legal analysis, taking account of the ever-present level of culture-specific ideas and value systems, including religion. In Chiba's model, these so-called 'legal postulates' are found in constant interaction with what he calls 'official law' and various 'unofficial laws', and we are left in no doubt that the Western assertions of secular universality are merely an ideological tool, an assertion of predominance, rather than an element of comparative methodology.

While it may make sense to group legal systems into families, based on certain criteria, I am therefore not convinced that using the label 'religious systems' is of any use at all. It merely seems to indicate that, from a European perspective, such systems are somehow 'traditional', 'backward', and thus dismissible as deficient.

It is also no coincidence that in these 'religious systems', the *millet* system of personal laws is very widely practised and in operation even today. This type of legal organisation is widely treated among lawyers as evidence of backwardness and lack of development, leading to arguments in favour of a consequent need for secularising legal reform.

Coming back to Hindu law specifically, one needs to start by noting that the level of public and scholarly ignorance about Hinduism and Hindu law is depressingly amazing, not only in Western Europe or North America. Political interferences provide ammunition for constant sniping: Many Muslims view Hindu polytheism as either a creation of the devil or definite evidence of backwardness. Western commentators love to dwell on colonially-inspired stereotypes and prejudices about primitive forms of religion and its alleged manifestations, like *sati* and the now topical issue of 'forced' marriages, on which a recent commission in the UK had really nothing useful to say because the illustrious members could not even agree on the most basic definitions. But one potential wider purpose was served, in that the legal behaviour of Asian people in the West continues to be in the spotlight as culturally backward and unacceptable in terms of human rights. All non-Western traditions are tarred with such brushes in a constant barrage of critique for the sake of criticism, not in a spirit of critical analysis.

Many outside observers have only been willing to credit Hindu religious and cultural manifestations with some form of legal quality if they appeared in the form of codes or, perhaps preferable from a London-based perspective, in the shape of British-style case law. Leading Hindu scholars duly obliged, ever since the British employed more or less learned *pandits* as advisors after 1772, eventually reacting defensively to such challenges by simply asserting that the Hindus have long had what Western observers would recognise as laws. P.V. Kane's monumental *History of Dharmasastra*, written in five volumes towards the end of colonial rule, and originally published between 1930 and 1962, has as its major ideological agenda to prove to the colonial power and later to the world, once and for all, that Hindus have always had laws in a form recognisable by Western lawyers – and were therefore indeed able to govern themselves. Reading Kane, it is thus very important to understand what this great scholar did not say, but how can one do this for long without being accused of constructing one's own images of the subject?

As one of only a few surviving academics in the field, I have learnt to take accusations that I am dangerous or erratic and portray Hinduism or Hindu law in my own idiosyncratic fashion as confirmation that somewhere a raw nerve has been hit and that I must have got it right.[10] One faces similar problems when dealing with 'learned' Hindus, who insist that their views of Hindu tradition should bind my interpretations, whereas I have found many supposedly illiterate Hindus 'on the street' to be much more open to comparative analysis and cross-cultural comparison. Semilearning is positively dangerous, wisdom is evidently not a scholarly prerogative, and complex understandings of 'truths' are clearly not restricted to those with bookderived knowledge. When it comes to Hinduism and

Hindu law, too, we undervalue the elements of orality and traditional internal plurality and seek to indulge our Western fixations with scriptures, certainty and uniformity.

To make it all worse, attempting to explain Hinduism from within, whether to Indians or outsiders, one is today invariably stereotyped as a Hindu revivalist. Especially post-Ayodhya, in the BJP era of modern Indian politics, one is immediately lumped together with *Hindutva* fanaticism, in other words, with various forms of Hindu fundamentalism. So there is even less reason to dedicate precious time to work on Hindu law, it seems, and it is certainly not for the faint-hearted.

HINDU LAW AND RELIGION

As a classically trained indologist turned modern lawyer, working in a British law school,[11] I have always remained deeply uncomfortable about the wonderfully tempting notion that simplifying short labels can be applied to complex concepts like 'religion' and 'law', and that the two can be neatly segregated. I also kept a cautious distance from the idea that what we call 'Hinduism' somehow covers all Hindus and their ways of life and beliefs in any coherent form. Consequently, I would argue here that the notion of Hinduism as a 'religious legal system' is a dangerously simplifying poisoned bait. In the same way that neither 'religion' nor 'law' can be easily circumscribed and classified, the notion of 'Hinduism' as a 'religious legal system' only makes sense to me as a comparative lawyer in that it needs to be instantly rejected. Maybe that is what the organisers of the panel discussion wanted to achieve.

If we go step by step, we see first of all that the scholarly community of indologists broadly agrees nowadays that there is no such thing as one recognisable 'Hinduism'. An important conference panel on this topic in Heidelberg in 1986 resulted in an influential book.[12] If there is no such thing as one Hinduism, consequently there cannot be one religious legal system with the label 'Hindu' attached to it, unless of course we talk ethnically, in which case my task seems very easy: In modern Indian law, too, everything that is not Muslim, Christian, Parsi, Jewish, Sikh, Buddhist or Jaina is legally, according to various Acts on Hindu law and the Constitution of India, presumed to be Hindu. Such exclusive-cum-inclusive methods of defining Hinduness pinpoint the key role of pluralism: Hinduism is so many different things at once, and is internally so diverse that its definition as an identifiable '-ism' has itself remained open to question. Worse, modern Western languages cannot adequately express the holistic and pluralistic concepts of Hindu theory and practice and thus remain inadequate tools for our analytical task. How does one speak to comparative lawyers if one wants to be understood? Certain key elements of Hinduism like *dharma* simply cannot be translated into English without losing precision. *Dharma* is neither 'law' nor 'religion', and yet it encompasses parts of both. This simple, most basic example demonstrates that the internal categorisations of Hindu culture do not match neatly with those of other 'religious' traditions and must be understood in their own right. At the same time, I would resist the argument that, for this reason alone, Hinduism and Hindu law cannot be meaningfully compared and are entirely unique.

Some basic facts, which are too easily overlooked in theoretical discussions, need to be emphasised before we embark on any kind of comparative analysis involving Hindu religion, culture and law. First, Hinduism is today the living tradition of more than 800 million people. One can hardly expect that so many people, even if they live largely in one particular part of the world, would all follow the same religious or legal set of norms to the letter, more so since there is no definitely binding definition of who or what is a Hindu.[13] This, indeed, distinguishes Hinduism from Islam and Christianity, where we find an internally binding, central strand of monotheistic belief that distinguishes a Muslim from a Christian or a Jew, and marks adherents of these faiths off from those of several other world religions. Beyond the very basics of monotheistic belief, faith and submission, however, uniformity of religious and legal manifestations is not really a fact for Islam, Christianity or Judaism either, and thus makes them comparable again to all other religions. In this sense, then, all legal systems of the world are internally plural and diverse, which makes life troublesome (or exciting, depending on your capacity for stomaching diversity) for these '-isms' as well as for all those who want to stereotype in the fashion of the colonial administrator: Muslims believe in one God, Hindus have many, and so on. There is clearly much more to be said about the various laws than the familiar claim that Islamic law, for example, is just God's law.[14]

Second, Hinduism as a historical entity spans more than thousands of years and, in a sense, takes us right back to the origins of the world. It projects past, present and future in an interlinked continuum which is not assumed to explode finally in a big bang, nor arose as such, but which has been ever-present and which appears to renew itself periodically. The cosmic vision, in that sense, is of an everlasting process, which may be cyclical but is certainly not just linear. None of all that Buddhist dreaming about the end of suffering and so on – there is no ramp to Heaven or *nirvana*, despite the alleged importance in Hindu thought of salvation (*moksha*). Still, to make the story more complex, let us be aware that Buddhist (and Jaina) ideas have of course influenced Hinduism, too.

Third, the many different perspectives taken about Hinduism and Hindu law tell us much more about the subjective views and perceptions of those who make those statements and assumptions than about the objective plural realities of Hindu law and religion. From an internal Hindu perspective, the '*dharma* complex' is the central element, with the expectation that all beings should ideally do the right thing at the right time and follow their individual *dharma* to promote and support universal harmony and well-being. Given such holistic conceptualisations, the distinction of 'law' and 'religion' is pretty meaningless and the poor individual soul is, *prima facie*, left to itself to sort out what is right and wrong in any given situation. This, as a terribly onerous individual obligation, reflects the real internal perspective of Hindu law, in which gods and fellow humans may offer guidance to the searching soul, but the final decision is inevitably that of the individual. There is no effort to pretend that the state could come in as the final arbiter, hence legal positivism is not among the available options. *Dharma* requires a method of self-controlled ordering which is based on internal control mechanisms, not external force, which only comes into the picture, conceptually linked but later, as the punishing rod (*danda*) of the ruler, whose primary function is not punishment, but deterrence.[15] Similarly, even Muslims recognise that on Judgement Day, it is not a good enough excuse to defend oneself by pointing to misguided advice by others: There is a never-ending duty and an ultimately individualistic obligation on every believer to find the right path (*shari'a*) for oneself. Scholars may offer useful guidance, but are not the final arbiters in conflict situations, *everyone* may only try their best, and the state plays at most a peripheral role in all of this, in Muslim terminology through the concept of *hadd* punishments, which also have deterrent force for the sake of strengthening selfcontrolled order, rather than immediate punitive application. Hence, from a certain perspective, there must be legitimate doubts about whether the ideally self-controlled types of purely classical Hindu or Muslim law are properly classified as law at all.

It is therefore crucial for the understanding of traditional Hindu law and religion to note that the concept of individual conscience (*atmanastushti*), which first appears in the classical *shastric* literature, becomes the central element of Hindu legal culture, linked to the limitless universal cosmic superstructure with its visible and invisible manifestations. This key concept of Hindu law as a living system rather than a theoretical construct was promptly dismissed by leading legal scholars, in particular Lingat, as outside the realm of the law, because according to Lingat[16] this element of 'individual conscience' was not an entity outside man, and thus not properly a legal factor. Professor Lingat, whose learning in Hindu law is otherwise impeccable and highly illuminating, here used an assumed universal conceptualisation of law, which turns out to be culture-specific and, let us face it, positivistic. Hence, his analysis of how Hindu law 'ticks' is based in the main on a dominant Western understanding of the nature of law and its interrelation with religion and fails to grasp the culture-specific Hindu essence of informal, even invisible, processes of lawmaking. This key example of classical textual interpretation seems to tell us persuasively that Hindu law, too, should be perceived to be about the secular domination of man by law, rather than about man's religious internal selfcontrol, but I fundamentally disagree with Lingat and his manifestly Western assumptions about the universality of legal centralism and of positivist power. For my analysis, the selfcontrolled order of the individual is just as potentially secular as Lingat's assumed outside force that impacts on the Hindu individual.

It is evident that Hindu law, like African laws, Chinese law and even Muslim law, does not start from the assumption that law is in essence state law. Hence such laws do not accept the centrality of a positivistic 'rule of law'. To say the same thing differently, the Hindu 'rule of law' may be similar to natural law approaches in that there is no generally applicable man-made rule, which everyone has to follow, but there is nevertheless a higher concept that pervades everything. Such juggling with words demonstrates our problems as comparative legal analysts with Hindu law material, since the cultural and textual evidence appears to slip all the time into the realms of 'religion' and of 'positive law'. This is quite arbitrary, however, since the eurocentric debates about natural law, and ultimately modern human rights, are presumed to be based on rationality when it is manifest that 'natural law' is also linked to superhuman basics. In contrast, the moment we talk about Hindu law, there is an automatic assumption of religious input, and thus irrationality. I do not think that such arbitrary distribution over the rationality/ irrationality spectrum is value-free or entirely accidental. In other words, the comparative academic analysis of Hindu law as 'law' has been impeded by the *a priori* assumption that every Hindu must have a religious dimension, while somehow Christianity-based laws were able to make distinctions that other systems are presumed not to recognise, so that they could 'progress' to higher levels of development than the 'traditional' religious legal systems of the East.

But how does one express totally holistic diversity in key terms or in a few words, if what is assumed by one culture-specific legal theory to be universal is dismissed by another culture-specific legal theory as non-existent? How do we envision a limitless never-ending continuum which is in constant flux and inter-minable dialectic interaction? Or, to take a simpler and more familiar image, how do we provide a real picture of the huge elephant called Hinduism (not to speak of Hindu 'law') if all we can do is argue about certain details that we think we see and know? In the words of a Somalian proverb, agreement about any of this is as rare as a he-mule with tits! It is in fact worse, as the Islamic principle of 'tolerated diversity' (*ikhtilaf*) explicitly recognises: No human could ever understand the last final detail of that higher entity called 'religion', here manifest in the words of God. Ancient Hindus realised this very early on and wisely agreed to disagree. Hence we have, thousands of years later, a religious tradition that is unwilling to define who should belong and who should not, the upshot is that the entire world is encompassed in the Hindu cosmos, only most people do not know this. Significantly, Hindu ideology has much less trouble justifying this globalising perspective than Islamic globalism, which is so manifestly dependent on the individual commitment of those who believe. In contrast, whether we believe in macrocosmic Hindu ideology or not, it exists and we are part of it because the sun shines for all and the moon is there for all to see. In that respect, *everything* in Hindu culture may be treated as religious, and secularism is perhaps just a learned illusion. But that is definitely not the end of the story.

THE KEY ISSUE OF DIVERSITY

The aforementioned 1986 Heidelberg Conference was motivated by the increas-ingly tricky problem of capturing the never-ending diversity within Hinduism from different perspectives, questioning whether the central notion of Hinduism made any sense at all within an interdisciplinary forum. One could ask similarly whether it makes sense at all, therefore, to speak of Hindu law. The panel organisers in Heidelberg found, very soon, that the idea of a coherent notion of what Hinduism means would have to be abandoned. Simply put, we collectively re-learnt an ancient Hindu lesson: Hinduism itself cannot be circumscribed or defined in any binding and universally valid sense, unlike Islam, in which belief in one specific God, and submission to His will, is assumed to unite all Muslims. The global foundational elements asserted themselves over the minute detail of human existence. In view of such 'big issues', is there any hope that we may understand segments like the nature of Hindu law?

Invariably, Hindus and non-Hindus alike have certain ideas about Hinduism as a religious legal system. Thus, we tend to envision a theistic religion with some Godlike figure, if not a specific God, to be 'in charge' of the world, which is in itself a remarkably positivistic assumption. This is contradicted by Hindu representations to the effect that all gods are themselves subject to a higher order, coupled with doubts over whether there actually is one God at all. Hence while for many scholars polytheism and monotheism cannot see eye to eye, Hinduism manages to make allowances for both and has even allowed the One to be defined as a biochemical or otherwise metaphysical entity rather than a personal God-in-charge. From a Hindu perspective, belief in one God can easily be seen as irrational, even dangerous and risky, while acceptance of plurality alone might be treated as a rational consequence of lived human experience. From such basic pluralities flow many others, to which outsiders have given disparaging labels: polytheism, superstition, blind belief, and the like.

But those very same 'rational' outsiders fervently believe (as do many Hindus as a result of being taught by such 'rationalists') in myths of a Hindu Ur-man called Manu who made laws for all Hindus. There are many humanly constructed, religiously inspired legal pretensions to the effect that human law-making based on divine inspiration is the foundation of Hindu law. The inevitable result is the construction of Hindu law as a positivistic, ultimately statecentred legal system in which wise old men lay down rules for all others, as happens in properly structured systems of 'rule of law'. Such assumptions constantly deny the situation-centred, culture-specific and innately religious elements of Hinduism any legal relevance and merely search for familiar, inherently positivistic manifestations of law in the shape of Austinian carbon copies. What sort of comparative endeavour is that? In my view, this is no comparison at all, it is a redefinition of 'the other' in our terms, which that other would not recognise without the civilising efforts that have been made globally to carry Christian values around the globe and preach the virtues of modernistic development. I am not surprised that modern Hindus are so confused, I see them all the time in my classes, often gasping in disbelief. However the present discussion is not the place to elaborate on what may happen when Hindus rediscover 'their' identity.

At a more sophisticated level of ignorance, commonly perceived to be characteristic of Hinduism, recognition of the divinely revealed status of the Vedas, belief in reincarnation, the doctrine of *karma* and the caste system are highlighted as conceptual foundations of that cultural and legal tradition. But we know very well that many Hindus reject all or some of these so-called key elements, and it has remained impossible to posit – as can be done for Islam – that adherence to certain absolutely fundamental basics of belief is common to all Hindus and marks out their adherence to Hinduism as a religion. Thus, if we are faced with a collection of religions here[17] rather than one coherent religious system, how can this nonsystem lead to something that we recognise as a religious legal system? Within the overarching religious framework of Hinduism, there is much more scope for secular analysis and development than most analysts can imagine.

LEVELS OF HINDU LAW AS A RELIGIOUS LEGAL SYSTEM

As indicated earlier, I find that the categories of 'religion' and 'law' itself are highly problematic in themselves. By definition, it would appear that a religion can never be a law, otherwise what would be the point of using two words for one and the same thing? The term 'religion' has remained troublesome not only because of the complexities of 'religion' itself, but also because in modernist discourses religion has been defined politically and ideologically. 'Religious law' means thus, first of all, a law made by religious authorities masking as legal authorities, so that both 'religion' and 'law' represent different forms of potentially competing ultimate authority. No wonder, then, that positivist discourse is so hostile towards religion: it masks a headon competition for power within the same social field. In another sense, 'religion' is identifiably religious if it is beyond the control of man, while 'law' is portrayed as secular, man-made, and open to constant modification and manipulation by so-called legal processes rather than superhuman writ.

The trouble is, of course, that these categories have not remained uncontaminated entities and that, in Hindu law as well as in many other traditional systems, any particular secular sphere seems still more or less entirely part of a wider religious complex, which law can declare 'extra-legal', but which does not thereby disappear from the scene and becomes legally irrelevant. In that wider sense, all of Hindu existence is religious forever, and in that spirit I originally wanted to title this paper along those lines. Religious authority of this type can easily be presented and represented by men (and sometimes women), making the claim that it should unquestionably be higher than 'law' and thus often challenging any particular legal, secular claims to dominance. Hence the common argument that religion is a source of law, even *the* source of law, a phrase that Muslims these days seem to carry on the tip of their tongue whenever it suits them politically,[18] and which some Hindus, too, have learnt to copy. However, such tempting arguments collapse as soon as one reminds the Hindu claimant of the internal plurality of deities, which no reference to the ultimate oneness of all superhuman manifestations can make irrelevant or nonexistent. For Muslims, too, a reference to the ultimate impossibility of ascertaining God's word in the Qur'an, even for the most learned individuals, has the same effect. The Qur'an is not merely 'the law', but a *source* of law which needs to be found and applied by man, and hence law inevitably extends to the realm of human reason rather than simply and purely to divine revelation. Had it not been so, then the history of Islamic law would have been very different indeed. In the same way, the Vedas are for Hindus never just the words of a defined God, but manifestations of a nutshell of superhuman truth that man may forever attempt to decode, but will never crack. This recognition of the ultimate limits of human endeavour distinguishes Eastern from Western traditions, and hence makes it questionable whether Islamic law should really be counted in the same group as Christian and Jewish laws. Does Islamic law rather belong to a wider non-Western category in which man is not perceived to be in ultimate control of ordering even the most microcosmic spaces? In other words, is it perhaps correct to put Hindu law and Muslim law into the same basket of 'religious laws'?

Like Islamic law, Hindu law is not entirely or exclusively religious law. Hinduism in its long history has, not surprisingly, been tempted to some extent to argue along basically positivistic religious lines, namely that *shruti*, in essence the Vedas, as the divinely revealed law, is supreme and therefore must of necessity be the source of all legal rules. It is impossible to argue that this approach has been influenced by Muslim techniques of interpretation, since the *Mimamsa* schools of thought in Hinduism which insist on Vedic predominance and divine status certainly predate Islam. Hence the reverse is possible: Have Muslims been inspired by Hindu techniques of asserting the power of divine revelations? All of this is speculation and goes too far here.

The Hindus themselves, probably very early on, realised that in the absence of agreement over who created the world, and hence the absence of one God who gave them their revealed collective knowledge in the shape of the Vedas, any argument that the Veda equals Truth, which equals supernatural power, which then equals law, was just like a giant magic mushroom-induced hallucination. Given the tenuous stories and mythologies about how the Vedas were created and transmitted, it has been theoretically impossible for Hindus to rely on a uniform central doctrine to the effect that a creator-God gave them their system in ready-made form and that all one had to do was to submit to that God's law. *Mimamsaka* approaches to Hindu law have therefore remained a highly sophisticated intellectual pursuit of little legal relevance, and they are practically dead today.[19] This confirms my central point that Hinduism, because of its pluralistic internal history of construction, could never become a religious legal system beyond the higher level of macrocosmic ordering, but became an essentially secular, man-made microcosmic conglomerate of both religion and law. The Hindus could use this as they pleased – but at their peril, given the all-pervasive *dharma*-complex as a supervening conceptual entity, which constantly drags everything back into the realm of the religious, as we shall see a little further below.

If Hindus agreed to disagree about religious beliefs a long time ago, did this give Hindu religious law less power? What is Hinduism as a constructed religious system, if it is not a religious *legal* system? Hinduism is, first of all, manifestly a collective term, derived from a slightly modified label for the people living on the other side of the river Sindhu, applied to several different forms of religions which originated in South Asia. The term itself is much younger than the religions it encompasses, which is why many indologists do not like to use the term 'Hinduism' for early forms of the tradition. However, all Hindu systems have at their core a holistic awareness that the universe as a whole is interconnected (the *rita* complex), that every living microcosm is linked together visibly and invisibly, and that this system will carry on regardless of what you and I, and hundreds of millions of Hindus and all the other living beings, are going to do with their lives. Call this essentialising, but that is the essence of ancient Hinduism in a nutshell.

Such a globalised worldview is hardly a ready-made basis for a particular legal system, since it seems to imagine a limitless plurality of interconnected existences that are somehow held together by the cosmic containers of *rita*, macrocosmic order, and *dharma*, microcosmic order, hence the key concept of duty.[20] Significantly these key elements exist whether we are aware of them or not, so from a Hindu perspective everyone is a Hindu, they just don't know it. This is the mildest form or, you might say, the most deeply fundamentalist manifestation of universalising Hinduism. From a Hindu perspective, therefore, Hinduism does encompass all the non-Hindus as well, they are just unconscious and unaware of *rita* and *dharma*, and are thus incapable of making informed decisions about their own actions in the light of Hindu interconnectedness. Lingat would have said that they are therefore unable to enjoy the fruits of their deeds in the next life[21], but many Hindus do not even believe in a next life. The point is, to take it a step further, that Hindus do not have to believe anything, it seems, they simply have to accept that they are subject to – and are therefore certainly intrinsically part of – the universal order which is manifest all around us. This is not necessarily a matter of acceptance, it may well be treated as a matter of fact.

If ancient man had been able to solve the riddles of life and death, then Hindu law would have developed differently, but clearly this was not possible, and the wise ancient men agreed that they did not know the ultimate answers as to where and how life begins, and how and why it ends. The resultant unending plurality of Hindu views and lifestyles is not as chaotic as many people assume, it is systemically coherent. Because cosmic existence is taken as a fact, it is neither a 'religious' nor a 'legal' requirement among Hindus to link oneself constantly to the universal order in any particular way – that is down to circumstances and to individual discretion in line with customs and traditions. Both religion and law, then, are treated as human constructs within the wider context of a superhuman structure that cannot be explained, but that is there, whether we like it or not. Hence, the mere fact of existence inescapably submits everything and everyone to this supervening order. To that extent, Hinduism became not a matter of belief, nor explicitly of submission, but a way of life. Not surprisingly, many Hindus are therefore atheists, and belief in biochemistry and metaphysics can be as good as (or may be combined with) worship of any cow, crow or deity.

In that most fundamental sense, then, Hinduism can indeed be seen as a religious legal system. No amount of formal legal definition and redefinition, or modernist legal reform, can take this away from any Hindu, because this is *prima facie* a matter of fundamental existence as well as freedom of religion, and not a question of law. However, how do we define a 'religious legal system' if reference to *rita* and *dharma* works primarily on the individual conscience, and not through the state as a maker of laws?

Analysts seem to be fascinated by the image of the Hindu 'holy man' who stipulates legal norms, the long shadow of Manu, the proverbially bogus Hindu lawgiver. Saffron-robe-clad dropouts roaming around in modern India give exactly that impression, but do you realise how widely they are held in contempt, especially if they wanted to declare the law, or now even have themselves elected as legislators? If the Bharatiya Janata Party in modern India seems *sadhu*-friendly, are the laws they make thereby religious law, or is it a form of state law that cleverly seems to exploit religion to legitimise itself, but in fact promotes its own political agenda?

To answer this, let me illustrate the dilemma of the ancient Hindu king or ruler, the *raja*, which is still reflected in modern Indian forms of governance whose understanding continues to elude us. Western model concepts of the positivist type assume that the classical Hindu ruler was a more or less despotic autocrat with the power to make rules as he pleased. Yes, such a ruler could try and abuse his powers, but he would not be seen as a good and lawful ruler, since Hindu tradition does not subscribe to or underwrite primitive despotism. The discovery early in the twentieth century of the *arthashastra*, ancient India's Macchiavellian handbook for rulers, as some have called it,[22] proved for many observers that India had a secular tradition of law-making, embodied in the concept of *artha*, focused on worldly goods and possessions, which here includes naked power. But such analyses have overlooked important unspoken – or invisible – assumptions within Hindu cultural traditions, with which insiders like the author of the *arthashastra* and his audience were familiar, so that there was no need to highlight them or mention them in so many words. Overlooking this element of purposeful textual silence, outsiders have remained in the dark, including many indologists who were just grammar-focused philologists and understood neither the ways of ancient Hindu society nor its laws.

Visibly, the Hindu ruler is in charge of his realm. Invisibly, however, the Hindu ruler is never a master of his own making, he remains a servant of *rita* and *dharma*. Hence, the superficially evident conclusion that *artha* must be secular, because we treat 'law' and 'power' as secular entities, is manifestly incomplete and misguided. Since *artha* remains at all times a sub-category of *dharma*, which every Hindu knows but outside observers overlooked, the Hindu ruler may make law, with the higher aim of promoting *rita* and *dharma*, but not for his own narrow benefit, and certainly not because he wishes the law to be in a particular form. Legislative intent, if it existed as a concept at all, expressing the free will of the ruler, had to be grounded in *dharmic* necessity. There will have been much lawlessness in ancient India, but legal absolutism was most definitely a theoretical as well as practical aberration, which could not justify and legitimise pompous assertions of power.

The ancient Hindu ruler therefore had a most demanding and difficult job as servant of *dharma*. Being a ruler meant having enhanced obligations rather than inflated rights, it meant accountability at all levels. While many rulers must have been tempted to overstep the limits of their *dharmic* brief and made rules as they pleased, rulers who subordinated justice to their whim, as we are told even in the *arthashastra* itself, might not survive in power for long. While secular concepts of law assume that the ruler is accountable to a body politic, however defined, the ancient Hindu ruler was first and foremost responsible to nobody in particular, but to the cosmic whole and the *dharma* complex. We may well see here parallels with the Daoist concept of the Mandate of Heaven and with African conceptual-isations of what it means to be in charge of a group of people or a certain territory. The Hindu ruler's responsibility to the cosmic whole is not only expressed in the intensely competitive link of ruler and Brahmin, but also in the limited authority that the Hindu ruler actually had over making rules. Far from being empowered to make law for his people, as we know only too well, his main function is to create – and more so, maintain – an environment in which all citizens are assisted in the fulfilment of their own personal *dharma*, thus promoting what we know to be the conceptual ideal, namely a system of selfcontrolled order. The ruler's *dharma*, the *rajadharma*, is therefore to protect other people's space for develop-ing their *dharma*, not to lay down rules for the subjects. Thus, religion remains a source of law here only in the sense that it legitimises and virtually requires the state's non-intervention in the substantive legal rules that people have been creating for themselves at lower levels.

This example shows that religion and law co-exist for Hindus and strengthen each other, *we* are the ones who put them in binary opposition. From a Hindu perspective, the practical emphasis is on custom as a source of law, where *sadacara*, acting in line with what one's social group considers as appropriate, is the major source of Hindu law. There is unequivocal agreement between Professor Derrett and myself[23] about *sadacara* as the major source of Hindu law, in daily practice being placed higher than religious authority in the form of any holy man laying down the law, or state law in any form, for that matter. Hence, in case this needs to be said again in view of whole issues of modern journals concerned about abuses,[24] there is no democratically sound conceptual legitimation from within Hinduism for godmen and other 'inspired' forces to lay down the law for the state or for any individual. Any form of Hindu religious authority merely has guidance value, no more, it is not and cannot be prescriptive, since no two people have the same *dharma*. *Hindutva* in India today, therefore, looks like a bogus positivist neo-Hindu growth that violates the basic norms of traditional Hindu society in misrepresenting the power of male-focused authorities.

But, you will say, is it not a fact that the ancient Hindu ruler, as people's leader, had the power to make laws as he pleased? Yes, of course, but in his temptation to make rules that pleased him, rather than his people, he did what all persons in position of authority are constantly tempted to do, he abused his position and overstepped his powers. The ancient *shastric* texts are full of evidence to the effect that such abuse was possible, and could be legitimated by emphasising only the visible strain of political power and its consequences. By leaving out the invisible, by secularising Hindu law, in other words, scholarship has removed the internal, invisible self-control mechanisms of Hindu law and has been helping, therefore, to legitimise abuses of power. I have long found this immensely dangerous, also because it has enormously helped all those who like to argue that Hinduism and Hindu law are intrinsically religion-centred and hence 'traditional' and medieval, undemocratic, and more recently, violative of human rights norms.

All of this is ideologically constructed and purposely tailor-made scholarship that does not even bother to capture the spirit of Hindu law but works from convenient, externally-oriented stereotypes with a view to achieving certain political aims. Hindus themselves, the silent majority, are often too polite to explain this to the misguided outsider, or, like Rajeev Dhavan, who tried to write about this in the 1990s,[25] they are too brainwashed by Western legal education to have maintained the capacity to express the invisible elements underlying all forms of Hindu and in fact Indian laws.

MANIFESTATIONS OF 'RELIGIOUS' ELEMENTS IN MODERN HINDU LAW

Muddled debates over whether Hindu laws are 'religious' or 'secular' have continued into our days. Two brief examples here must suffice to illustrate the resulting confusions about our interpretations of modern Indian law and its relationship with 'religion' and 'Hindu tradition'. First, Mrs. Gandhi in 1975, in her anguish over the continuing lack of democratic development and the abuse of the post-colonial Indian legal system by the elite, remembered and realised that she was not only Prime Minister of modern India, but also a successor to the ancient Hindu tradition of the *raja*. Most political analysts saw only the brutal dictator, who brought about India's only emergency, visibly a dictatorship, which seemed to extinguish all proper legal processes. Invisibly, though, as Ramchandra Guha has recently confirmed[26] she also wanted to bring her country's legal system back to the recognition of *dharmic* basics about interconnectedness by increasing democratic accountability and implementation of fundamental human rights. Suspending the Constitution, and thus withdrawing power from the abusers of legal privileges, she reminded the whole nation that hundreds of millions of

Indians had no access to the Constitution and its wonderful basic guarantees. In a nutshell, she made everyone face up to the reality that it was necessary to rethink why and how the basic modern legal rules had become so inequitable. Indira Gandhi promptly amended the Indian Constitution in very significant ways, increasing access to justice and highlighting the element of duty over that of rights. More or less indirectly, this constitutional re-orientation has given rise to phenomena like public interest litigation, which have yet to be analysed comprehensively as Hindu-inspired techniques of safeguarding holistic balances in an intensely politicised and competitive socio-legal environment. Thus, my argument here is that Indian public law has been invisibly reconstructed along Hindu lines through the Emergency of 1975–77 and in its aftermath. This was not a matter of Hinduism becoming 'the law of the nation', but a selective use of Hindu concepts for constructing a post-modern, post-colonial South Asian legal system in which it is actually irrelevant whether a rule is legitimated by religion or by law, since the higher intrinsic value of justice and 'appropriateness' is still the focal concern. Hence it is situational justice that counts most in modern Indian legal hierarchies of values, not the mere letter of the law.

Second, the current reconstruction of post-modern Indian family laws also displays the same trend towards situation-specific justice and has been strangely unconnected to any particular government in charge. While successive Indian parliaments have been too busy with their own survival, the new legal developments have to a large extent been judge-driven, which reflects further on the use of underlying invisible Hindu elements in modern Indian law. Rather than constructing a formally uniform, legislated secular legal system for all Indians, the judges as a collective body have developed the existing personal law system on a case-by-case basis, to a point where all the various concurrent rule systems operate more or less along similar lines. Remarkably, the culturally familiar 'unity in diversity' is maintained in this pluralistic way also within the formal legal system. In terms of substance, too, the most recent family law developments systematically place duties on those who have control over resources, manifestly to ensure the survival of those who require support.[27] Such support, like in ancient India, is not directly given by the state itself, so that the Hindu definition of the post-modern welfare state envisages and operates a system that creates conditions in which no individual should fall through the welfare net. In other words, *sadacara*, self-control mechanisms at societal level in the form of social welfare, rather than provision of centralised state welfare, is the desired and actually achievable result. We see here Indian, and to some extent self-consciously Hindu, models of sustainable contemporary development that feed on ancient religious concepts which have lost none of their relevance and validity today, but must not be talked about as 'religious' for reasons of political correctness.

If we, as theoretical analysts with our own political agenda, wish to argue for the irrelevance of religion as a source of law in the modern world, we will therefore not be totally happy with the complex evidence from ancient India and probably deeply dissatisfied with modern Indian law for failing to follow Western secular models. Ancient Indian law appears to have placed 'religion' in the widest sense above 'law', while yet leaving 'law' – within the basic model of self-controlled order – to sort out daily realities in an outwardly secular fashion. Modern Indian law uses the concept of secularism as a means to strengthen respect for all religions, demanding their equal treatment in a Hindu-dominated state. Further, it has also built the central but invisible elements of Hindu religion into modern legal structures and demands constant accountability to a higher entity from all those who claim to rule in any form, and even of all citizens.[28] Nothing much seems to have changed in comparison to ancient Hindu laws, therefore, and even in modern Indian law the *dharma* complex is still a focal point of legal reference, now interacting with an outwardly dominant formal system of legislated law and Hindu case law. In that sense, modern Indian law has remained more strongly imbued with Hindu values and more local or indigenous (*deshi*) in nature than anyone would wish to admit.

CONCLUSIONS

Perhaps the basic Hindu concept that everyone should at all times be accountable for all their actions is not actually just Hindu, it is a universal concept, in harmony with natural law ideas of justice. In fact, it may be one of those elements of universal law that we find so difficult to implement in practice but love to venerate in principle. Put differently, within a holistic framework of reference and with a focus on justice, whether with Hindu cultural characteristics or not, the distinction of 'religious' and 'secular' is perhaps actually meaningless. If one accepts that all secular activities in all legal systems occur within a wider framework of religious assumptions, which may well include the absence of God, as the Hindu case so clearly demonstrates, then what is the point of writing books on law and religion? Given that we cannot define religion or law universally, that all forms of belief must be seen as religious, and that secularism becomes then also a form of religion, where is the scope for classification, distinction, and lengthy discourses? None of this is new to Hindu lawyers – they had enormously complex debates about such issues several thousand years ago, but they did not think they were lawyers, they probably assumed they were striving to understand *dharma*. The manifest evidence is that the ancient Hindus effectively turned away from such debates to a large extent, imbibed the holistic key messages in their ways of life, and let them be filtered through the ages in cultural osmosis. No miracle we are so confused today and find Hindu law so difficult to disentangle.

To return, finally, to the possibilities of finding answers for the questions asked in this volume about law and religion, I shall continue to evade firm commitment to the so-called secular agenda, since secularity appears to be merely an alternative religion. It follows that dividing the laws of the world into families of law may be useful, provided they are really related, but what about intermarriages, trans-migrations, or transfers of concepts that muddy the waters? The conventional division of common law and civil law has long ceased to impress me, given that already the colonial Indian system was a subtle mixture of Scottish and English law, and hence most definitely not just pure 'common law'. It may be useful to consider in more depth how different culture-specific legal systems may be grouped together. But then, at the end of the day, all legal systems are culture-specific on their own terms, and hence all laws are culture-specific elements that invite comparisons but may not provide much comparative illumination. I am not saying that comparison is useless, but the history of comparative legal effort is so tainted by politicised abuse that I have preferred to devote more effort to exploring culture-specificity here than to speculation about possible legal comparisons. Perhaps it is right to assume that being a regional specialist and becoming a comparativist do not go together easily.

As for 'religious systems', nobody will presumably want to argue about the inherently religious nature of Hindu law, which has been co-existing with secularity in the realm of customary as well as state-made Hindu laws. But what about debating the extent of cultural-cum-religious influence on so-called secular legal systems? If I am right on that count, and I take strength from Chiba's analysis in that regard, then efforts of classifying any member of any legal family as 'religious' law are simply meaningless for comparative purposes and merely disclose the ideological inclinations of those who propose such classifications.

NOTES

1 There are historical layers of such purported irrelevance even within Hindu law itself. Thus, the largely forgotten Vedic foundations of Hinduism, revered on the one hand and ignored on the other, have led to an ambivalent scholarly relationship between tradition and modernity within Hinduism and its various manifestations. See further: Werner Menski [1997]: *Indian Legal Systems Past and Present,* Occasional Papers No. 3 (London: SOAS Law Department, 1997).
2 René David and John E.C. Brierley, *Major Legal Systems in the World Today.* 2nd ed. (London: Stevens & Sons, 1978).
3 Konrad Zweigert and Hein Kötz, *Introduction to Comparative Law.* Translated from the German by Tony Weir, 3rd rev. ed. (Oxford: Clarendon Press, 1998).
4 H. Patrick Glenn, *Legal Traditions of the World. Sustainable Diversity in Law.* (Oxford: Oxford University Press, 2000).
5 See further: Werner F. Menski, *Comparative Law in a Global Context: The Legal Systems of Asia and Africa* (London: Platinium, 2000).
6 id.
7 Antony N. Allott, *The Limits of Law* (London: Butterworths, 1980).
8 On religion in Chinese law see further Menski, *supra* note 5, at 439–532.
9 Masaji Chiba, *Asian Indigenous Law in Interaction with Received Law* (London: KPI, 1986).
10 For an example see Werner F. Menski 1998 'Sati: A review article' *Bulletin of the School of Oriental and African Studies* 61: 74–81.
11 Even the term 'British' now no longer reassuringly means what it used to imply, as the recent Runnymede Report highlighted to widespread howls of dismay: Bhikhu Parekh, *The Future of Multi-ethnic Britain* (London: Profile Books, 2000).

125

12 Gunther-D. Sontheimer and Hermann Kulke (eds), *Hinduism Reconsidered* (New Delhi: Manohar, 1989).

13 See further: J. Duncan M. Derrett, 'The Definition of a Hindu'. In: *Supreme Court Journal*, Journal Section II: 67–74 (1966); J. Duncan M. Derrett, 'Unity in Diversity: The Hindu Experience' *Bharata Manisha* 5: 21–36 (1979).

14 Michael King (ed.), *God's Law versus State Law* (London: Grey Seal, 1995).

15 Terence P. Day, *The Conception of Punishment in Early Indian Literature* (Waterloo: Wilfred Laurier University Press, 1982).

16 Robert Lingat, *The Classical Law of India* (Berkeley: University of California Press), 6.

17 Heinrich von Stietencron, 'Hinduism: On the Proper Use of a Deceptive Term' 11–27 of ed. Sontheimer and Kulke, *supra* note 12.

18 It is not a new concept, however: see Noel J. Coulson, *Conflicts and Tensions in Islamic Jurisprudence* (Chicago: University of Chicago Press, 1969).

19 Significantly, radically 'fundamentalist' Muslim schools of thought such as that of the Zahiris, arguing along similar lines, have died out as school traditions as well but continue to exert a powerful ideological influence. See further: Menski, *supra* note 5, at 209–324.

20 Surya P. Subedi, 'Are the Principles of Human Rights "Western" Ideas? An Analysis of the Claims of the "Asian" Concept of Human Rights from the Perspective of Hinduism' *California Western International Law Journal* 30: 45–69 (1999).

21 Lingat, *supra* note 16.

22 R.P. Kangle, *The Kautiliya Arthashastra* Part II (Bombay: University of Bombay, 1972).

23 J. Duncan M. Derrett, *Religion, Law and the State in India* (London: Faber and Faber, 1968); Menski, *supra* note 1.

24 See now *Ethnic and Racial Studies* Vol. 23 No. 3 (May 2000).

25 Rajeev Dhavan, 'Dharmasastra and Modern Indian Society: A Preliminary Exploration' *Journal of the Indian Law Institute* 34: 515–540 (1992).

26 *India Today* (3rd July, 2000: 34–35).

27 See further: Werner F. Menski, *Modern Indian Family Law* (Richmond: Curzon Press, 2001).

28 See Article 51-A of the Constitution, the 'Fundamental Duties'.

8

BUDDHIST LAW AS A
RELIGIOUS SYSTEM?

Andrew Huxley[1]

Karl Marx, looking back on his first attempt to elaborate a philosophy of law, complained that it was 'replete with tripartite divisions'.[2] He would have hated this chapter on Buddhist law: I divide Buddhism into three traditions (Tibetan, Chinese and Pali); I divide the history of Pali Buddhism into three periods (formative, classical and bricolage); and I analyse Buddhist law from three points of view (of monks, of kings and of the laity). Is this trichotomising forced on me by the phenomena I describe? I hope so, but I cannot shake the suspicion that I am unconsciously reading into Buddhist law something I have picked up from Roman law. I do not want, at any rate, to irritate Karl Marx's ghost: I require his assistance to get past Max Weber, who blocks the entrance to Buddhist law growling 'Go away! There's nothing here to study'. Or, as Weber puts it, 'Ancient Buddhism' was a 'specifically unpolitical and anti-political status religion'.[3] His version of Buddhism was acted out by a few anti-social monks deep in some Indian jungle; it never made much impression on the rest of society. With the sole exception of John Wigmore,[4] comparative lawyers have accepted Weber's word. The latest survey of legal traditions around the world, for example, tells us that 'Because of Buddhist teaching there aren't many lawyer Buddhists',[5] and that 'Buddhism emerged... essentially in protest against the (legal) formalism of hindu teaching'.[6]

Before I sketch the evidence which persuades me that Weber and his followers are wrong, let us consider the plausibility of his proposition in the abstract. Where the people have chosen Buddhism as their particular opium (where Buddhism acts as 'the sigh of the oppressed creature, the comfort of a heartless world'[7]), how was their repression organised? In the absence of Buddhist law and Buddhist politics, what kind of legal and political superstructure supports the dominant class in Buddhist countries? What would Marx have said? Surely a state organised on Hindu or Confucian principles could have little purchase on the hearts and minds of a Buddhist populace. Under such circumstances, how will the ideologues of the ruling class manage to bind the lower classes in ropes of religion and law? Yet this was Weber's position. He described *dhammasat* and *rajasat* (the mainland

Southeast Asian legal literature of the last thousand years) as 'a law of Hindu origin modified in the direction of Buddhism'.[8]

Weber misinterpreted Buddhism because he coincided with the birth of European Buddhology. He knew only the first thirty years of work on ancient Indian Buddhism (400 BCE–200 CE). A lot has been rediscovered since then, in particular, for those trying to understand law and government around 200 BCE, Kautilya's *Arthasastra* in 1905. Weber knew only the first ten years of research on the Southeast Asian Buddhist legal tradition (1000–2000 CE). We now have about ten times as many pre-colonial lawtexts as were available to Weber's informants. In particular, for those interested in the beginnings of the tradition, we can now understand the copious epigraphy of twelfth-century Pagan. Those of us who have studied Buddhist Southeast Asia as it was in 1870 CE at the start of colonisation tend to find more law and politics in the ancient Indian texts than did the pioneers. The premise of this chapter is that we can bring modern Southeast Asia together with ancient Indian Buddhism and label the combination 'the Pali Buddhist legal tradition'.

This chapter delivers less than its title promises: it is restricted to Pali Buddhism, one of the three major sub-divisions into which contemporary Buddhism divides. Over 2,500 years many Buddhist traditions have risen to fame, and nearly as many have drifted back into obscurity. Each tradition preserved its own particular literature, often in its own language and script. While Islamic, Chinese and Jewish law texts prefer to be written in the Arabic, Chinese and Hebrew languages, Buddhism can display no such preference. The common core of Buddhist literature (which ranges from the legalisms of the *patimokkha* and the dry psychological lists of the *Abidhamma* texts to such literary masterpieces as the *Sutta of the Great Decease*) is preserved in about fifteen different languages and about thirty different scripts. We have learnt to adopt a postmodern disregard for absolutes in our discussions of this common core. Claims that 'Sanskrit texts are more authentically Buddhist than Tibetan' or that 'Chinese texts have preserved the earliest form of Buddhism' will start arguments, maybe fights. Each Buddhist tradition typically seems to have preserved a literature that was three parts common core to one part unique texts. There is no complete agreement on what constitutes this common core, but most Buddhologists would, I think, agree with these two generalisations about Buddhist law. First, traditions which preserved their own *vinaya* text survived longer than those which didn't.[9] Second, the Tibetan, Chinese and Pali trichotomy can be expressed as three living *vinaya* traditions. Chinese and other East Asian monks follow the *Dharmagupta vinaya*, Tibetan and other Central Asian monks follow the *Mulasarvastivada vinaya*, while Southeast Asian and Sri Lankan monks follow the *Pali Vinaya*.[10] Over the last twenty years, a significant amount of work has been done on legalism in the Pali tradition.[11] As a result, Pali Buddhism now seems predominately historical, meditative and legalistic. Whereas Tibetan and Chinese Buddhism seem more concerned with deconstruction and theology. If such a thing as Buddhist law exists, it follows that we are most likely to find it in the Pali tradition.

Table 8.1 sketches the three periods into which I divide Pali Buddhist legal history. To allow comparison with the familiar, I have juxtaposed the landmarks

Table 8.1 Romano-Buddhist legal chronologies

Roman law	Pali Buddhist law
Formative period: 500–50 BCE	*Formative period*: 500–50 BCE
450 BCE *XII Tables*	400 BCE ob. Gautama Buddha
198 BCE *Tripertita*	250 BCE King Ashoka's *Rock Edicts*
82 BCE ob. Q. Mucius Scaevola	50 BCE *Vinayapali* written down
Classical period: 50 BCE–1000 CE	*Classical period*: 50 BCE–1000 CE
43 BCE ob. M. Tullius Cicero	50 *Parivara, Milinda's Questions*
100–223 Golden age of *responsa*	430 the vinaya commentaries: *Sp, Kkh*
310 Constantine	489 *Sp* translated into Chinese
530 *Corpus Iuris Civilis*	
Bricolage period: 1000–1900 CE	*Bricolage period*: 1000–1900 CE
1120 Irnerius at Bologna	1165 'official' sub-cty on *Sp* [SL]
1140 Gratian's *Concordantia*	1200 Pagan dhammathats [SEA]
1180 *Libri feudorum*	1500 Chiangmai law-texts [SEA]
1500 Budaeus	1605 Lawyers in Burma
1625 Grotius	1770 Burmese law-texts flourish
1690 Jean Domat	1805 *Three Seals Code* [Bangkok]
1750 Robert Pothier	1840 Khmer law-texts flourish

Notes
All dates are approximate; Buddhist dates are approximate and controversial.

of Roman Legal development. I have applied the same periodisation to the two traditions, but at the price of using the familiar term 'classical' in an unfamiliar way. By the *formative* period of Roman law, I mean especially the last two centuries of the Republic, following S. Aelius Paetus' *Tripertita*. The textual redaction associated with Justinian marks the peak of the *classical* period (as I use the term). Justinian and Trebonian edited the wisdom of the past into a textual package that could survive into the future. During the *Bricolage period*, European lawyers adapted this *Corpus Iuris* to new ends, producing such Romanoid inventions as Canon law, tracts on feudal law in Latin and the Grotian *Law of Nations*. There are parallels between Justinian and the fifth-century author of the *vinaya commentary* and *patimokkha commentary*. Both men reordered the material at their disposal so as to make it of maximal utility to other legal specialists. Both men were working in a new cultural centre (Constantinople, Anuradhapura) with a legal tradition that had originated elsewhere (Rome, Northern India) and both were concerned with the relationship between languages of rule (Greek, Sinhalese) and the international language of their material (Latin, Pali). There are further parallels between Irnerius and his successors and the Southeast Asian bricoleurs. Roman law under Justinian still ruled an empire, while for Irnerius, it had become a classical law (that is, a repository of best ancient practice) to be studied, theorised and quarried for raw materials. The authors of *dhammasat* and *rajasat* treated the Pali vinaya literature as their classical law. They mixed it with other Buddhist sources and with a pinch of Hindu legal material to create a law for the ordinary rice-farmers.

In sketching the Pali Buddhist legal tradition, I shall compromise between the diachronic and the synchronic. In order to persuade Weberian waverers, I must provide an historical account of the tradition's development. In order to elucidate the complex relationship between law and religion, I would prefer to treat it as a whole, independent of its history. What follows is divided into three sections. They deal with three periods in the development of Buddhism, while also dealing with three different consumer groups for Buddhist law. The first section, which treats the last five centuries BCE, looks at Buddhist law as it applies to monks. The second section, which describes the first millenium CE, examines the Buddhist law for kings. The third section, which summarises the second millenium CE, concentrates on Buddhist law for the laity.

FORMATIVE PERIOD (500–50 BCE): IS THE *VINAYA* RELIGIOUS LAW?

On 22nd March, 1807, King Badon of Burma prefaced one of his formal orders with the following:

> The Buddha's teachings comprise scriptures, practice and insight. Let us start with the scriptures. Learn the *suttas*, obey the *vinaya* and work progressively at the *abidhamma*. [ROB 22-3-1807][12]

The *suttas*, which we must learn, are the Buddha's sermons, primarily on ethics and psychology. The *vinaya*, which we must obey, is the set of rules and procedures that define how monks live together. The *abidhamma*, at which we must work progressively, are the texts that accompany meditation. Buddhism is the combination of these three pursuits – does that make it a religion? If I could cram the essence of Buddhism into a single sentence, then you would be able to answer this question for yourself. Bob Marley came nearest to doing this: 'Every need got an ego to feed'.[13] The Buddhist *diagnosis* of human suffering is that need (or grasping, or desire) causes our illusion of ego (or consciousness, or subjective personality). We suffer because we mistakenly think we have an ego. The Buddhist *cure* reverses this chain of causation: To end suffering we must remove the illusion. We do this by psychosurgically removing our mental need-functions, a process requiring intense meditation, impeccable moral behaviour and total chastity. In both the Confucian and Aristotelian traditions, virtue takes most of a lifetime to acquire. Buddhism takes even longer: it takes several hundred lifetimes before those brain-functions are completely shut down, and nirvana is fully achieved.

Notice the importance of causation in this analysis. If the practice of Buddhism is largely meditation, doctrinal Buddhism consists largely in the analysis of causation. The Buddhist creed mentions only the theory of multifactored causation (which the nineteenth-century translators called 'codependent origination'). At the centre of Buddhism, then, is the belief that, of all the causes that coalesce to bring about an effect, no single one can be singled out as *causa efficiens* or *causa sine qua non*. One of the many causes of Abraham Lincoln's demise was that John Wilkes Booth pulled the trigger of his gun. But we must not privilege this over any other cause, such as the President's decision to go to the theatre that night. The Buddha will not allow us to evaluate the relative strengths of these causes. The reality of the moment can only be grasped by appreciating all its effective causes (and all the effective causes that gave rise to John Wilkes Booth and theatres and guns, and so on in infinite recursivity). To grasp the reality of the moment in its sublime complexity, we must cut off all distractions. Hence the need for meditation: we won't be able to grasp it while landing a jumbo jet.

Is the *vinaya* law? Not if you insist that law should have sovereign and sanction. But yes, if you will apply the word to an intricate system of rules that are binding only on those who wish for the time being to be bound. A monk can resign his status whenever he wants: there are no golden manacles in this social contract. Whether or not you call this law, I would like to persuade you that the vinaya specialists think like lawyers. To do so, we must look at the contents and use of the *vinaya* in more detail. Tradition tells us that the Pali scriptures were handed down as memorised texts before being committed to writing around 75 BCE in the *Alu* monastery in Sri Lanka. In this recension, the canon divides into three baskets (*pitaka*), which I list together with the number of volumes in the *Pali Text Society* English translations.

1   *vinaya* (rules and cases about monks and monasteries), 6 volumes
2   *sutta* (sermons about *dhamma*), 39 volumes
3   *abidhamma* (ontologies of causation for meditators), 11 volumes

The *Vinaya commentary* describes their respective contents like this: *vinaya* is about offences and non-offences, *sutta* is about ethics and meditation, *abidhamma* is about name and form.[14] The six volumes of the *vinaya* basket divide into three separate works:

1   *khandhaka* (rules telling monasteries how to act collectively)
2   *suttavibhanga* (rules telling monasteries how to deal with offences)
3   *parivara* (analysis and specimen problems for students)

The *parivara* is undoubtedly a late addition to the canon, written or edited by a monk named Dipa at the end of the formative period.[15] The *vinaya* proper comprises the *khandhaka* (meaning *Heaps of Stuff*) and the *suttavibhanga* (meaning *Rule-Analyser*).

In the beginning were two legal lists. By a long process of encrustation these lists had, by the first century BCE, turned into the *khandhaka* and *suttavibhanga*. The original lists were reefs, onto which clung the limpets of explanation, the mussels of analysis, the barnacles of case-law and the animal-flowers of scholastic playfulness.

The monks who first wrote down the *vinayapali* edited this exuberant textual eco-system into a form sufficiently organised to be usable. They were more ruthless than their rivals: compared with the other seven recensions of the *vinaya* which survive in whole or part, the *vinayapali* is shorter, and more selfconsciously literary.

The list behind the *suttavibhanga* is the recitation of 227 offences known as the *patimokkha*. Its public recitation at least once a month is the only truly obligatory monastic duty.[16] The *patimokkha* can be seen as a fortnightly social contract: 'Let us go on living under these constraints until the next time we meet together'. It divides each of the 227 forms of individual misbehaviour into one of eight *genera* of accusation-handling procedures. We move from the most serious accusations (the four *offences of defeat*, which lead automatically to the end of monastic status) to the least (the seventy-five lapses in *politesse* which don't merit any specified punishment). The four *defeats* are: killing, having sex, thieving and misclaiming meditative prowess. Two of the seventy-five *impolitesses* are: Don't tiptoe in public; Don't urinate standing up.[17] Peter Birks, who condemns the inefficiency and inconvenience of a criminal law system 'organised around imprisonment, fines, probation, and other responses', would find this structure irrational.[18] True, you will not find all the sexual transgressions a monk can commit within a single chapter. You must look in the first list for penetrative sex, in the second list for masturbation, in the third list for unchaperoned (and therefore ambiguous) proximity to a member of the opposite sex, and so on. But the organisation is rational, if we start from a particular confession or accusation within the *sima*. Having classified the alleged offense into one of 227 pigeon-holes, the monks can read off the procedures that are to be applied.

Behind the *khandhaka* is an ill-defined list of between twenty and forty *kammavaca* (deed-speech). *Kammavaca* are the verbal formulas put to the monastic community in formal assembly for their approval. The monastic community in formal enclave is known as the *sima* (defined as all those monks and hermits who live within the parish boundaries of a particular monastery). Nothing whatsoever in the entire *vinayapali* envisages any formal organisation above the *sima*.[19] Its attention is entirely concentrated on practical problems within the *sima*: how is it to distribute blankets, ordain new recruits, fix the calendar, discipline transgressors?

Different *kammavaca* have different functions, and hence require different quorums and approval techniques. The *khandhaka* organises them into twenty-two chapters. Some chapters contain *kammavaca* on related topics such as probation and nunneries; others contain miscellaneous collections of formulas; others deal with the meta-theory of *kammavaca* – their conditions of formal validity, and the possibility of declaring them void or voidable. The *khandhaka* establishes the *kammavaca* as templates for how various issues and tasks are to be discussed and carried out. The underlying assumption is that the *sima* cannot improvise new procedures to deal with new problems. Only when it follows a specific *kammavaca* described in the *khandhaka*, using the right words and having the right quorum, are its collective actions valid. Each formula must be spoken in a Pali that is scrupulously correct: 'down to the correct pronunciation of single sounds;

pronouncing... labial *m* instead of nasal *m* in the word *sangham* would result in... invalidity'.[20] If we take Administrative Law and Constitutional Law as our models of legalism, then surely we can call all this legalistic? Unless we label the rules which govern formal public discourse (the kind of thing that interests Jürgen Habermas[21]) as rhetorical rather than legal?

There are three major differences between the Pali *khandhaka* and the other recensions. At 950 pages long, it is shorter than the other Buddhist *khandaka*. Unlike them, it is divided into two Books: the *Greater* and *Lesser Chapters*. And unlike them, it upgrades the accounts of the first two Councils from mere appendices to fully fledged chapters.[22] This treatment of the Councils implies a claim about orthodoxy within the generation that followed the Buddha. It is reminiscent of the Christian decision to afford the *Acts of the Apostles* the same standing as the *Gospels*. Or the Muslim decision to treat hadith on an equal footing with the Qu'ran. Pali Buddhism, like Christianity and Islam, emphasises the ongoing tradition as well as the exemplary life.

We can see how this works in detail by sampling the opening and closing words of both Books. The *Greater Chapters* start thus:

> Just after achieving enlightenment, the Lord Buddha sat cross-legged under the Bodhi Tree at Uruvela on the banks of the river Neranjara. For seven days he did not move, as he experienced the bliss of freedom. [V i 1][23]

Without the enlightenment, there would be no *khandhaka*. Gautama's words only have authority because he is a Buddha, an enlightened one. By the end of the *Greater Chapters*, however, we are already contemplating the problem of authority within the *sangha*. Even before the Buddha went to his great decease, it was apparent that his replacement would need *vinaya* expertise, as well as a high level of intra-personal skills. Chapter ten tells how the monks at Kosambi got so wrapped up in a *vinaya* dispute that they escaped the Buddha's control. It climaxes with the text of the *kammavaca* for establishing unanimity in a fractious order. Then the Buddha tells Upali how to distinguish between unanimity based on the letter and spirit, and unanimity based on the letter alone. [V i 357] Upali replies with a paean to future generations of vinaya experts, who will be trained to extract the spirit of the vinaya from its letter. Upali rose to his feet, draped his robe across one shoulder, saluted the Buddha with joined palms, then recited the following poem:

> What kind of man do we most need to lead our Order's business?
> What virtues equip a monk for leadership?
> First he must be moral, a paragon of self-restraint,
> One against whom accusations will not be credible.
> Second, he shall not be shy to speak in public:
> Without stutter or digression, he will get his point across.

He is able to respond to objections:
He knows when to speak, when to let others speak.
He respects all Elders, while standing by his own Teachers,
He shows judgement, knows his lines, and can join in debate.

Master of dialectic and teacher of multitudes,
He wins the debate without hurting opponents.
As ambassador on our Order's behalf
He follows his brief without getting big-headed.
He knows whether what you've done counts as an offence:
If it is, he knows how to remove your stain.

He can analyse the grounds for probation and restoration.
He shows equal esteem within each generation –
The elders, the seniors, the middle-aged, the youth.
Our leader should be clever and a helper to many. [V i 358]

This poem gives a good indication of the extent to which the *vinaya* codifies discourse as well as behaviour. *Vinaya* expertise is only part of this paragon's qualifications. He will also know how to influence his fellows, how to judge the climate of opinion and how to change it. He is, in a sense, a lawyer, but he is also a spin doctor intent on persuading the *sima* towards the right decision and, above all, he is a glad-hander, treating everyone in the *sima* with respect.

Compare this idealised picture with the passage that starts the *Lesser Chapters*:

> The fully-awakened Lord was staying at Savatthi in the monastery given him by Anathapindika. A group of monks under the influence of Panduka and Lohatika[24] were stirring up contention, quarrels, litigation, trouble and strife amongst the *sangha*. These monks encouraged each other with talk like this: 'Don't let them beat you. Keep on arguing loud and long, for you are wiser, cleverer and more learned than they are. Keep up the struggle, and we will be on your side.' Their language created quarrels where none had been before and pumped up small disputes into serious feuds. [V ii 1]

How can the *sima* deal with a serious feud? Because the *khandhaka* discusses no decision-making body higher than each *sima*, it cannot give us a legal mechanism for resolving schism within the *sima*. But it can tell us stories of actual schisms, from which we can infer the various possible outcomes. Chapter 10 *Kosambi* is one such. So is Chapter 17 *On splits in the order*, which concludes with the Buddha and Upali discussing the boundary between dissension and schism. They agree that if, in a *sima*, seven monks disagree with one monk, there is dissension, but eight against one is schism indeed. Such disputes tend to revolve around the validity of *kammavaca*. Let us see how it works, by examining an imaginary dispute of this kind.

Suppose that the *sima* has just expelled a monk called Ananda. He has any number of grounds on which to argue that the act was void. He can claim that one syllable in the formula of expulsion was mispronounced, or that Sariputta (a monk living within the *sima*) was not present at the expulsion, or that Revata (who was present) is not a valid monk. If the *sima* rejects his challenge, he must leave the neighbourhood. If the *sima* accepts his challenge and reinstate him, then Revata, who thinks Ananda's expulsion was valid, must himself leave the neighbourhood: Ananda's presence would henceforth invalidate all future *kammavacas* which the *sima* purports to make. Whichever of them leaves will remain convinced that he is still a monk, and will try to convince monks elsewhere that this is the case. If Ananda or Revata can persuade enough other monks to join him, they can form their own *sima* and ordain their first postulants. They must be prepared to rebut any suspicion of their credentials by repeating the details of the vinaya dispute that led to the split and explaining why their interpretation of the *khandhaka* was correct. Over the last five centuries in Southeast Asia, this has given birth to a particular genre of *vinaya* work: the text that records the dispute that led to the lineage's foundation. These works – *lineage charters*, if you will – resolve the original dispute by turning it into the foundation stone of a new *sima*.

The final words in the *Lesser Chapters* specify a particular edition of the *Khandaka* as the authentic one, and explain its provenance. Chapter 22 chronicles the *Council of Vesali* (a century after the Buddha's great decease), and its resolution of ten *vinaya* controversies. Revata acts as chairman, putting the disputed questions one by one to the venerable Sabbakama, the only monk still living who knew the monks who knew the Buddha. Sabbakama used to share a cell with Ananda, the Buddha's valet and chief-of-staff. The final words of the *Khandhaka*, as Revata addresses the assembled monks, are these:

> 'This legal dispute, is ended, your reverences. What is settled is well-settled. Any more questions?'
>
> Such were the ten issues as Revata put them, and the venerable Sabbakama's answers. Because there were exactly 700 monks present, this speaking-together of vinaya subsequently became known as the *700 monks text*. [V ii 307]

So the last words of the *Khandhaka* identify itself with a particular edition of the *vinaya*, and, by implication, a particular lineage that preserved that edition. All versions of the *vinaya* claim the authority of Upali, whom we might call the patron-saint of *vinaya*. But this *700 monks text* claims the authority of Ananda, via the single transmission of Sabbakamma. Some opponent of the Pali tradition must once have asked 'What's so great about Ananda, anyway?' because Buddhaghosa's commentaries provide an answer: Ananda accepted his appointment as personal secretary to the Buddha subject to conditions. One of these was that the Buddha was to repeat to him any doctrine taught in his absence.[25] He became, in effect, the walking data-base of the Buddha's words, the repository (and hence the validator) of all Buddhist doctrine.

We are now 2,400 years further removed from such companions of the prophet as Upali and Ananda, yet the essential *vinaya* problem remains the same. A monk's hopes of enlightenment depend on getting the formalities right. How can he be sure that the lineage which he inherited from the monk who ordained him is correct? Do other lineages, other *sima*s, preserve a more accurate orthopraxy than his? In the absence of a Rome or Canterbury that can guaruntee the apostolic succession – if necessary by force – each monk has to answer these questions for himself. Not all Buddhist monks are interested in the validity of *kammavaca*. I have tried to persuade you that those who become fascinated by it are describable, for cross-cultural purposes, as the Buddhist lawyers.

CLASSICAL PERIOD (50 BCE–1000 CE): DOES BUDDHIST POLITICS EXIST?

The Pali texts of the classical period were still written by monks, but many classical authors seem as familiar with the royal palace as with their own monastery. In the canon there is some 'fairly extensive but scattered'[26] material on *rajadhamma* (the proper behaviour of kings). In the classical age, this was concentrated into particular texts. In this sense, we can say that the classical period saw the birth of a Buddhist political philosophy. The *dramatis personae* of such classical works as the *Great Chronicle* of Sri Lanka and the *Ten Last Jataka* (#538–547 of the *547 Jataka*) are kings and queens, ministers and generals, wicked usurpers and resourceful ex-princes. In all of his last ten incarnations, the Buddha was born either as a prince, a royal counsellor or a pretender to the throne. Real kings who heard such material would inevitably draw lessons from it. The *Ten Last Jataka* was to Southeast Asian lay Buddhists what Homer was to the Hellenistic age. Like the *Iliad* and the *Odyssey*, the *Ten Last Jataka* is about kingship. Like them, it is about much else besides. The familiar written stories could work their power communally when performed by puppet shows or live actors. Even the rowdy, half-drunk audience at a three day festival would be reduced to tears at the weepy bits – as when in #547 Vessantara gives away his wife and children out of excess of generosity. Then the mood switched to Chaucerian slapstick – as when in #546 Mahosadha's wife sends an importunate suitor down the chute into the shit. Interspersed with all this are short talks on dhamma. Amongst the tragedy and slapstick will come a sudden moment of Faustian clarity when the cosmos can be glimpsed as a whole:

> On either side of the Great Tunnel clever painters made all manner of paintings: the splendour of Sakka, the zones of Mt. Sineru, the sea and

the ocean, the four continents, Himavat, Lake Anotatta, the Vermilion mountain, Sun and Moon, the heaven of the four great kings with the six heavens of sense and their divisions – all were to be seen in the Great Tunnel. [J vi 432]

The *Ten Last Jataka* is Pali narrative at its most sophisticated. But is narrative literature compatible with serious political science? The European tradition believes so: the classical roots of our political science are in theory (Aristotle and Cicero) and narrative history (Thucydides and Suetonius). When events move us to political reflection, as in mid seventeenth-century England or late eighteenth-century North America, we seek guidance by applying classical theory to the case studies preserved in classical history. I believe the Pali Buddhist experts in *rajadhamma* treated the *Jataka* as we used to treat Thucydides, though I would rather speak of the Pali scholars as applying a *structure* to the narratives than applying a *theory*. While Aristotle's theory was a matter of definitions and classifications, the Buddhist authors structured what they knew by remembering *lists* (which define the qualities of a concept, or the sub-components of a complex idea) and *lists of lists* (which provide a taxonomy of the discipline). The field of Buddhist politics is defined by the political lists. The three most important political lists all make their first appearance in the classical literature.

The *four solidarities* (*sangahavatthu*) defines the sub-components of the political economy. The *four roads not to take* (*agati*) analyses due process and fair procedure. The *ten royal virtues* (*rajadhamma*) lists desirable royal character traits. These lists form part of the descriptive language of the *Jataka*. Two different kings are described by the same formula: 'Shunning the *four roads not to take* and following the *ten royal virtues*, he ruled his people in righteousness'. [J i 260, 399]. Elsewhere king Bharata is one who 'practiced the *ten royal virtues*, won the people by the *four solidarities*... and gave great gifts to the poor, the wayfarers, the beggars, the suitors and the like' [J iii 470]. Following these lists was the key to a successful legal system: 'Brahmadatta ruled righteously in Benares... and he kept the *ten royal virtues*. This being so, his court of justice became, so to say, empty'. [J iv 232] Just as these lists are woven into the narratives, the narratives may themselves be woven into the lists: Siamese monks of the eighteenth century correlated each of the *Ten Last Jataka* to one of the *ten royal virtues*.[27] And the lists can be bundled into taxonomies of political science as a whole: a nineteenth-century Siamese source summarises *rajadhamma* as *twenty-four forms of princely knowledge*, consisting of *four crafts, five arts, eight merits* and *seven means of action*.[28]

The *four roads not to take* are first expounded in the *Cemetry Dog Jataka* [Jat #22]. The future Buddha, born as leader of a pack of wild cemetry dogs, was unjustly accused of eating the royal bridle and harness. He reveals the true culprits by administering an emetic to the palace lap-dogs. Then he barks a sermon to the king on the avoidance of 'the *four roads not to take* of partiality, dislike, ignorance and fear... For kings, when trying cases, should be as unbiased as the beam of a balance'. [J i 177] Jat #332 versifies this message:

> Wise men, O king, of partial views beware,
> Hear both sides first, then judgement true declare.
> ... The warrior prince a well-weighed verdict gives
> Of righteous judge the fame for ever lives. [J iii 173][29]

The *ten royal virtues* get their first enumeration in the *Three Birds Jataka* [Jat #521]. Once the future Buddha was born as a parrot, who became the pet of a king. Along with the owl and the mynah-bird (his fellow-pets) he instructed the king in the arts of kingship. The future Buddha squawked a sermon on the *ten royal virtues* to the human king. [J v 123] The *four solidarities*, as a political list, comes from Buddhaghosa's fifth century CE commentaries on the *sutta basket*, in a passage comparing them to the four Vedic sacrifices:

> Among them, the *hay-sacrifice* was taking the tenth part from the grain that had been harvested;... The *human sacrifice* was the providing of six month's food and wages to great warriors;... The *wedge-throw* was taking a written chit from poor people and providing them with money, in the amount of one or two thousand, for three months without interest;... The *soma sacrifice* was speaking gentle words such as 'Daddy' and 'Mummy'. [Mp iv 69; Spk i 144][30]

Buddhaghosa is stealing the prestige attached to the Vedic list, and attaching it to his own list on kingship: such list-larceny is standard practice in the Pali canon. What is remarkable about this passage is the economic detail in which the relationship between people and king is portrayed. The rice growers will give the king 10 per cent of their harvest (*hay-sacrifice*), no more and no less. In return the king will redistribute the common wealth as loans to tide the rice-farmers over their bad times (*wedge throw*). When mobilising the *corvée* labour force, the king must provide a subsistence allowance (*human sacrifice*). Steven Collins has pioneered our understanding of the Pali texts as political ideology, 'a discursive, textual world available to the... agrarian societies of Southern Asia'.[31] I have argued against his view that the formative period texts contain any social contract theory,[32] but I concede his point in relation to the classical *four solidarities*. Once the terms of the deal between paddy-farmers and kings have become as explicit as this, we might as well refer to it as contractual.

Southeast Asian Buddhists lapped up anything to do with Buddhist politics. Some of the earliest epigraphy from Southeast Asia refers to the *Ten Last Jataka*.[33] More recent literature regards the stories and lists of the *Jataka* as the starting point of all political speculation. A special Burmese genre *Myitta sa* was written by monks for kings, expounding the lessons to be derived from a selection of *Jataka*.[34] Another genre *Rajovada* did the same, but in prose rather than verse. In eighteenth-century Burma's most important *rajasat*, the passage on kingship starts thus:

> The *Great Goose Jataka* gives the *10 rajadhamma*. Practice them. In addition learn the lessons from *Jataka*s and histories . . . [ROB 21-8-1785]

and follows with a bravura passage giving ten lists on kingship in ascending numerical order. Thirty years earlier, the *Ten Last Jataka* had provided a standardised negotiating move in international diplomacy. In 1756, Alaungpaya of Upper Burma's army was pressing hard into the king of Pegu's territory. On 13th December, the Pegu king wrote suggesting 'an alliance following the example of the *Bhuridatta Jataka*'. What he meant was 'marry my daughter and don't sack my city'.[35]

Karl Polanyi has bequeathed us a term to describe this model of political economy. When the king siphons wealth up from his farmers in tax and passes it back down by acting as lender of last resort, Polanyi terms it a *redistributive economy*.[36] Such an economy favours the poor (who have no cushion to see them through bad times) over the rich. The *Great Chronicle*'s description of king Buddhadasa recognizes this. He won over 'his subjects by the *four solidarities* . . . He fulfilled the wishes of the poor by gifts of money, those of the rich by protecting their property and their life'. [Clv 37: 105] One of the *Ten Last Jataka* gives an idealised picture of a redistributive king. The future Buddha appears in all his glory to convert a king who had fallen in with nihilists and believers in predestination. Hovering in the sky, he explains to king Narada the sacred text and its meaning:

> Let your courtiers take food in their hands and proclaim to the city: 'Who is hungry or thirsty? Who deserves a garland? Who needs ointment? Would naked men please step this way, so we can dress you in jewel-sparkling garments? Anyone fancy a sunshade and soft delicate shoes for their travels?' [J vi 125]

The *four solidarities* gives us the practical details by which such idealism should be implemented. How much? For how long? On what security? By the eighteenth century this list is found all over the Southeast Asian legal literature. E Maung, Burma's greatest legal historian, discusses its prevalence and concludes that the eighteenth-century Burmese jurists had moved from 'moral exhortations to legal obligations binding on the ruler'.[37] He was commenting in particular on this passage from a mid-eighteenth century *dhammasat*:

> If a person has incurred debts beyond his means of paying, and his family are unable to assist him . . . he shall make a petition to the king, who will say 'On conditions, give him an advance' . . . In three years the

king may take back the advances. This he may do in accordance with the laws of [the *solidarities*].[38]

A new edition of the same work, written in 1782 and rediscovered 200 years later, adds:

The Buddhas reveal the *four solidarities* to every world, so that every king may practice them. Those kings who have founded their kingdoms and practised these *four solidarities* should admonish their subjects in accordance with the law in the *dhammasat*.[39]

If the *four solidarities* are not themselves legalistic, they certainly urge legalism (in the sense of following the *dhammasat*) on the king.

What milieu produced this flowering of classical political science? What was the seat-in-life of the *Ten Last Jataka* and the *Four Solidarities*? I suspect that we can project back into fifth-century Sri Lanka the conditions that prevailed more recently in Southeast Asia. In the capitals of Burma and Siam, the palace and the chief monasteries collaborated closely in providing a decent classical education for as many boys as wanted it. Starting as an inky eight year old schoolboy, you could stay in the education system until you became a twenty-eight year old postgraduate specialist in the sutta, the abidhamma, the jataka or the vinaya. The kings supported monastic schools and universities which taught the full range of Pali literature as a path either to the monkhood or to royal service.[40] The kings built monasteries with enough sleeping space for pupils, provided enough rice, ink and paper to keep them going, and made sure that their own pre-teens and adolescents attended and did their homework. In the *Ten Last Jataka* king Janaka sums up his interest in education:

Those ministers who misadvise my son
(when he in turn stars in this royal drama),
who teach him wrong in thought and word and deed
will earn themselves some pretty nasty karma. [J vi 34]

The king's immediate retinue of ministers usually included a couple who were still monks: some of the others might have dropped out of classical education at the age of fourteen, but most would have 'graduated' (that is, taken full ordination) at twenty-one and gone on to study for a year or two in the specialist 'post-graduate' monasteries. In my view, the Buddhist political science of the classical age came out of a Sinhalese educational system analagous to what I have described in Southeast Asia.

Classical vinaya literature – the *Parivara* and the great *vinaya commentary*, called *Samantapasadika* (The Thoroughly Enlightening) – gives us glimpses of this. The *Sweat-inducing Suttas* of the *Parivara* reek of tertiary education. A series of moot-points and paradoxes are separated by the refrain 'These questions are devised by experts'. Surely the following three examples are from the lecture theatre, rather than the courtroom: Can one be guilty of matricide and patricide if one's parents have both changed sex between the birth and the murder? [V v 217] Can one lose one's celibacy with a headless and limbless person, whose eyes and mouth are located on her chest? [V v 216]. If a monk embraces a group of women simultaneously, how many 'offences of touching fingers and hair' does he commit?[41] [V v 218] Norman Calder has identified similar 'normative and virtuoso patterning' in the early Islamic law texts. It can, he says, act as a 'primary generator of change and development in legal theory'.[42]

An anecdote in the *vinaya commentary* gives us some clues as to how these *vinaya* colleges operated. It tells of an early first millenium specialist, Upatissa, who had two outstanding pupils called Mahasumma and Mahapaduma. Each year Upatissa took his students through the entire *vinaya* and its extensive commentaries. Mahapaduma heard the course eighteen times, and is willing to go on hearing it until Upatissa drops dead, and he can take over his teacher's role. Mahasumma, at the end of his ninth year, went off beyond the River Ganga (presumably to set up practice on his own as a *vinaya* specialist). Evidently the course varied somewhat from year to year. Because of his early departure, Mahasumma missed hearing Upatissa's incisive and authoritative answer to the question 'How decomposed must a female corpse be, before interfering with it can no longer constitute an act of necrophilia?'[43] I surmise that the pupils of Mahapaduma debated this question[44] with the pupils of Mahasumma, and that their knock-down argument was to cite the authority of Upatissa, who featured as an ancestor in both lineages.

Can we refer to the emergence of vinaya experts and vinaya universities as a 'professionalisation' of Buddhist law? Since the vinaya forbids monks to handle cash, no monk can, as Cicero did, earn his living from lawyering. Weber's masterly treatment of the emergence of legal reasoning shifts the focus away from the legal professionals onto the amateurs who preceded them. It is these amateurs – the *rechts-honoratioren* – who give each legal tradition its distinctive look and feel.[45] We should think of the authors of the *Great Chronicle* and the *vinaya commentary* as amateurs (in this Weberian sense) of law and politics. Since nothing ethical was alien to them, they colluded in a general widening of reference for the word *vinaya*[46]. The jataka consistently use the word *vinaya* to describe such ethical phenomena as the law of the land or the policies of a law-abiding king.[47] Buddhaghosa describes the *Advice to Siggala sutta* as *gihivinaya* (vinaya for the laity), because it lays down the discipline to be followed by a lay householder. Many Buddhist ethical texts subsequently have adopted this title.[48] The author of the *vinaya commentary*, meanwhile, happily included a detailed village irrigation code.[49]

BRICOLAGE PERIOD (1000–1900 CE): IS *DHAMMASAT AND RAJASAT* BUDDHIST?

Cambodia, Thailand, Burma and the states of the Middle Mekong all adopted the Buddhist kingship model of government. They treated Pali literature as their classical literature, they taught Pali in their schools and they used Pali as their language of international diplomacy. These kingdoms also shared an interlinked tradition of *dhammasat* and *rajasat*, written in a mixture of Pali and the vernacular. The family resemblances between these law texts suggest descent from a common ancestor. I have argued that the common ancestor was not a single *ur-dhammasat* but a group of texts circulating in twelfth-century Pagan.[50] I use the gallicism *bricolage* to suggest that the early *dhammasat* authors built a new genre out of odds and ends that were lying around their book-chests. Lists, stories and technical terms from obscure Pali texts were recycled to perform new functions in a new legal context. I adopted the term to distinguish Southeast Asia's adoption of Buddhist Law from the eighteenth and nineteenth-century colonial receptions of law.[51] But the term *bricolage* can pinpoint a similarity as well as a difference: the routes by which *vinaya* fed into *dhammasat* are at least as complex as those that led from the *Corpus Iuris Civilis* into the Romanoid legal systems of Europe. If the Southeast Asian legal authors were *bricoleurs*, then so were the European heirs of Irnerius.

Dhammasat and *rajasat* are law, even by John Austin and Hans Kelsen's restrictive definitions. They contain rules and precedents for the guidance of the populace, they lay down punishments for non-compliance and they assume a hierarchy of power stretching up from the rice-grower in her village to the king in his palace. In Burma there was even a profession of lawyers who wore distinctive robes, had their fees regulated by government, and swore to restrict their arguments within the parameters laid down by *dhammasat* and *rajasat*.[52] The problem, then, is not whether mainland Southeast Asia had *law*, but whether it had *Buddhist* law. Max Weber, as we have seen, thought that *dhammasat* and *rajasat* were Hindu law which had been hastily repainted in Buddhist colours. Modern comparative lawyers, to my dismay, echo Weber's line. Unfortunately, this is sometimes also true of specialists in the region. Anthony Reid's *Southeast Asia in the Age of Commerce* is the most distinguished regional contribution of the last fifteen years. Yet even he speaks of 'The Indian law books, especially the Code of Manu' being 'copied, translated and incorporated into local law codes, with stricter adherence to the original texts in Burma and Siam'.[53] How can such a widespread misconception ever be corrected? For the last fifty years, legal historians have stated that the texts contain far more Buddhist than Hindu legal materials.[54] Since I started writing on the *dhammasats*, I have published six articles expounding the detailed evidence of Buddhist influence. Though I have enough unpublished material for six more, this chapter will not be one of them. For present purposes how outsiders such as Weber assess the relative contribution of Buddhism and Hinduism to Southeast Asian law is a side issue. More relevant is how Southeast Asian insiders assessed the relationship between Buddhism and law.

I shall summarise the position for the period and country I know best. How did the kings, monks and lawyers of eighteenth-century Burma (who between them wrote most of the surviving sources) conceptualise the ethical terrain on which they worked? Did they think of *dhammasat* and *rajasat* as being part of the *Buddha-teachings*? Yes, though perhaps the lawyers were less convinced of this than the monks and king. Did *dhammasat* rules apply universally, rather than merely locally? Yes, said lawyers and monks. No, hinted the king. Was the king bound by the rules of *dhammasat*? Yes, agreed all three, though kings went on to minimise the extent of their obligation. Could the king exercise any *vinaya* authority? All three constituencies agreed that the king could enforce *vinaya* rulings made by monks, but was not competent to decide such issues himself. In reality, however, kings who were interested in vinaya matters did support their preferred interpretation by promoting 'their' monks to national influence. From this headnote summary, you will gather that much of the ethical terrain was contested. I have just identified the contesting rivals in institutional terms.[55] But the sources are rich enough to support other analyses of eighteenth-century intellectual history. Supporters of rival monastic lineages seem to have had differing conceptions of ethics. There may still have been regional differences in approach between Upper Burma and the old Mon territories to the south. Certainly different kings had different conceptions of ethics, and in the case of King Badon [1782–1819], different conceptions at different stages of his long and well-documented reign. The closer we look, the more diversity we find.

CONCLUSIONS

So far I have paid more attention to describing what Buddhist law is than to discussing whether we should treat it as a religous legal system. I now address the question posed by my title. If Buddhism is a religion, then Buddhist law is religious law. Let us examine the conditional clause step by step.

First, is Buddhism theistic? Buddhism puts no clear water between the gods and other sentient beings. God-hood, rather than being a transcendent state, is an office to be performed, a job that someone has to do. Anybody who accrues enough merit in this lifetime can be reborn as Indra in the next incarnation. And after that, they will very likely return again as human. To the extent that Buddhism is theistic, it is an Andy Warhol theism in which *Everyone can be God for 15 minutes*. Better to call it atheistic, in recognition that *nibbana*, Buddhism's transcendent principle, was designed to be as different from Vedic polytheism as Jehova was from the polytheism of the Middle East. Second, does Buddhism involve an attitude of reverence? Certainly, Buddhists revere the Buddha. But reverence by itself cannot define religion. Though medics revere Hippocrates of Cos and Stoics revere Zeno of Citium, neither Hippocratism nor Stoicism is a religion. We commonly reverence the ancient authors who engendered our tradition. Southeast Asian authors of the precolonial age treated the Buddha more as an intellectual authority than as a God. Buddhists, when writing, are more like Stoics than like Christians.[56] Third, is the Buddha invoked as an authority on ethics? Yes, the Buddha is regularly invoked to argue that one branch of ethics is more firmly grounded in truth than another. The Buddha has ethical significance and is revered, but these two facts do not combine to make him a religious figure. A modern Aristotelian, such as Alisdair MacIntyre, does not worship Aristotle, though he reveres him as the arbiter of ethical truth. Not all intellectual traditions appeal in the last resort to religious revelation: the appeal might be to a great logician such as Aristotle, to a great grammatist such as Panini, or to a great poet such as Lao-tzu.

Thus far, Buddhism looks more like a philosophy than a religion. But when we study the way Buddhists act in public, the emphasis shifts. The fourth question, then, is whether Buddhist ritual activity resembles more closely a philosophers' colloquium or the rite of Holy Communion? The Burmese authors may have written as if the Buddha was Euclid of Alexandria or Chrysippus of Soli, but they behaved in their public acts of ritual as if the Buddha were Jesus of Nazareth. A single hair plucked from the Buddha's head eight days after his enlightenment is enshrined within Rangoon's *Shwedagon Pagoda*. Its presence in the middle of the Lower Burmese wet-lands has, since the 1st millenium, anchored the local Burmese Buddhist identity. The relics of the Buddha (as well as his footprints and statues) are treated as objects of boundless power. The European equivalents are not such antiquarian curios as Flaubert's parrot, Newton's apple and Diogenes' tub, but the fragments of the true cross.

As ritual practice, Buddhism looks religious. As a written literature, Buddhism looks more like classical knowledge. How does Buddhist law fit in? Is law part of written theory or part of ritualised social practice? It is, of course, both, which means that it simultaneously is, and is not, a religious legal system. This conclusion contains less clarity than I would have wished. Perhaps, though, it is the question itself which is at fault.

Because of a quirk of European intellectual history, Europe draws a sharp distinction between the knowledge embedded in the pagan classics and the faith revealed by the church fathers. There was no such distinction in Buddhist Southeast Asia nor, as far as I can see, in the Hindu and Chinese traditions. In most of the world, ancient knowledge came in one traditional package. In Europe post-Constantine, it has been divided into religious knowledge and classical knowledge. The word *religion* is weighed down by this idiosyncratic history. The further we travel from Europe, therefore, the less useful *religion* becomes as a comparative tool.[57]

NOTES

1 My thanks to Oskar v. Hinüber for correcting errors in an earlier draft.
2 Donald R. Kelley, 'The Metaphysics of Law: An Essay on the Very Young Marx' *American Historical Review* 83: 350–367 (1978), 354. Compare: Henry Goudy, *Trichotomy in Roman Law* (Oxford: Oxford University Press, 1910).
3 Max Weber, *The Religion of India* (New York: Free Press, 1958), 206.
4 John Henry Wigmore, *A Panorama of Legal Systems* (Washington: Law Book Co., 1928), 224–279.

5 H. Patrick Glenn, *Legal Traditions of the World* (Oxford: Oxford University Press, 2000), 292.

6 Glenn, *supra* note 3, at 252.

7 Karl Marx and Friedrich Engels, *Werke* (Berlin: Dietz Verlag, 1957), Vol. 1, 378.

8 Max Weber, *Law in Economy and Society* ed. M. Rheinstein (Cambridge: Harvard University Press, 1954), 236.

9 Charles S. Prebish, *A Survey of Vinaya Literature* (Taipei: Jin Luen Publishing House, 1994), 46.

10 Tibetan and Chinese monks read their *vinaya*s in their own languages, but Pali Buddhists read it in Pali. Hence their education is dominated by learning how to read ancient literature in a dead tongue.

11 J.C. Holt, *Discipline: the Canonical Buddhism of the Vinayapitaka* (Delhi: Motilal Banarsidass, 1981); Oskar v. Hinüber, *Selected Papers on Pali Studies* (Oxford: Pali Text Society, 1994); Oskar v. Hinüber, 'Buddhist Law According to the Theravada Vinaya – a Survey of Theory and Practice' *Journal of the International Association of Buddhist Studies* 18: 7–45 (1995); Andrew Huxley, 'The Vinaya – Legal System or Performance Enhancing Drug?' *Buddhist Forum* 4: 141–163 (1996). Over the last five years, the Tibetologists have begun to catch up: Rebecca French, *The Golden Yoke: The Legal Cosmology of Buddhist Tibet* (Ithaca: Cornell University Press, 1995). But there is still scarcely anything published on what influence, if any, Buddhism had on Chinese law. Peerenboom's chapter in this volume cites what little there is.

12 References in this form are to Than Tun, *The Royal Orders of Burma AD 1598–1885* Vol. 1–10 (Kyoto: Centre of South East Asian Studies, 1984–1990).

13 Bob Marley, 'Pimper's Paradise' *Uprising* (London: Island Records, 1980).

14 David Kalupahana, *Buddhist Philosophy – A Historical Analysis* (Honolulu: University Press of Hawaii, 1976), 94.

15 Oskar v. Hinüber, *A Handbook of Pali Literature* (Berlin: Walter de Gruyter, 1996), 21.

16 The Buddha exempted himself from this requirement a few years before his great decease. I'm not sure why. I surmise it was something to do with the shimmer of his approaching great decease.

17 The eighth list doesn't quite fit: it analyses (in a rudimentary way) the possible ways in which a dispute could end. The final item of this list of seven (and thus the last of the 227 items in the *patimokkha*) is *covering it up with grass*: What the farmer does with a fresh deposit of bovine faeces should be taken as a model for ending monastic disputes. The general drift of this suggestion is obvious enough, but what exactly are the specifics being recommended?

18 Peter Birks, 'Definition and Division: A Meditation on *Institutes 3.13*' in ed. Peter Birks *The Classification of Obligations* (Oxford: Clarendon Press, 1997), 30.

19 No rules for constituting it or ascertaining its will is given. It is merely an imagined community.

20 Oskar v. Hinüber, *supra* note 11, at 19.

21 Given the *khandhaka*'s concern to provide the minimum conditions under which unconstrained discourse can take place within a community of volunteers, we might want to label it as *Habermasian*. See: Jürgen Habermas, *On the pragmatics of communication* ed. Maeve Cooke (Cambridge: MIT Press, 1998).

22 Prebish, *supra* note 9, at 83.

23 These are the first 37 words of the 84,000,000 that traditionally make up the Pali Canon. Citations to Pali literature follow, except for some modifications of punctuation, the conventions laid out in the *Critical Pali Dictionary* ed. V. Trenckner (Copenhagen: Royal Danish Academy of Science and Letters, (1924) 1: 37–69, as modified by Oskar v. Hinüber, *A Handbook of Pali Literature* (Berlin: Walter de Gruyter), 256–257. Unless otherwise noted, translations from Pali are my paraphrases, aiming at maximum

accessibility to the nonspecialist. Since I am far from being a skilled Pali linguist, the wary reader will want to check them against the official *Pali Text Society* translations. Not that these are wholly reliable: See the warning of the recently retired President of the Pali Text Society: K.R. Norman, 'Pali Studies in the West: Present State and Future Tasks' *Religion* 24: 165–172 (1994), 168.

24 Two of the *chabbaggiya* (group of six): 'A group of Monks, Contemporary with the Buddha, Frequently Mentioned as Being Guilty of Various *Vinaya* offences.' G.P. Malalasekera, *Dictionary of Pali Proper Names* 2 volumes, Indian Text Series (London: John Murray, 1937), 1: 926.

25 Malalasekera, *supra* note 24, at 1: 23.

26 Prince Dhani, 'The Old Siamese Conception of the Monarchy' *Journal of the Siam Society* 36: 91–106 (1947), 96.

27 Elizabeth Wray, Clare Rosenfield and Dorothy Bailey, *Ten Lives of the Buddha: Siamese Temple Painting and Jataka Tales* (New York: Weatherhill, 1972), 16.

28 James Gray, *Ancient Proverbs and Maxims from Burmese Sources, or the Niti Literature of Burma* (London: Trübner & Co, 1886), 40.

29 Translation by H.T. Francis and R.A. Neil.

30 Steven Collins and O.v. Hinüber have both helped with this translation from the Pali.

31 Steven Collins, *Nirvana and other Buddhist Felicities* (Cambridge: C.U.P., 1998), 18.

32 Andrew Huxley, 'The Buddha and the Social Contract' *Journal of Indian Philosophy* 24: 407–420 (1996).

33 For seventh century Korat (N.E. Thailand), see: Nai Pan Hla, *The Significant Role of the Mon Language and Culture in S.E. Asia* (Tokyo: Institute for the Study of Languages and Cultures of Asia and Africa, 1992), 26–27. For thirteenth century Pegu, see: Maung Mya, 'Exploration in Burma' 195–204 of ed. C. Fabri *Archaeological Survey of India Annual Report 1930–4* (Delhi: Manager of Publications, 1936). For a possible reference to Jat.#538 in seventh century Sri Ksetra, see: Charles Duroiselle, *Archaeological Survey of India Annual Report 1927*, 173.

34 Lu Pe Win, 'The Jatakas in Burma' 94–108 of ed. Ba Shin, Jean Boisselier and A.B. Griswold *Essays offered to G.H. Luce* (Ascona: Artibus Asiae, 1966), 106.

35 Yi Yi, 'Additional Burmese Historical Sources 1752–6' *Researches in Burmese History* 3: 103–130 (1968), 105.

36 Karl Polanyi, *The Great Transformation* (Boston: Beacon Press, 1944), 43–55, 269–273. Karl Polanyi, 'The Economy as Instituted Process' 243–270 of ed Karl Polanyi, Conrad Arensberg and Harry Pearson *Trade and Markets in the Early Empires* (Glencoe: The Free Press, 1957). Michael Aung-Thwin has argued for the usefulness of Polanyi's analysis in understanding twelfth century Pagan: Michael Aung-Thwin, *Pagan: the Origins of Modern Burma* (Honolulu: U. Hawaii Press, 1985), 171.

37 E. Maung, 'Insolvency Jurisdiction in Early Burmese Law' *Journal of the Burma Research Society* 34: 1–7 (1951), 6.

38 *Manugye* iii 74. D. Richardson, *The Damathat, or the Laws of Menoo* (Moulmein: American Baptist Mission Press, 1847), 106.

39 Ryuji Okudaira and Andrew Huxley, 'Political Science in the Court of King Badon: Eleven Burmese lists on kingship from 1782' *Bulletin of the School of Oriental and African Studies* 64: 248–259 (2001).

40 'Examiners in religious exam shall produce a ranked order of candidates: when there are equals, give precedence to one who has done more lecture courses, or who attempted more questions on the canon rather than on the commentaries and *tika*s, or whose teacher is senior to the teacher of a rival'. (ROB 27-5-1836)

41 Answer: As many as there are women in the group, not as many as there are fingers and hairs.

42 Norman Calder, *Studies in Early Muslim Jurisprudence* (Oxford: Clarendon Press, 1992), 199.

43 P. Bapat and A. Hirakawa, *Shan-Chien-P'i-P'o-Sha* (Poona: Bhandarka Oriental Research Institute, 1970), 200.

44 This is not necessarily a hypothetical question for classroom discussion. See: *Sydney Morning Herald* 5 April, 1994: 'Phra Dharmamatanobhas said to the press conference in Bangkok: "People should understand the temptations we monks must endure in the modern world . . . Many of us use rotting corpse contemplation to surmount lust, and I agree with the prosecution that the monk who was caught having sex with a corpse did wrong. But do not tar us all with the same brush"'.

45 Weber, *supra* note, at 332.

46 Or perhaps a return to the meaning *vinaya* had before the Buddha appropriated it as a technical term. We know next to nothing about the pre-Buddhist Middle-Indic vocabulary in the various languages related to Pali.

47 Kanai Lal Hazra, *Pali Language and Literature, volume one* (New Delhi: D.K. Printworks, 1994), 138.

48 A late example: In 1830s Burma the monk U Budh wrote a Pali collection of *niti* with full Burmese translation called the *gihivinaya sangahaniti* (Collected Wisdom Verses as vinaya for the Laity).

49 S. Paranavitana, 'Some Regulations Concerning Village Irrigation Works in Ancient Ceylon' *Ceylon Journal of Historical and Social Studies* 1: 1–7 (1958).

50 Andrew Huxley, 'Thai, Mon and Burmese dhammathats: Who Influenced Whom?' 82–131 of ed. Andrew Huxley *Thai Law: Buddhist Law* (Bangkok: White Orchid Press, 1996), 111.

51 Andrew Huxley, 'The Reception of Buddhist Law in S.E. Asia' 139–237 of ed. M. Doucet and J. Vanderlinden *La Réception des Systèmes Juridiques: Implantation et Destin* (Bruxelles: Bruylant, 1994), 199.

52 The Burmese lawyers must have existed in the sixteenth century [ROB 23-6-1607]. They may well be older. See: Andrew Huxley, 'The Burmese Legal Profession 1200–1880' in *Receuils de la Société Jean Bodin* 58:155–187 (1996).

53 Anthony Reid, *Southeast Asia in the Age of Commerce 1450–1680, Volume One, The Land Below the Winds* (New Haven: Yale University Press, 1988), 137.

54 E. Maung, *The Expansion of Burmese Law* (Rangoon: Royal Printing Works, 1951). Shwe Baw, *The Origin and Development of Burmese Legal Literature* PhD, School of Oriental and African Studies (1955). Kyin Swi, 'The Origin and Development of the Dhammathats' *Journal of the Burma Research Society* 49: 173–205 (1966). Dev Raj Chanana, 'Social Implications of Reason and Authority in Buddhism' *Indian Economic and Social History Review* 3: 292–310 (1966), 295.

55 As I did at greater length in: Andrew Huxley, 'Buddhism and Law – The view from Mandalay' *Journal of the International Association of Buddhist Studies* 18: 47–95 (1995), 73ff.

56 Sir John Jardine, the first English scholar of the *dhammasats*, was the first to make this connection: 'The laws of Burma can no longer be understood without regard to Buddhist ethics. They are in as close touch with it as the Roman law was with Stoic philosophy and the law of nature during the reigns of the Antonine Caesars.' John Jardine, 'Buddhist Law' *Imperial and Asiatic Quarterly Review*, 3RD SERIES, 4: 367–375 (1897), 375.

57 If you require deeper knowledge of the last thousand years of the Pali Buddhist legal tradition, may I recommend the annotated bibliography appended to: Andrew Huxley, 'Studying Theravada Legal Literature' *Journal of the International Association of Buddhist Studies* 20: 63–91 (1997). For more information on the ancient Indian texts of Buddhist law, try the works cited in *supra* note 11.

9

RELIGIOUS LAW: A DISCUSSION

The Panel

ANDREW HUXLEY WRITES: This discussion began in the pub immediately after we had given our papers. It has continued since then by email. In offering it as a conversation inter praesentes *I have necessarily taken some editorial liberties.*

ANDREW: When Comparative lawyers talk of *religious systems of law*, they typically mean the monotheistic religions of the book: Judaism, Christianity and Islam. If we did anything new this afternoon, it was to introduce the usual suspects (Calum, Silvio, Bernard and Lynn) to representatives of other religions (Werner, Randall and myself). Did the experiment work? Is the word *religion* wide enough to cover the faiths and philosophies that have flourished east of the Urals?

SILVIO: Jewish law, Canon law and Muslim law are based on a divinely revealed law. Is that something which affects the way these monotheistic laws work? And they aim to give the faithful eternal life. Is this aim a characteristic feature, of religious laws? It seems to me that nobody has yet tried to explore whether (and eventually how) such divine foundation and supernatural orientation work. Up to now nobody has really tried to compare religious laws: we need to study a lot more.

WERNER: I remain doubtful. The term *religious systems* has been tainted by the use to which Europeans have put it: it denotes the legal systems they thought of as traditional or backward.

SILVIO: We need definitions which can distinguish religious law from secular law. True, there are religious components in secular laws and vice versa, so we cannot draw a sharp dividing line. But we can base our distinction on the predominance human groups have given to either religious or secular (political, ethnic, artistic, etc.) elements. Sometimes the same group acts in both capacities. In such case we should be able to say which is the main focus. Where religious components are more central than secular, I am inclined to call the group *religious* and its law *religious law*.

BERNARD: Silvio is undoubtedly correct in stressing the need to define *religious* (I am equally keen to define *law*). I am not entirely happy with the definition he proposes; for the ancient period, in particular, I would find it difficult to form a judgement as to whether the "main focus" of a particular group was religious or secular. I think it is better to remain close to the evidence we actually have – the texts. If these texts claim a religious origin, in some form of divinity, then we are dealing with *religious* texts. I fear this may sound simplistic – but at least it is operational.

ANDREW: Perhaps not so operational east of the Urals. The Pali Buddhist texts will leave you in a real quandary as to whether *nibbana* is some form of divinity. As I read them, they are less religious texts, and more like philosophical texts, do-it-yourself guides to meditation and ethical narratives. If Buddhism can rightly be called a religion, it is because of ritual activity rather than doctrine – what people do at pagodas rather than what people have read in the canon. I would much rather evade this question by finding some portmanteau word that embraces religion, philosophy, science and ethics.

WERNER: Like "-isms".

ANDREW: That will do nicely. You distinguish an "-ism" from everything else by the motivation of the student. Whether it's a religion, a philosophy or a science, the student is driven on by *libido sciendi*, the lust to know things. Whereas a secular student of law is prodded by the wish to learn a trade (at the Beirut law school or at Lincoln's Inn) or simply to acquire a skill that might occasionally be useful (as in the case of Chinese mandarins).

RANDALL: First we should expose our purpose in discussing the semantics of *religion* and *law*. On that depends how we define the terms, and indeed whether we need to define them. As a devout pragmatist asked to write on religious law in China, I would want to define religious law in a way that allows me to discuss what I consider to be the relevant issues with respect to the Chinese legal system. What did the Chinese mean by *religion*? By *law*? What were the particular issues at stake? Was transcendence an issue? Were rituals significant? Was the distinction between rituals (*li*) and law (*fa*) significant? The terms will gain significance through an explanation of how law and religion relate in China. That said, we must use words in ways that our readers will understand or, if not, we must explain the sense in which we are using them. This necessarily introduces some element of comparison, but we need not religious law for all systems, all places, all times. Indeed, to do so would require a level of generality that would make it difficult to explain our particular tradition. But someone reading this book will probably be able to create several different categories of *religious law*. Chinese law is religious in this way…, Jewish law in that way…, Islam in the other way…

THEORIES – WEBER, HART, DWORKIN

ANDREW: Most of us round this table see ourselves as regionalists first, theorists second. Which encourages an eclectic approach to theory: we use whatever happens to work on our data. At yesterday's panel there was a long discussion on what Comparative Law could learn from Legal Sociology and Jurisprudence. Their conclusion – putting it crudely – was that Max Weber is of much greater relevance than Hans Kelsen or Herbert Hart. Any comments?

CALUM: I am not surprised. An astonishing degree of artificiality characterizes the theories of Hart and Kelsen. They are too much in love with classification, too little acquainted with reflection.

ANDREW: Yesterday David Nelken said that comparatists should 'concentrate on problems of meaning, identity and tradition... develop their sensitivity to legal history' while sociologists concentrate on the here and now 'explaining the "law in action."' On that basis, Weber seems more like a comparatist than a sociologist.

BERNARD: It should be both/and, not either/or. They clearly have different objectives. A social theoriest like Weber will describe a factual universe, the processes of history, etc. Jurists like Hart and Kelsen will seek to describe the normative assumptions of legal systems. Both types of question are appropriately posed in relation to the *religious systems of law*. My concern is with the extent to which popular versions of the jurisprudential theories are implied and communicated by our very use of the language of *law* in relation to these religious traditions. Jurisprudence becomes useful when it helps us to "unpack" more precisely the underlying assumptions of our modern legal language. Only when we make these tacit understandings/claims explicit can we ask the historical question: whether we can appropriately apply modern legal language to any particular period of the tradition.

ANDREW: Can I try a thought experiment on you? If you were forced at gunpoint to spend six months doing a comparative study of our seven legal systems, what theoretical approach would you find most helpful out of Weber's legal reasoning, Hart's rules of change or Dworkin's principles?

Personally, I'm a great fan of Weber's approach to legal history. He tells us that reading these old texts to extract rules is not enough. We should also be reading them to extract information on who wrote them, who preserved them and how they were argued over. In particular we should ask 'What motivated the early legal specialists?' From these questions emerges his analysis of how *rechts-honoratioren* change into professional lawyers. We can usefully apply all this analysis to the monks, priests, rabbis, erudites, gurus and qadis who wrote our religious law texts. But I think we should use Weber selectively. Because Roman Law was his central-case, he got badly hung up on law providing clearly stated rules in a well-organised field. If Roman Law is peripheral to our religious concerns, then we can avoid the elephant-trap of formal rationality.

In the paper published herein David Daube draws an interesting distinction between Roman and Jewish law: "Coming to argumentation and presentation, Roman law proudly displays specialized refinement... Jewish law is vulgar all along... not lawyers' law." His idea is that under certain conditions vulgarity (or popular appeal) aids survival. I find *vulgar* v. *refined* much more useful than

formal-rational v. *substantive rational* for discussing how lawyers thought.
What Daube mentions as signs of vulgarity (judgement-tales, debates and
popular anecdotes about clever judges) feature prominently in the Buddhist
material. It pleases me to think of my research as one great wallow in vulgarity.

CALUM: I am not sure that it is vulgarity that aids survival. Daube's point is that
the chaotic character of the Talmud compels curiosity in it. The distinction
between the Jewish and Roman legal systems turned on the distinction
between the masses versus the non-masses, or rather, the somewhat undiffer-
entiated nature of Jewry and its small numbers over against the large numbers
under Roman control in the hands of an elite.

BERNARD: I think we need to be careful about Daube's distinction. Certainly, the
literature of Jewish law, and particularly the Talmud, is the stuff of learning,
in which non-experts are encouraged to engage. But this goes back to the
close connections in the Bible between law and wisdom, and the very etymology of the word Torah as 'instruction'. This should not blind us to the fact
that when this same literature is used for the purposes of halakhic decision-
making, the views of only the most highly-regarded specialists will be taken
into account. It's hardly surprising. The same text can be used for a variety
of different purposes, and can be read at a variety of different levels. Though
we might expect that a *religious* system of law might adopt such a didactic
function more naturally than a *secular* system (perhaps correlated with the
view that the religion speaks directly to each believer, whereas a modern,
secular system speaks primarily to specialists, and uses them as intermediaries
to the public). But don't forget Cicero's story that in his day schoolchildren
learnt the Twelve Tables by heart. In some secular societies, 'civics' education
focuses upon foundational texts. It is not the character of *religious* as against
secular legal texts which prompts the distinction between *vulgar* as against
professional use, but rather the ideology of the society concerned. Justinian's
Digest is immensely more accessible than the Talmud.

ANDREW: I take your point. The bits of the Vinaya that recount the Buddha's
biography are central texts of popular Buddhism, but the specialists still
manage to squeeze abstruse legal points from them. And I accept that as
a distinction *vulgar* v. *refined* is not well-specified. But it's a better starting
point than Weber's tainted concept of rationality. Perhaps we could improve
on Daube by asking further questions, such as: [a] is case-law and biography
mixed into the lawtexts? [b] do the lawtext authors see chaos as a challenge
to their interpretative skills, or as an affront? [c] are there attempts to impose
a systematic arrangement on legal material?

The Hart approach: rules of change

ANDREW: The legal positivists criticise religious laws for their unchangeability.
If a text emanates from God, or from an enlightened being, then mere
humans can't alter it. Hart, with his secondary rules of change, gives the

clearest version of this attack. Unchangeable law texts, he says, are socially inefficient. Proper grown-up legal systems must contain rules of change. Has Hart inadvertently given us a diagnostic tool? Can we decide such borderline cases as Roman law and Buddhist law by looking for *rules of change*: 'Roman law could be changed by imperial rescript, therefore it was not religious. Buddhist *vinaya* was unchangeable, therefore it is religious'.?

SILVIO: In my chapter I drew attention to the fact that Canon Law specifies its *rules of change*. And to the example of usury which show them being used. But Canon Law is not unique in this. Surely all religious laws change their content? For example, Jewish marriage is no longer potentially polygamous (as it was in biblical times). The real task is to find out what the *rules of change* are. Do they vary between each religion? Are they different from the *rules of change* we find in 'secular' systems? If the religious law distinguishes a core of divine revelation from a husk of lesser revelation, do different *rules of change* apply to each part? There's a whole research program me for you!

BERNARD: Jewish law does indeed contain Hartian *rules of change* – which, as Silvio correctly observes, make distinctions between different parts of the system. But we must not neglect to ask, in my view, whether these *rules of change* themselves change, both as a factual (historical) question, and as a normative question: whether there is authority within the system to change the *rules of change*.

CALUM: Let me pick up the point about Canon law and usury. Jewish law can raise the similar issue. For example, Hillel's *Prosbul* neutralized a biblical rule requiring the release of debts every seven years by enabling a loan to be enforced even after the seventh year. In the original biblical context the rule solely and reasonably applied to dealings with the poor.

ANDREW: Some critics of the Catholic church mock the change of stance on usury. Did Jewish law lose any face?

CALUM: We are in the dark as to whether or not Jewish law's reputation suffered because of the change. It would doubtless depend on someone's stance at the time. Those involved in the system would see the development as progressive and those looking in from the outside might see chicanery at work. Daube makes the telling point that a religious system such as the Jewish might claim to be unchangeable but in reality be perfectly capable of making changes. Contrariwise, even in a secular system such as Roman law, the Emperor Justinian went to great lengths to keep his code of Roman law unchangeable.

RANDALL: Any set of rules or principles is necessarily subject to interpretation, and hence to change, whether one pretends so or not. How far can change be achieved through interpretation, as opposed to outright amendment or over-rule? This is significant for the human rights activists, some of them feminists, who are trying various hermeneutic strategies to historicize passages they dislike. A good example is Norani Othman's attempt to reconcile Islamic texts and practices with the contemporary rights of women envisioned in international rights documents. She counsels that 'the vast social changes that span the time between the establishment of the first Islamic community and the emergence of the contemporary world order require a creative and historically sensitive interpretation.' Using this method, one could limit the text to the period – much as judges isolate the judgement in a particular case they disagree with by limiting it to its specific facts. But Othman's historicizing might not be available to all the interpretative sub-traditions. My colleague, Khaled Abou El Fadl, tells me there are seven schools of Islamic jurisprudence, each with its own hermeneutic principles.

To return to China and my own area of expertise, the old view was that Chinese law saw little change because around 70 per cent of the Tang statutes (*lu*) were still part of the Qing code. Closer examination has shown that the degree of change over the years has been significant. Draftsmen created substatutes (*li*) that ostensibly interpreted the *lu* and applied it to particular circumstances. This interpretative process went in cycles. Every now and then, there would be so many *li* (and many of them contradictory) that they threw them all out and started over with fresh *lu*.

ANDREW: I'm happy to accept that all legal systems *de facto* change through time. Hart is asking about the *de iure* position: does the law formally acknowledge ways in which change may be brought about? And rightly so. Whether or not the system officially accepts *rules of change* impacts on the kind of debate that the system can tolerate. To take a Buddhist example, vinaya practice has changed over 2,500 years, because most governments now seek to impose a national hierarchy on their monks. Because the vinaya does not specify any *rules of change*, this remains controversial. Twentieth-century governments have claimed that their omnicompetence extends to vinaya matters. The purist monks (whose side I take) argue straight past them: 'We are ruled by the text of the vinaya: the government hierarchy has no standing.' If Buddhism had *rules of change*, the nature of the debate would be quite different: both sides would be lobbying for or against some specific legislative or constitutional change.

CALUM: Hart's argument has little value: it makes too sharp a separation between what the rules are and why people obey the rules. The claim that a text has a divine origin is an attempt to lend *authority* to the contents of the body of law in question. And that involves an *augmentation* of its rules. Both words share the same root: *auctoritas* is from the verb *augere* (to increase).

The Dworkin approach – rules and principles

ANDREW: Is there a religious answer to the question 'Do we express our norms primarily through rules or through principles?' I'm assuming that we use Dworkin's distinction between *rules* (all-or-nothing application, not transferable across subjects, easy to apply mechanically) and *principles* (differing weight of application, relevant to many subjects, can't be applied mechanically). I'm not sure how far Dworkin is prepared to go as a comparative lawyer: he makes a general claim that all legal systems embody *rules* and *principles*, but I don't know if that claim includes religious systems. Suppose for a moment that his general claim is false: his distinction might then be useful to us for diagnostic purposes. If religious law connects with high-level ethics and bold generalisations, we might expect it to favour *principles* over *rules*. I've seen it claimed of both Islamic law and Canon law that they are long on *principles* and short on *rules*. Is this true? And is it true of other religious laws?

RANDALL: It would surprise me if all systems were not some combination of *rules* and *principles*, at least in practice. Certainly the Chinese system has both. Even if there were a *rule*, as we all know, the indeterminacy of language permits a range of interpretation, thus blurring the line between *rules* and *principles*. That is not to deny that some provisions are more *rule*-like and some more *principle*-like, just to suggest that an actual empirical comparison of different systems along this dimension would be hard.

ANDREW: I endorse that. So far as I can see, there are vanishingly few *principles* to be found in the Vinaya. But I don't know whether to blame the Buddha for this, or to blame my own conception of how *principles* differ from *rules*.

SILVIO: With this issue we are moving quite far from the core of religious law. It may well be that other, non-religious, cultural influences bear on the presence or absence of *principles*. If this is so, I would expect to see a wide range of different models. The New Testament, for example, has many divine *principles* but few divine *rules*: according to Helmut Pree 'Jesus himself never enacted a law, not even in the most clear, valid and binding principles such as the claim for marital fidelity.' But it is surely possible to find a law in the Old Testament or in the Qu'ran. The distinction between *rule* and *principle* affects the system's scope for change and adaptation. A *rule* can be applied (if sufficiently defined); a *principle* cannot be applied without first being interpreted.

CALUM: I don't think that it is a question of more or less room for interpretation. I see it rather as one of reticence. In Jewish Law the many *rules* to be observed take for granted profound beliefs and higher ideals. The question is why these *principles* are not spelled out more often. A major factor why they are not is that Judaism has not, by and large, gone in for missionary activity. Hence there has been no need to spell out to outsiders what the religion is about. Then again, it might not be desirable to spell them out, because the body of *rules* may be a cover for some dubious stance. Biblical incest rules, for example, reveal an anti-foreign bias on critical examination. Better that this underlying *principle* remains unspoken. Mind you, even when *principles* are expressed, they can still act so as to conceal undesirable attitudes.

BERNARD: Dworkin describes his Hercules as 'a lawyer of superhuman skill, learning, patience and acumen'. I have commented that Hercules 'indulges in a hermeneutic holism of truly Rabbinic proportions'. By that I meant that everything within the system is potentially relevant to everything else, precisely because (according to the Rabbinic understanding) it is the product of a single divine author, who is capable (beyond any human author) of using literary means in order to justify the use of (often analogical) reasoning in relation to matters entirely diverse both in substance and textual expression. In this sense, Rabbinic assumptions transcend even those of Dworkin (at least that version of Dworkin which Andrew has provided): arguments based upon *rules* in one area may indeed be used in order to justify conclusions in relation to *rules* in a quite different area – and without, necessarily, invoking *principles* in order to do so. The justification may reside in purely literary features of the biblical text. Nevertheless, constraints have in practice been adopted in various periods; we need to study the historical and sociological factors which have produced such constraints.

Prospects for future research

RANDALL: I don't think there is a generic answer to the question what is a religious system. If you want to require a transcendent dimension, go ahead. That just means you have another category of something else that is not transcendent but relies on moral principles defined in terms of ultimate meaning or whatever. To me, the question is rather: assuming some legal systems rely on a transcendent normative order and some don't, what are the implications for law? Is law more likely to be respected in one than the other? Is one more supportive of a natural law human rights tradition? Of civil disobedience? Is legal reasoning likely to be any different? And so on.

ANDREW: I'm thinking of calling this book *Religions, Laws, Traditions* so as to hint that if *Religion* fails us as a comparative concept, there's always *Tradition* to fall back on.

SILVIO: Many comparative law scholars (Constantinesco, Mattei, etc.) put religious law in the same box together with traditional law. Maybe they are right but what does tradition mean? If we mean old law, law based on the past, what about the legal systems of the new religious movements? Religions (and religious laws) are born and die every day: it is a dynamic phenomenon, rooted in the present as well in the past. Jehovah's Witnesses law, the law of the Church of Scientology, Mormon law ... There are a lot of new religious movements and some of them are not young offspring of old religions but something really new. If we mean law based on custom, what about canon law, where custom has now a negligible importance? Moreover the faithful do not obey a religious law because it is old or because it has been obeyed by their ancestors: they obey it because they think it is God's law and/or because they think it is a good way to get happiness here and eternal life later.

ANDREW: So instead of the seven cases we came together to discuss, there are fifty religions? Or five hundred? Or five thousand?

SILVIO: There are five thousand religions and five thousand religious laws. But do you think 'secular' laws are fewer? Comparative law scholars have reduced the 'secular' laws to order: why should we not manage to do the same with religious laws? Maybe it is just a dream, but why should we discard the possibility we are now at the same point the scholars of secular legal systems were just before the 1900 Paris Exposition Universelle, that is at the beginning of a fruitful and long scientific experience? Nobody has yet seriously tried to compare religious laws. Maybe at the end we shall discover it was not worthwhile doing it, but how can we know without trying?

10

JEWISH AND ROMAN
PHILOSOPHIES OF LAW

David Daube

CALUM CARMICHAEL WRITES: *I have put together this piece from notes left by David Daube who died on 24 February 1999. As he states at the outset the topic was not to his liking, but it was the one on which York University, Toronto, asked him to speak (March 14, 1983, a Leonard Wolinsky Lecture on Jewish Life and Education under the auspices of the Faculties of Arts and Education with the cooperation of the Toronto Board of Jewish Education). I have taken the outline of his talk from different versions and, arranging matters as best I could, I also added footnotes from jottings where I thought they might help. By and large, I have retained Daube's characteristically elliptical way of communicating. Although this talk does not provide an example, one of his major qualities was his capacity to read texts closely. I sometimes think that he resorted to his cryptic style because, in part, he wanted his readers to pay as close attention to what he had to say as he demonstrated in reading any text that came his way. Walter Weyrauch, to whom I showed this piece, wrote, 'It occurs to me that David is writing like a seer who is speaking in tongues. Mostly this is less visible than in this essay, but it is always present. One does not think of contemporaries as prophets, thus this quality of David tends to be obscured, but it explains part of the hold he has over people.'[1] On the occasion of his lecture at York University, Daube began (tongue in cheek): 'I always thought that comparative law could be taught in four short sentences. In England, anything is allowed that is not forbidden; in Germany, anything is forbidden that is not allowed; in Russia anything is forbidden even what is allowed; and in France, anything is allowed, even what is forbidden!'*

For reasons unknown to me, my hosts at York University absolutely wanted me to lecture on this subject though I pointed out to them that I am no philosopher. In despair I thought up a question which, while just defensible under the title, avoids the usual demanding themes: if we look at the areas traditionally dear to jurists – such as property, business deals, torts – in the epoch traditionally chosen for comparison – the Talmudic one, coinciding with that from Cicero to Justinian – wherein lies the true, substantive difference between the two systems? I shall, however, start with a few wider-ranging reflections.

In their *Major Legal Systems in the World Today*, René David and John Brierley exalt three great families of law: the Romano-Germanic, the common and the socialist.[2] The first might just as well be called Roman since nothing in the body of the discussion filters out anything peculiarly Germanic. Conceivably, this epithet is added with a view to pleasing an important constituency among the readers. If so, it is a small price to pay; after all, *captatio benevolentiae* has an old and honored place in argumentation. Anyhow, besides these three, they say, we find normative edifices like the Hindu, Muslim, and Jewish which are religious or philosophical rather than juridical. It is doubtful whether they are 'law' at all.

I am not concerned about nomenclature – provided its basis is reasonably intelligible. If you choose to speak of 'law' only where there are rules fixing the temperature of zabaglione, or indeed if you define 'law' as an elephant with three legs, that is alright by me. In the case under notice, the sense is not clear. Confronted by structures strange and troublesome, the authors avoid real analysis by narrowly focusing on and exaggerating disqualifying features. They make no reference to the enormous role of creeds and isms in their own territory – say, in regard to marriage, concubinage, incest, children, Sunday observance, treatment of old age, notions of sanity, valuation of ownership, status, freedom, life human, animal, plant, metallic.

Nor do they acknowledge the extent of the juridical on the other side. It is true that they purport to supply a criterion by accepting the verdict that over there no rights of the individual are recognized, only duties. But, on the one hand, it is hotly debated whether classical Roman law had the concept of a subjective right.[3] On the other, I have suggested elsewhere[4] that the ancient Hebrews – some of them – had a conscience without a word for it, and the Greeks worshipped many gods before Philo, alien observer, coined the designation 'polytheist.' Just so, despite the lack in Scripture of a word for an individual's right – or, for that matter, duty – something like it did exist. The cave of Machpelah 'is ensured to Abraham for a possession for a burying place.' (Gen. 23: 17ff.) Esau 'sells Jacob his first-bornhood' (Gen. 25: 33). Naboth bravely puts his sacred ancestral ties above accommodation with the king, yet he would obviously be entitled to make over his vineyard: his is a genuine dilemma (1 Kings 21). 'He was riding on a beast and saw a lost object and said to a fellow, "Give it to me." The latter took it up and said, "I have acquired it." He has acquired it; if it was after he gave it to the former that he said, "I have acquired it," he did not say a thing.' (*mishnah Baba Metzia* 1:3).

In the face of these samples, how meaningful is it to state that Bible and Talmud know of no rights of the individual, only of duties? Curiously, the third of the great families, the socialist, in strictness deserves its ranking less than the rejects. Insofar as a regime has achieved full socialism, it avowedly denies state and law, rendered needless through perfect economic conditions. Maybe there is here yet a further effort to show and gain goodwill, directed to a different group from that adverted to above.

Of course, David and Brierley cannot be blamed for continuing the time-hallowed contrast between societies where law is a branch of religion and societies where it is independent. This is the usual division and, according as the inspector is piously traditionalist or liberal, he accords praise and censure in opposite ways. Nor am I denying that the degree of conscious subordination of the legal order to first principles varies hugely between various countries and periods. It was very high, for instance, among Babylonian Jewry of the fifth century A.D., in Geneva during Calvin's reign – yes, the phenomenon is not confined to the Orient – and in Germany under Hitler.[5] It was higher in early twentieth-century Austria and Spain than Sweden. That a system with a rather steady inclination one way will come to differ from a system with the opposite tendency is obvious. Only we must not overwork this aspect, at the expense of principles or factors effective without being formulated.[6]

Roman religion influences such matters as marriage, concubinage, incest, children, burial grounds, *dies fasti ne fasti* [days on which court hearings are held and days on which they are not] – all this goes on even in the Empire. The pontiffs, according to Kunkel, are jurists in the Republic longer than we thought. But take Julian: he is a pontiff and the curator of sacred buildings. One of his Emperors, Marcus Aurelius, is deeply religious and active in legal matters (11.1.2): 'A property of the rational soul is the love of our neighbor, and truthfulness, and modesty, and to prize nothing above itself – all of which indeed befits the law.' (Cf Mark 8: 36: 'For what shall it profit a man if he shall gain the whole world and lose his soul?') Or (2.1): 'Say to thyself at daybreak: I shall come across the busybody, the thankless, the bully, the treacherous, the envious, the unneighborly. All this has befallen them because they know not good from evil. But I, in that I have comprehended the nature of the Good that is beautiful and the nature of the Evil that is ugly, and the nature of the wrongdoer himself that is akin to me, not as partaker of the same blood and seed but of intelligence and a morsel of the Divine, can neither be injured by any of them – for no one can involve me in what is debasing – nor can I be wroth with my kinsman and hate him. For we have come into being for co-operation, as have the feet, the hands.... Therefore to thwart one another is against Nature, and we do not thwart one another by having resentment and aversion.' Perhaps it is more like a Reform Rabbi or a Bishop of the Church of England than a Lubavitcher or Oral Roberts.[7] But it is good enough and neglected unjustly, but I won't go into the reasons.

It may be more interesting to concentrate on unduly neglected aspects: first, the enormous difference between successive periods through which Jewish and Roman law passed, and, second, some fundamental down-to-earth dissimilarities in outlook and function between the two in the sector and period commonly thought of when we compare them, private law 250 B.C.–550 A.D. (Hellenistic and Talmudic centuries on the Jewish side, pre-classical, classical, and Justinian jurisprudence on the Roman), dissimilarities obscured by, hiding behind, the simplifying antithesis sacred-lay.

First, as for Jewish law under God, actually, in an early biblical stratum, he is hostile to culture, including legal progress. The paradise story shows him trying to prevent man's access to knowledge and punishing him for breaking through regardless (Genesis 2, 3); and at Babel, universal co-existence and mutual understanding is prevented (Gen. 11: 1–9). In a way, the latter legend already touches the concerns of law. Certainly, at Sodom, we meet the problem of collective responsibility. God starts with it but Abraham manages to wrest a higher principle from him (Genesis 18). Similarly Abimelech wrests another in regard to wrongdoing in error (Genesis 20). All four tales are intended as signposts for mankind: they cover pagans as well as Jews. But even after Sinai, man has to persuade God to advance, though the tone is easier: in Num16: 22 something like the Sodom problem recurs, if this time intranational, and in Numbers 27, also an intranational affair, inheritance rules are changed in response to an argument of the daughters of Zelophehad (amended in Numbers 36). Needless to say, in the end – and we must not conceive of it as a straightforward development for things move at varying speeds in different contexts – God demands ideal justice and sets an example, for example, he condemns the indirect murder of Uriah. Job constitutes an elaborate wisdom treatment of the dilemma as to God's standing in the matter, vindicating his perfection in the face of all that we experience.

A Greek parallel to the paradise myth is that of Prometheus. The God taking no account of subjective innocence or impasse is represented by the Erinyes as they persecute Orestes; and their participation in the establishment of Areopagus parallels the Biblical solution. We may recall also that in regard to Homer's gods some side with Troy, some with Greece; in Aeschylus, all unite for justice. There is less at Rome of the ancient stage, not surprising considering dates; but according to Numa and the XII Tables, the gods have still to be appeased for unwitting homicide by the offer of a ram (cp. how Jacob in Gen. 28: 18 has to dedicate a pillar with oil because of his unwitting trespass on sacred ground). Pagans can more easily juggle new versus old because they can distribute positions among several gods; Jews must get it all into one. The ultimate explanation of this evolution from a hostile to a friendly deity is that originally nature felt as inimical, was gradually tamed, even becoming helpful. As at present, with disease, hunger, radiation, etc., threat once again comes to the fore. Satan is being reintroduced as a mighty force.

Second, as to the solid differences during the famous period of private law: Roman law is by and for an elite, Jewish law is relatively undiscriminating. W. Kunkel, *Herkunft and soziale Stellung der römischen Juristen* (1952), 38ff., 271ff., demonstrates that Republican jurists for long came from the leading nobility, towards the end from knights-money aristocracy; from Augustus they belonged to the senatorial class which he preferred for this purpose as less mercenary and as tradition-true; since Hadrian the knights again prevailed. Throughout differences are tied to politics. If Sadducees had won, maybe the Jewish side would be closer. But Pharisaic lawyers, despite the weight of old houses, were more widely spread. Such eminent ones as Akiba, Meir, Simon ben Laqish were plebeian, not to mention a host of minor ones. Much Roman law was never meant for the mass. The *filiusfamilias* of lowly background is not, in effect, propertyless: that is unenforceable. Augustus boasts: 'To each member of the plebs of Rome I paid out 300 sesterces – $25 – under my father's will; in 12th year of my tribunate I paid 400 a third time; the distributions never reached fewer than 250,000.' They could not enquire whether a guy had a grandfather living. Propertylessness applied only to the haves.

Consider Guardianship: among excuses ignorance of law, *nominatio potioris* [nomination of a more powerful person] – cannot concern the slums. There is no such split in Jewish law. A momentous factor is that Jewry has no 'mass' like Rome and the Empire. Augustus enacted that men must marry and procreate between 25–60, women 20–50. Note the penalty: no outside inheritance and second at inauguration as consul. In Jewry, which adopted the duty about that time (Rabbis, Philo), it is religious, general, with divorce recommended for the childless. Augustus includes women, quite free in his circles; Jewish law does not, they are not to be liberated, *pace* Johanan ben Beroqa.[8] J.M. Kelly, proves that in findable-out-about Roman suits plaintiff is superior or at least equal to defendant;[9] an inferior would have no chance.[10] He adds, on Kunkel's authority,[11] that separation *honestior-humilior* [upper class-lower class], dominating the criminal law of the later Empire, basically reaches into the Republic and is outside the criminal law. Picture the Praetor with an album at the outset of a lawsuit. While not denying the biases in the Jewish field, I submit that all this indicates a gulf. An incident reported in the Talmud brings out Roman Law's stress on clubability. Bana'ah ca. 220 combats the exclusion from a judgeship of one who sued even without good cause.[12]

In Roman gentlemanly, 'manly' evaluation condemnation for *dolus* [fraud] in *actio doli* brings infamy, but not on the ground of *metus* [fear]. Killing a child is tolerated longer than selling him. A Roman gentleman does not personally engage in trade generally, so the latter *a priori* dubious. I daresay in much Jewish diaspora rating, a threat of crude violence would be worse than a bit of cheating. The story of Samson still goes with the Roman evaluation. His wild deeds are admired; the unfair way in which his companions acquire the solution of his riddle is despised, and he triumphantly gets the better of them by, once again, a brutal enterprise though on this occasion he himself rivals them, outdoes them, in 'cleverness' – he procures the garments by slaying their fellow-countrymen. With the attitude in good Roman society to *dolus* and *metus* chimes a well-known contrast in the field of *patria potestas* and *manus*. A father who sold his son three times lost his *patria potestas*. Not a father who beat him up three times; and even the right to kill him persisted a long time. Similarly, to sell your wife (married with *manus*) became a no-no well before a hitting or even a putting to death. Significantly, Samson does finish his wife and all hers once he judges them involved in adultery. Abraham accepts gifts for Sarah's services at Gerar.[13]

Coming to argumentation and presentation, Roman law proudly displays specialized refinement. Unlike Jewish, it is not to be intelligible, arguable about, broadly. The remoter branches of *condictio* and the handling of agency/no agency in contract highlight this.[14] Post-classical law, which drops those branches and simplifies agency, is called 'vulgar'. Jewish law is vulgar all along. You can at a glance tell Julian from a Rabbi. Yet it is good law, only it is not lawyers' law. The difference is like that between a good folksong, or poetry v. Beethoven's string quartets, or T.S. Eliot. Some can do both. Shakespeare could sing both low ('When daffodils begin to peer') and high (the sonnets). Likewise Rilke: compare *Brüh-derlein muss immer fragen* with *Duineser Elegieen*. Bob Dylan and the Beatles stay folksy, Stefan George goes up. Law affects people without their choosing, unlike music or poetry; something to be said for folk-law – but this is my bias.

Let us, however, be clear about the social implications of the classical. It is significant that the Gemara [the contents of the Talmud] records proceedings, debates, but the Digest only quotes final works. Just a few passages in Digest, e.g., 12.4.4, 12.6.12, do show that in the post-classical era such debates were recorded somewhere: which only underlines classical elitism, preferred by Justinian. Such popular anecdotes as those about clever judges (Solomon, Bana'ah, Sancho) are foreign to Rome from early on.[15] Whereas even the legal tractates of the Talmud are full of Haggadah [teaching designed to guide but not strictly binding]. As is well known, the Palestinian, around 400 AD, contains far less Haggadah than the Babylonian, 500 AD. The reason is not only different dates of completion, but also perhaps primarily the greater closeness of the Palestinian to the Roman world, of the Babylonian to the Oriental. Ironically, it is the 'vulgar', down-to-earth nature and the chaotic formulation of Jewish law to which its continued, wide attractiveness throughout the centuries is largely due. To this day, those interested, scholars and non-academics, assemble Saturday afternoon, not for Maimonides' Mishneh Torah, but for Babylonian Gemara. Alas, in the past 200 years there has occurred a breakdown in commonsensical input, owing to the lack of practical testing, hence the failure of Talmudists in 1948 and, except for marriage law – which did go on in the real world – foreign law was adopted by the new State of Israel.

Undoubtedly Jewish law is more influenced by religion than Roman. But as to contents or quality, this means not nothing but less than might be expected.[16] Either can be open or nasty to aliens, children; for or against wars. Even in respect of immutability – the Sadducees were no less religious than the Pharisees but would admit more direct freedom; the Pharisees – *petits bourgeois* – desired security, yet where changes were urgent did manage them, via interpretation. The secular Romans often moved very slowly; Justinian prohibited even commentaries on his legislation in order to keep it fixed. His image is Christian but there is no real change in the character of the law. Where I sense possible value in a religion-oriented system is not in detail but in constant general consciousness of a realm beyond the momentary and the petty. Of course, the opportunity entails dangers, as always. At any rate, the striking cases of religious influence are nearly all outside private law (counting marriage as public); and indeed, if many are blind to the religious element in Roman law, even its full extent in Jewish is yet to be appreciated – largely because much remains buried that researchers find embarrassing.[17] An illustration are the Talmudic methods of execution, explicable (as, using some of Adolf Büchler's results, I have tried to work out) by a conflux of two forces: the limited rights of Jewry in the matter of capital punishment and – religion – the wish to keep the skeleton intact in deference to bodily resurrection.[18]

Private law is, as I have outlined, distinct by its social thrust. A charming instance of religious intervention in private law is met in *mishnah Baba Qamma* 6.6 [and *babylonian Baba Qamma* 62b]. A camel laden with flax passes a shop, some flax gets inside where an open light burns and a fire ensues; the cameldriver owes reparation. The same case but this time the light is kept outside the shop and the fire gets going in this way; the shopkeeper owes reparation. Ah, says R. Judah, except if it is the Feast of Maccabees, for then it is incumbent on you to kindle a light in the open, because it is the proclamation of God's saving power. The moral of this lecture is then: don't drive a camel with flax through a narrow street on Hanukkah.

NOTES

1 *Editorial note*: Walter Weyrauch, letter on file; see now: Walter Weyrauch, 'Nonrational Sources of Scholarship. Remembering David Daube (1909–1999)' *Rechtshistorisches Journal* 19: 677–681 (2000).

2 René David and John Brierley, *Major Legal Systems in the World Today: An Introduction to the Comparative Study of Law* (London: Stevens & Son, 1968), 9.

3 M. Kaser, *Das römische Privatrecht* 2nd. ed. Erster Abschnitt (Munich: Beck, 1971), 195.

4 David Daube, *Ancient Jewish Law* (Leiden: Brill, 1981), 123ff.

5 Bernd Rüthers, *Die unbegrenzte Auslegung: zum Wandel der Privatrechtordnung im Nationalsozialismus* (Tübingen: Mohr, 1968).

6 It is ironical that the term [religious] used for the non-law systems is Latin. In fact, the oldest etymology of it we have is from Cicero: *relegere*, to read over and over again. Hillel uses *shana*, to repeat, for to study; Bacher pointing out that it comes from the constant repetition of orally transmitted teachings.

7 *Editorial note:* Recall Oscar Wilde's quip, 'The Roman Catholic Church is for saints and sinners alone. For respectable people the Anglican Church will do.'

8 David Daube, *Collected Works, Vol. 1, Talmudic Law* ed. Calum Carmichael (Berkeley: Robbins Collection, 1992), 143–152.

9 J.M. Kelly, *Roman Litigation* (Oxford: Clarendon Press, 1966), 61ff.

10 *Editorial note*: On Daube's evaluation of such word formations as 'findable-out-about' see 'Word-Formation in Indo-European and Semitic' in ed. Michael Hoeflich *Lex et Romanitas: Essays for Alan Watson* (Berkeley: Robbins Collection, 2000), 15–19.

11 Wolfgang Kunkel, *Untersuchungen zur Entwicklung des römischen Kriminalverfahrens in vorsullanischer Zeit* (Munich: Abhandlungen der Bayerischen Akademie der Wissenschaften, phil.-hist., 1952), 56.

12 Daube, *supra* note 8, at 221–222.

13 The medieval Jewish killing of children during crusades hardly includes adult ones (though wives?). See: David Daube, 'Three Footnotes on Civil Disobedience in Antiquity' *Humanities in Society* 2: 69–82 (1979), 82.

14 *Editorial note: Condictio* is a type of action alleging a civil law debt without mentioning any cause of action, available not only as a contractual remedy, but also on a quasi-contractual basis, where unjustified enrichment could be shown.

15 David Daube, 'Fraud on Law for Fraud on Law' *Oxford Journal of Legal Studies* 1: 51–60 (1981), 59.

16 Capitalism is said to spring from protestantism!

17 David Daube, *Collected Works, Vol. 2, New Testament Judaism* ed. Calum Carmichael (Berkeley: Robbins Collection, 2000), 531.

18 Daube, *supra* note 7, at 620–622.

11

RELIGIOUS LAWS AS SYSTEMS
OF LAW

A comparatist's view

Jacques Vanderlinden

Some contributors to the W.G. Hart 2000 panel on *Religious System of Law* declined to tackle the three fundamental questions which Andrew Huxley posed in his *Call for Papers*. Some even implied that such comparative questions should be left to a comparatist, and restricted themselves to a detailed description of their specialist legal system. Hence my presence at the end of the volume. I have been asked to come in as a *concierge* after the party is over, to empty the dustbins, change the light bulbs and sweep up. You do not expect an intellectual firework display from a concierge – only that he cleans up quickly and efficiently. Nor would you expect the concierge to claim his methods to be objectively superior to all others. I have performed my chores in a highly subjective and, accordingly, relative way. Tidying up mental categories is an intellectual game that I enjoy. Like most so-called scientific approaches, it is a pure construction of the mind. The more so, in that it rests on premises which are the result of other intellectual games. I refer to the definitions of law, which are intended to apply in very different cultural, economic, political or social surroundings. These premises, unlike those on which some other sciences rely, are of an incommensurable nature.

IS IT USEFUL TO CLASSIFY THE WORLD'S LEGAL SYSTEMS INTO FAMILIES?

I still answer yes to this first question, though aware that some colleagues have come to consider taxonomy as unfashionable. When confronted with a plurality of objects, it is convenient to distinguish between them, sorting them into groups according to one or more of their respective features. This activity fits into our more general organisation of the world around us. Classifying legal systems is similar to reorganising the books in our library, or the knives in our kitchen. My attempts at the latter have occasionally conflicted with my wife's doctrines of kitchen organisation. The ensuing marital disharmony suggests that, as a general rule, different taxonomies should meet in a spirit of mutual deference and *politesse*. And we should extend the same spirit to those who refuse to taxonomise, those who espouse a so-called 'disorderly take on life'.

Calum Carmichael is correct to label taxonomy as 'overly restrictive'. Taxonomy (indeed, comparison itself) must be a reductive exercise, because it focuses on single characteristics. The anthropologist and historian crave thick description and deep detail. Because only thin description and shallow detail can apply to two taxa at once, the comparatist and taxonomist must adopt a different approach. The former try to 'understand' the Other, in space and time, as deeply as they possibly can.[1] Should the latter try this approach, they would find nothing but a list of specificities and a few minimal similarities – scarcely enough foundation on which to establish a family. These different approaches are not mutually exclusive: I am an anthropologist, a comparatist and a historian, sometimes simultaneously and often in relation to the same data. If you find contradictions in what I am about to expound, please ascribe them to my split disciplinary personality. I like to impose a certain amount of order on my life, though the state of my desktop may give a different impression. At the same time, I aspire to go as deep as possible into the so-called 'reality' of things perceived.

I have difficulties with Huxley's uncharacteristically Benthamite phrasing of his first question. His appeal to utility imposes undue constraints on our discussion. Academic activities, including taxonomy, ought not to be subjected to a criterion of usefulness. Let us not condemn those colleagues who enjoy taxonomy by suggesting their pastime is useless! Taxonomy, like everything else we do as lawyers – from defining legal concepts and distinguishing precedents to inventing tax loopholes – is a mental exercise. All comparatists, to the extent that they like to keep their desks tidy, must also be taxonomists. I recognise that there are as many *comparative laws* as there are *comparative lawyers*.[2] What I have to say is one view among many. It may be met with respect by some. It will be met with derision by others.

I shall approach this first question under three headings: *about law*; *about systems*; *about criteria of classification*. Since I am interested in the classification of legal systems, I must clarify what 'systems' are and what 'criteria' I shall use to classify them. But the adjective 'legal' is also in play, and requires a preliminary discussion.

About law

Werner Menski's chapter indicates how difficult it is to identify law, once we have left the secure ground of positive law (as we must when examing religious laws). B.Z. Tamanaha in a recent article suggests a way to avoid these difficulties: he proposes to consider as *law* whatever is called law, droit, recht, derecho, direito, diritto by the speakers of these languages.[3] As the papers in this volume are all in English and all refer to *law*, this approach could easily settle the matter. But I fear that Tamanaha stands on shaky ground: his proposal cannot cope with

Buddhist, Chinese, Hindu, Islamic or Jewish law.[4] Though we call these systems *legal*, we cannot declare, with our hand on our heart, that the English word *law* represents something identical to what it conveys in Thai, Chinese, Hindi, Arabic or Hebrew. These languages have words which, we believe, mean something similar to *law*, but the precise range of their meaning is difficult to determine. Let's examine three 'classical' definitions of Arabic *Shari'a*, which is often taken as an equivalent of English *law*:

> The *Shari'a* is the path laid down by the creator; in following it men will find both moral and material well-being. The *Shari'a* regulates in great detail the dealings of individuals with each other and with the community; it encompasses all man's duties to God and his fellow-men.[5]
>
> Floating above Muslim society as a disembodied soul, freed from the currents and vicissitudes of time, it represented the eternal valid ideal towards which society must aspire.[6]
>
> The sacred Law of Islam [*shari'a*] is an all embracing body of religious duties, the totality of Allah's commands that regulate the life of every Muslim in all its aspects; it comprises on an equal footing ordinances regarding worship and ritual, as well as political and (in the narrow sense) legal rules.[7]

It is clear from these that *Shari'a* is not coterminous with *law*.

Joseph Schacht goes on to elaborate what is '(in the narrow sense) legal', but this turns out to be those parts of *shari'a* which entail punishment (*hadd*), in other words, penal law. Much of what Europeans call private law would fall outside this restrictive definition: this illustrates the latent positivist influence on Europeans who approach Islamic law. Such a narrow perception of law raises serious issues at a time when radical pluralists are willing to consider as law whatever socially controlled behavioural constraints are accepted by the members of any type of society. For radical pluralists, the individual ceases to be exclusively an object of the law; he becomes a producer of law on the same footing as the chief who produces legislation, the judge who produces caselaw, the learned man who produces legal science, the people at large who produces custom, and, of course, God who produces revelation. This approach to the concept of law shifts us from the exclusive consideration of State-like societies to taking all types of society as our subject matter. It widens the field of law to such an extent that some have complained that 'it sees the law everywhere'. However that may be, the legal taxonomy I offer here is grounded in radical pluralism, which is where I find myself fifty years after I first poked my head through a small window in my positivist European upbringing.[8] It is as a radical pluralist that I consider the claims of the systems discussed in this volume. Huxley claims that the systems he has chosen are those to which comparatists have chosen to apply the tag *religious laws*. For my part, I suspect that his choice was motivated more by considerations of who would be good company around the conference hall and restaurant table.

About systems

Let us assume – *per impossibile* – that we have achieved a non-essentialist identi-fication of law. We must now deal with the fact that each comparatist has his own view of what is meant by *systems*.[9] I start with the *Shorter Oxford* definition: 'either an organized or connected group of objects or a whole composed of parts in orderly arrangement according to some scheme or plan'.[10] In this sense of system, Huxley's invitations have preempted the problem. This volume presents us with Buddhist, Canon, Chinese, Hindu, Islamic and Jewish law as a connected group. Are such *religious laws* the same as *religious legal systems*? Up to a point. Indeed, I would prefer to keep the word *system* to designate the families as such rather than their components, the laws. Thus we would have *laws* such as the Buddhist, Canon, Chinese, Hindu, Islamic or Jewish laws which would be part of a *family* or *system* in the same way that we speak of a romano–germanic (which common lawyers would call *civil*) system including Austrian, Belgian, French, German, Italian and Portuguese laws and of a common law system including American, Australian, English and Nigerian laws. By this convention, *system* would be equated to *family*, so our task is to determine the criteria by which we define a system or a family of laws.

One more fundamental caveat before we proceed. *Systems*, as specific arrange-ments of the sources of a given law, are not static through history. They appear, develop, flourish, and disappear in an overlapping cavalcade. Many comparatists, adopting a historical perspective, consider that each stage of a law's historical development belongs to the same system, that is, to the same arrangement of the sources of law. This is obviously not the case. I have shown, for example, that Roman law of the time of monarchy is not, insofar as its production of laws is concerned, that of the Republic, nor that of the Empire.[11] In terms of dominant source, we travel from revelation to legal science and on to legislation. Likewise, French law has passed through at least three systems during its history. Until the seventeenth century it was essentially customary. Then, with the growing influence of scholarly writings, it tended towards the doctrinal. Finally with the codification of 1805, it took a legislative turn. In the same way, English law has certainly not been judge-made ever since 1066. It only began to develop in that direction during Henry II's reign. Dutch law has been successively customary, doctrinal (during the heyday of the roman-dutch law) and code-based since the nineteenth century. These four European examples show that a law at different stages of its history might belong to different systems, provided one follows my definitional criteria.

About criteria of classification

I shall address the criteria of classification under two headings: *which criteria* and *how to apply them to the existing laws*?[12] First, which criteria? I justify my preferred criteria by appealing to three principles. First, the main criterion has to be legal. This is why, quite apart from other objections, I would not favour those economic, geographical or racial criteria which appealed during the first half century of comparative law. This also explains my general hostility to dividing laws into religious and non-religious families. Even if we could overcome the problems of distinguishing law and religion, and if we were then able to label some parts of the Buddhist, Chinese, Christian, Hindu, Muslim and Jewish traditions as legal, I would still prefer to apply legal rather than extra-legal criteria to their classification. It follows that a legal family based on religion is unnecessary. This negative conclusion is easy to reach; to suggest a convincing alternative is more difficult.

A second and more important point: the essence of the law lies more in how it is produced, than in the subject-matter it contains. Different laws organise the public and private sides of society in different ways. Such differences are merely contingent and cannot be the basis for primary families. I propose instead to adopt the formal sources of law as my main criterion by which to characterise laws. My basic assumption is that law is part of culture. Like religion and many other cultural creations, law is influenced by (and has influence on) the economic, geographical, political and social environment. Law is a product of men's mind, an intellectual construction. Mankind can only access it if it is made part of a communication. As the German codifiers of the BGB put it, there is a distinction between *der Willen* (the will), which is shaped in the mind but inaccessible, and *die Willenserklärung* (the declaration of will), which gives communicative form (gestural, oral or written) to the will. This latter is what I mean by a formal source of law. Most of the societies which I have studied have used six such formal sources. They are, in alphabetical order: acts, case-law, custom, legal science, legislation and revelation.

So that these sources can be identified both through time by historians and through space by comparatists, I define *act* as the law formulated by individuals (wills, contracts, marriages, and so on), *case-law* the law formulated by the one who adjudicates conflicts, *custom* the law formulated by the group through its collective behaviour, *legal science* the law formulated by people who have a reputation for knowing the law, and *legislation* the law formulated by the chief(s) of the group. As for *revelation*, it is the law as expressed by a supra-natural being whom by convention we call God. In real life, each actual instance of law-making will be a combination of elements of these non-exclusive sources. Thus, if we find that the customary mode of production to have been dominant in the laws of pre-colonial African countries, we should not infer the absence in Africa of revelation, legislation, legal science, case law or acts. What justifies the label 'customary' is the attitude pre-colonial Africans themselves have about the production of their laws. They explain that they do what they do because 'one has always done it like that'. From the same internal angle, the common law is 'judge-made', French law 'legislative', classical Roman law 'scholarly' and so on. In each case, that source which is dominant (an adjective which admittedly belongs to the realm of incommensurability) is far from being the only source of each of these laws.

My third principle is that the same criteria should be applied at the same level of our taxonomy. We cannot allocate law A to one family because it is 'judge-made' and law B to another because its economy is based on socialism. Of course laws can be classified according to the economy which underlies them; but then all our families must be economic. In an economic scheme which divided laws into capitalist, feudal, subsistance and socialist, we might use the distinction between judge-made law and codified law to draw second level distinctions between members of a legal family defined by their shared economic stance.

Let me admit immediately that I have drawn these principles from the environment in which I was educated and from whatever else I have picked up over the last fifty years. These few fragments I have shored up against what Professor Tamanaha would regard as my ruinous search for an essentialist view of law. Can any of one's theorizations be completely abstracted from one's own background? Can comparison or even history exist unless one has some rough ideas of what one is looking for? I shall illustrate the point with an anecdote. Some years ago, in my capacity as Secretary-General of the *Société Jean Bodin pour l'Histoire comparative des Institutions*, I had an argument with Professor Peter Sack, a colleague I very much respect. In the course of our preparations for a conference on Punishment, he objected in strong words, which I much resented when applied to me, to the 'definition' (in the sense of trying to circumscribe a common theme for a Conference) which I proposed to the members of the *Société*. He objected that my definition did not embrace the *self-punishment* practised by Trobriand islanders.[13] I found this Sack attack (that my scholarship was imperialist) particularly hurtful because I had just come across precisely such a case in the colonial society I was studying. I had just read the story of a European woman who had 'punished' her unfaithful husband by committing a public suicide outside where he was with his paramour. I have no doubt that this indeed inflicted terrible pain on the husband, (perhaps more than any formal punisment could have done). But, for the purposes of my conference, I believe I was right not to extend the legal definition of punishment to include it. Though any Trobriander who would organise a conference on punishment has my blessing to define punishment in whatever way seems most fitting.

This anecdote warns us that a comparative and historical investigation such as ours into religion, takes us into dark and controversial territory. We may well disagree as to what counts as religious law – would it, for example, include French revolutionary law under the protection of the Goddess Reason? – and our disagreements may well be passionate. I address myself primarily to non-believers (among whom I number myself). Even slight familiarity with contemporary Christian, Islamic or Jewish laws shows that their primary source is the word of God as expressed to His prophet. Often this is described not as Law but as the Way or Path that God wills us to follow. As Silvio Ferrari puts it, 'Canon law is . . . founded on divine law, which can be fully understood only through faith'. Whatever follows from revelation in terms of behavioural, oral or written legal developments, may be analysed as acts, case law, customs, legal science or even legislation, all man-made; the underlying revelation these communications attempt to express remains divine. This falls within the *Shorter Oxford* definition of revelation as 'something disclosed or made known by divine means'. If one believes in revelation as a source of law, one generally also believes that such law is higher than man's laws and that other sources of law (acts, case-law, custom, legal science and legislation) must be understood in the light of revelation.

For these reasons I am willing to consider the law of Pakistan, where a statute or court decision contrary to the *shari'a* can be nullified, as one based on revelation. But such cases seem rare in the early twenty-first century: perhaps Pakistan is the only one of its kind. Revealed law was to be found earlier in European legal history during the Middle Ages and among some activists of the Puritan Revolution and as a source it survived into the nineteenth century. Let us remember that the *Code Napoleon* allowed one of the parties in civil cases (where no decisive evidence could be produced by either party) to challenge the other to swear on a Bible that he was telling the truth – if he refused, he lost the case. Of course this should not lead us to put the *Code Napoleon* into the category of revealed laws. But nor should we do so with States which adopt occasional rules inspired by Islamic law, such as the recognition that a man may take four wives provided he can treat them equally. The system is characterised not by its contents but by its own estimation of its most characteristic source.

It is not too difficult to deal with Christianity, Islam and Judaism, the three religions which originated in the Middle East and then spread throughout the world. They clearly have a revealed corpus of fundamental legal rules which have emerged from the contents of books – the Bible (including the New Testament) and the Qur'an – which mix religious and legal precepts. Buddhism and the religions which Europeans have come to call Hinduism present more difficulty. The evident differences between Middle Eastern and Indian religions are almost enough by themselves to sink any religious family of laws. But let us not anticipate. Finally, I must underline that revelation is essentially a matter of belief. For the non-believer, revelation is merely an alibi enabling certain people to establish their domination over the gullible. Perhaps so. But the hundreds of millions who believe outnumber these non-believers.

I turn to my second problem: how should we apply the criteria to existing laws? Shall we apply them cumulatively or successively? Typical of the cumulative approach are Zweigert and Kötz, whose taxonomy employs no less than five criteria to characterise their legal families. They bring many criteria to bear simultaneously on the objects of their comparison, and thus tend to offer more families with less members. The more criteria you select, the more difficult to keep many laws within one family. Zweigert and Kötz scandalised René David by splitting his beloved romano-germanic family into distinct romanist and germanic families. I much prefer to operate the criteria successively, so as to produce a progressively more detailed classification of families. I give, as my single example, the family comprising the original French Napoleonic law and Russian socialist law. The common feature is that in each case the supreme courts have no power to solve an interpretative crux and must refer it back to the legisla-tor for solution. If we emphasise this similarity, the two laws belong together. If we emphasise their differences, say in economic ideology, they belong apart. So our main *legislators interpret the law* system spawns two sub-systems: *legislators interpret the capitalist law* for the French Napoleonic system and *legis-lators interpret the socialist law* for the Russian revolutionary system. No doubt there are other criteria, equally or more relevant, which can generate different sub-systems.

We must limit our criteria to a fairly general level of description. Otherwise we court incommensurability, as did Zweigert and Kötz in their inclusion of what they called the *style* of the system. If *le style, c'est l'homme*, then style is peculiar to the individual taxon, that is, incommensurable with other taxa. A comparison that admits style as one of its criteria must produce an atomized taxonomy. Not that we can wholly avoid incommensurability. The distinction between 'judge-made law' and 'codified law' is ultimately a matter of qualitative rather than quantitative judgement. There are as many statutes in *Halsbury's Statutes of England* as there are in the french *Petits codes Dalloz*. It is notorious that the *Cour de Cassation* produces much the same kind of judge-made law as the *House of Lords*. The adepts of globalisation deduce from this that all laws are converging on a common identity. I am unconvinced. What matters in the definition of a system is not the number of occurrences of each source, nor even the formal hierarchy of sources, but how the sources are perceived by those inside the legal system. On this basis there is little doubt that the common law is perceived as a judge-made law, that what I call the romano-germanic laws are considered as legislative ones and that the Roman-Dutch law is founded on legal science. Examples of custom may be found among the African pre-colonial laws and perhaps the law of Pakistan may serve as an example of revealed law.

SHOULD ONE OF THE FAMILIES BE LABELLED AS RELIGIOUS?

In order to answer Huxley's second question, I shall apply the Vanderlinnaean taxonomy of sources to each of the systems described in the chapters above. In the eyes of the people living under these so-called religious laws, which of my six sources prevailed? I will proceed in an analytical fashion looking first at each individual system before passing to my epilogue and conclusions. In the process, I shall express my reactions (often in the form of perplexities) to the presentation of my colleagues.[14] If a chapter provides a clear answer to classification into Vanderlinnaean categories, I will immediately adopt it and proceed to the next. This is not indifference, but necessity. Time presses, and there is no time for courtesies. But may I record in general terms that I have learnt much more on the so-called religious laws through the essays collected here than I knew before. My thanks to Huxley and to my fellow authors for providing such riches.

Buddhist law. I start with Andrew Huxley's paper, not out of respect for his *droit de patron* but because Buddhism comes first in an alphabetical order of topics. His conclusions provide me with a clear answer. Buddhist law is not a revealed system, but one, whose main formal sources is legal science. This legal learning was quite elaborate, and spread throughout many places. The individuals who found its norms and mechanisms of adjudication relevant, be they commoners, monks or kings, thought of themselves as guiding their lives by this legal science. For me, all the rest is silence.

Canon law. Silvio Ferrari describes Canon law as 'grounded on divine law, that is on a law revealed by God to men through Jesus Christ'. Hurrah! There is, *expressis verbis*, my dominant source: revelation. Unfortunately for my argument, he brings forward a second character relating to the purpose of Canon law which, due to my limited linguistic talents, I cannot distinguish from the first. On the one hand, 'The supernatural character of its main source makes Canon law a religious legal system'. On the other hand, 'This aim [salvation] gives Canon law its religious character'. I assume that these are not cumulative, but alternative views as to the nature of Canon law. And, if this is correct, the second character, being non-legal, interests me less than the first. Plainly, Ferrari feels otherwise. He writes 'The eternal salvation of spouses is paramount in Canon law'. Maybe so, but this is outside the field of law. We can return to it when we consider possible sub-systems. Let us now return to revelation.

My happiness proves to be premature. Insofar as Canon law is 'a law revealed by God' it rests on revelation, but insofar as it is natural law 'given to men by God through creation', it may not. Perhaps it does not matter whether the law has been 'revealed' by Him during man's life or incorporated in man from the moment humanity was created. Either way, God is still the ultimate origin of the law. But is natural law a source of law distinct from my five human sources, or can it be subsumed within revelation? The *Shorter Oxford* encourages me to do the latter by defining revelation as 'something disclosed or made known by divine or supernatural means'. If natural law is the normative understanding the human species derives from the world of nature, then the creation, a supernatural mean of bringing the human species into this world, was a necessary precondition.

Going further in this taxonomic exercise, one meets the four characteristics of divine law: completeness, superiority to human law, universality and immutability. Because these offer wide scope for comparisons between the laws covered within these pages, I incorporate them into my chart. Finally we must consider Ferrari's cautious suggestion in the final sentence of his introductory description of Canon law. He draws attention to 'the importance of what happens in *foro interno*' and asks whether '*the* [my emphasis] specific feature of Canon law as a religious system can be found here?'. Is this suggestion compatible with revelation? When one debates a legal issue in the internal forum, it is one's individual conscience – shaped, admittedly, by natural law – which disposes of the issue. Following Ferrari's analysis leads to a choice of paths: either we come back to revelation via natural law or we embrace radical legal pluralism by leaving each individual free

Canon law (as characterized by Ferrari)

Main characters	Secondary characters
Divine, i.e. revealed by God	completeness
	superiority to human law
	universality
	immutability
Pursuing salvation	
Favouring forum internum	

to determine his own set of values. Either of these options suits the scheme I am developing here. I summarise my discussion of Canon law in this table.

A final comment: neither the pursuit of salvation nor the importance of the *forum internum* appear to me as specifically legal. They are not, while revelation is, necessarily linked to the production of law through its formal sources.

Chinese law. Here we meet a geographical instead of a doctrinal term of reference. Why do we speak of Chinese law and not Daoist law, Confucian law or even Buddhist law (Chinese style)? Randall Peerenboom indirectly clarifies the issue by rapidly bringing Confucius to the forefront of his analysis, by referring to the Way (*dao*) as a social norm and by mentioning Legalism as a manner of looking at law. Let us then consider the triplet Buddhism, Confucianism and Daoism on the one hand and Legalism on the other.

Scholarship, the activity of learned people, appears to be the mode of legal production primarily associated with the first three. Confucius, Laozi and Zhuangzi and such Chinese Buddhists as Fo-t'u-teng were, first and foremost, scholars. I shall never forget what Professor René Dekkers used to tell us second year students in the faculty of law at Brussels University: 'When the steps to the school are worn out and weeds are growing in the courthouse, the land is in good health'. This linkage between scholarship and law is typically Chinese. Indeed Dekkers' sentiments have Daoist and Buddhist echoes. As for legalism, which is symbolized by the *fa* of the imperial bureaucrats and gave rise to the collections of imperial sources known as the Chinese codes, there is no doubt that the imperial command, legislation, is the dominant source in the law as the legalists conceive it. In that sense they may rightly be compared, from the point of view of systems, with the Western European State-controlled positivist model. Perenboom, however, does not focus on the different sources of laws coexisting in China. His exposition is more positivist: the only law is the *fa* and the rest is religion.

Hindu law. For any comparatist who has not, as I have, been subjected to Werner Menski's uncompromising look at things 'Hindu' for some decades, his contribution must appear devastating. Behind the phrase 'Hindu Law' does anything legal in fact exist? Menski displays ambivalence on this point. On the one hand, he presents himself, Fennimore Cooper style, as *The Last of the Hinduists*, while on the other hand he continues to refer to 'Hindu law'. I shall follow him down the latter track in order to suggest a slot in my analysis which might be hospitable to Hindu law as he portrays it. My suggestion is that Hindu law belongs to the family of the customary systems of laws, in that custom is ultimately the basic term of reference of people who live under that law. On this, Menski is perfectly clear: 'From a Hindu perspective, the practical emphasis is on custom as a source of law, where *sadacara*, acting in line with what one's social group considers as appropriate, is the major source of Hindu law'. If this is insufficiently unequivocal, note his agreement with J.D.M. Derrett as to the fact that *sadacara* is 'placed higher than religious authority . . . or state law in any form' . . . These statements preclude further discussion.[15] In the Vanderlinnaean scheme, then, Hindu law is customary rather than religious.

Islamic law. Lynn Welchman's paper, like Peerenboom's, examines a geographically defined area where many legal systems coexist and compete for supremacy, rather than what is usually called a religious law. Her view of Islamic law, like Peerenboom's of Chinese law, is more territorial than personal. She highlights the problems which I have mentioned in connection with Pakistan: How can revealed law be inserted into a legislative system? And can revealed law become the dominant source in such a system? Her portrait of Palestinian law at a particular moment in its development underlines the importance of specifying the time-frame of any legal description. In earlier phases of its history, Islamic law was probably less challenged by non-religious opposition than it is today. This would appear to be true of many systems, including the French. As the state develops, and as new pressures emerge for emancipation from clergy or church, the religious authorities are pushed to the side of the field of law production. Nothing in Welchman's paper contradicts my picture of Muslim law (which I distinguish from the law of Muslim states) as revealed law. Perhaps, as I have suggested, Pakistan is a Muslim state with revealed law. Are there others? Could Afghanistan, Saudi Arabia or Libya be placed in the same group as Pakistan? I doubt that we yet know enough about the Taliban state to answer for Afghanistan. An anecdote about the Saudi legal system suggests a positive answer. An individual (I believe he was a foreigner) who had been caught drinking alcohol managed to be absolved by the State court, only to be immediately sentenced by a religious court to physical punishment.[16] It would seem that the Qu'ranic interdict took precedence over the interpretation of State law by State courts. One of the first articles of the Libyan Constitution proclaims that the word of God is the only paramount law of the Libyan State.[17] Does this point to a revealed system, in which the majority of Libyans see God's word as the main source of the law that governs them?

But the most important aspect of Welchman's paper is her demonstration of how difficult it is to build a truly pluralist legal system when the Palestinian executives are aiming for full modern statehood and the Palestinian *ulama* for full implementation of the *Shar'ia*. I am most grateful to her for having revealed to me the 'triangle' of law producing sources to which Buskens and Menski refer in their recent works. This triangular analysis merits further investigation by comparatists or historians interested in how law is produced. I shall return to it briefly in my final summing up.

Jewish law. Calum Carmichael's chapter convincingly demonstrates the undue restrictiveness imposed by the comparative method and makes further useful suggestions for historians when looking at ancient (and also, in some cases, at modern[18]) laws. Implicit in his remarks is the complete impossibility of any analysis of families of law. He also brings forward an aspect of biblical law which can usefully be employed to generate additional legal subsystems: by showing that some biblical laws are what I would call 'mythically justified' or 'story-told', he focuses our attention on the other sub-system of non-mythically justified or non-story-told law.

Bernard Jackson's chapter leaves no doubt that, allowing for the contribution of the scholars who developed the *halakah*, Jewish law is God-made law. Those of us unfamiliar with the Jewish and Islamic law cannot but be struck by the similarities between God and Allah, Moses and Muhammad, and, finally, the rabbis with their not always unanimous teachings and the learned men of Islam whose writings divide Muslim law in its various schools.

EPILOGUE – COMPARING THE INCOMMENSURABLE

My job is done. I have answered Huxley's questions to the best of my ability and I have shown how the so-called religious laws can be subsumed within a typology of legal systems. Yet there are seven more points arising from these chapters which I would have pursued, had I been able to attend the Workshop. I shall take advantage of my role as concierge to sweep them together into one pile, before I close by summarising my arguments.

The reductive character of the classical -isms

Among the six 'religious laws' discussed herein, only one may claim to be rightly so called: this is the Canon law of the Catholic Church as presented by Ferrari. But Christianity, the religion, does not reduce to Catholicism, the Church. We must consider the wider family of Christian laws. Perhaps we can divide the family into Eastern and Western halves. And perhaps we must break each half down further, the Eastern into Russian, Greek, Nestorian and Coptic orthodoxies, and the Western into Catholicism and the various post-Reformation schisms (Adventism, Anglicanism, Baptism, Calvinism, Episcopalism, Lutherianism, Presbyterianism and Puritanism, to mention only a few.) Each of these -isms might have its own Christian law, though all claim a common ideological base in the revelation of God's will through the teaching of Jesus of Nazareth. Islam appears to be an equally reductive label, if one accepts the fundamental division between Kharijites, Shi'ites and Sunnites, and the further division of the Sunnites into the Shafi'ite,

Hanbalite, Hanafite and Malikite rites. All are Muslims, in that they believe in Allah as the one God, and follow at least four fundamental rules linked to charity, fast, pilgrimage and prayer. Let us propose, in counter-reductive mode, that Christianism is twofold (Eastern and Western), Buddhism (Chinese, Pali and Tibetan) and Islam (Kharijite, Shi'ite and Sunnite) are threefold. On Menski's account, Hinduism would be manyfold. And on Peerenboom's account, Chinese law occupies an entirely different dimension.

Americano-Europeocentricism

Menski and Jackson have excoriated the way American-European scholarship has (deliberately or negligently) misdescribed Hindu and Jewish legal culture. They are totally convincing in showing how not only jurists, but also anthropologists, historians and sociologists, have had their crafts manipulated to various unsavoury ends. It is the French scholarship of the last half-century which best exemplifies these fundamental misunderstandings. The evolution in the successive editions of David's *Les grands systèmes*, mentioned by Jackson, exemplifies that great comparatist's perplexity when confronted with other cultures. There are two more examples which caused me particular grief. He wrote that Ethiopians had no law – only customs – prior to the legislation early in Haile Sellassie's reign and, of course, prior to the codification movement of the second half of the century of which Professor David's *Code civil* is the best known monument! And, in his capacity as chief editor of a volume of the *International Encyclopedia of Comparative Law*,[19] he felt it necessary to justify Hassan Afchar's presentation of Muslim law by stating that Afchar's text had been submitted 'to the highest authorities of the Muslim world' who 'found no fault with it'. This is an incredible editorial intrusion. Can we imagine him submitting a contribution on German land law or Italian contract law to the approval of the highest authorities of the Western world? Yet David was the acme of global sophistication compared with his contemporary, Professor René Rodière. Rodière, having described briefly the common law, romano-germanic and socialist families in his *Introduction to Comparative Law*, allowed himself to stop there as obviously nothing existed beyond these three Christian-inspired legal families![20]

The ambiguity of the word 'source'

I prefer to avoid ambiguity by distinguishing *material* and *formal* sources of law. The former encompass every factor – cultural, economic, geographic, political and social – which bears upon the producer's mind when producing law. The latter are the precise forms that the legal product takes. For a strict observance lawyer only the formal source matters; for an anthropologist or sociologist the material source is essential to explain why the formal source stands as it is. I accept, however, that it is hard to maintain this distinction for societies where religion and law form a complex whole. A positivist would label religion as a material source and legal acts, case law, custom, legal science and legislation as formal sources. But what of revelation? How do we decide whether a norm originating from God is religious or legal, a material or a formal source? Should we even try to make this distinction? Had I been present at the Workshop, I would have liked to ask Welchman why the often quoted Qu'ranic verse on polygamy is regarded as legal, when the preceding and following verses are regarded as purely religious. I believe it may be possible to generate answers to these questions by a double pronged analysis combining a static point of view (the pluralist view of society) with a dynamic point of view (the competition between social networks).

How far can we push revelation as a source of law?

Can revelation as a source of law be extended beyond the monotheistic creeds? Could it be extended beyond Christianism, Islam and Judaism to the concept of natural law? To those who do not accept that natural law can have a 'natural' (meaning rational or religious) basis, it appears to be a foundationless belief. Could it, then, be classified as a form of revelation, though not necessarily coming from God? Were we to take this step, we might also include those very general sources identified as the 'general principles of law', 'natural justice', and 'good conscience'. My impression is that their only foundation is in a judge's personal revelation when he cannot find specific formal sources to apply, or when he dislikes the consequences of applying the formal source to the instant case. Hence I would rather classify the so-called general principles of law within revelation than among the other classical formal sources.

The pluralist view of law and society

I am a strong believer in a kind of pluralism, often called radical by those whose opinion differs from mine, in which the individual is at the meeting point of many social networks.[21] In my view the individual belongs not to one, but to many societies, each of which has its own set of norms. Positivist law (i.e. State-controlled norms and/or mechanisms of adjudication) has no exclusive right to produce the norms which govern human behaviour. Since man is a multi-social being, he must decide his priorities in cases where there is conflict between the norms or mechanisms of adjudication defined by each society. In his multiple social life he is faced with constant choices: law-shopping and forum-shopping are the central manifestations of pluralism as I understand it. Within a defined geographical area, therefore, we should not distinguish between proper law and informal law.[22] Peerenboom refers to Chinese 'guild regulations and communal practices and norms'. I would regard these as of equal legal status with the Han Emperors' criminal codes. He also refers to 'semi-formal means of settling disputes', which apparently involved imperial judges delegating their adjudicative power as a cost-saving measure. If I have understood him correctly, if these imperial judges gave semi-official recognition to other adjudicating authorities, then Han China exhibited a typical colonial pseudo-pluralism: its normative networks lacked autonomy vis-à-vis the State-controlled positivist law represented by the imperial judge. From my pluralist perspective, the important issue is whether legal norms can be distinguished from other norms. As long as we speak of *legal* pluralism, we must identify something corresponding to a concept of law. I offered theoretical means for identifying law at the beginning of this chapter. Let me add that in most practical cases, there is no room for controversy. Where social networks coexist or compete, lawyers can usually identify one of the networks as being legal.

The competition between social networks

Each social network generally has its own mechanisms to prevent or relieve disintegrative tensions. These mechanisms differ from each other and may compete with each other, putting the individual to the inconvenience or – why not? – advantage of law-shopping and forum-shopping. Some social networks – the modern State is the clearest example – may be ambitious to impose their own norms and adjudicative institutions on the others.[23] Welchman's chapter on the Palestinian state-to-be shows that social networks are in constant interaction and that such interaction is far from neutral. I shall mention three other examples involving the laws under consideration in this volume. First, consider the competition between Canon law and royal law in mediaeval France. In relation to family law, both networks tried to impose their control on the daily life of French men and women. Through various mechanisms, including brute force, royal law came to be substituted for Canon law on many points, but often this was old wine with a new label. In these cases when the royal law replicated the Canon law, its formal source ceased to be religious. But we must admit that its material source continued to be religious. Second, consider Jackson's paper on modern developments in Israel. As I read him, it seems that a 'traditional' society, based essentially on religion, and a 'modern' society, including both believers and non-believers, are competing to define the norms or adjudicative institutions applicable within Israel's boundaries. Mr Justice Elon proposes to reconcile these competitors by bringing them together into the positive law of the State of Israel, in which the former would serve as a fundamental norm for the latter. In my terms, the 'traditional' network would become the cultural material source of the formal sources of the 'modern' network. This solution would entail the law of Israel shifting from a legislative or judge-made system towards a system based on revelation, or divine command. It would leave ample scope for continued controversy: Would the members of the 'traditional' network be satisfied without a direct input to the positive law of the country? And would the non-religious Israelis accept that the fundamental values on which their positive law is built are derived from a religion which they do not espouse? Third, consider the evolution of Islamic law in Algeria under French rule. After some initial hesitations, a pseudo-pluralism was developed in which Islamic law was incorporated within, and closely controlled

179

by, the Algerian colonial network. In matters of personal status, Islamic law was accepted, but it was subjected to the control of the second division of the Court of Appeal in Algiers, specializing in Muslim affairs. What emerged was a judge-made French–Muslim law, which most specialists refuse to recognise as Islamic law. The competition for the control of the indigenous Algerian society gave birth to a new type of law. Perhaps Han China can be analysed along similar lines: Peerenboom refers to the selective incorporation of Confucian principles as reflected in the *li* into the positive law represented by the *fa*. If it is difficult to decide which source of law effectively serves as a foundation to the judges' decisions, it may be that a new type of law has evolved.

Radical pluralism and the individual

To regard the individual as the most important producer of law, rather than the State or the intermediary social structures, is to turn the processes of legal production upside down. I will be accused of anarchism, of encouraging the freedom of the individual to prevail over the interests of society. Not so. The human being who chooses between competing normative systems remains, and I cannot sufficiently underscore the point, a *social* being, but a multi-social one. Society exists at all levels, from the State down to a cohabiting couple. My version of pluralism accepts that on rare occasions an individual, such as a Trappist monk, might choose to be governed exclusively by one set of laws. But usually the individual chooses between laws. A professional sportsman will be more concerned with breaching the rules of his sport than the laws of his State. The anti-abortionist who kills a doctor chooses the law of God over the criminal law of the State. The essential pluralist point is that the individual is not just the anonymous object of State law, but also the autonomous subject who chooses between the various laws of the social networks to which he belongs. Understood thus, pluralism is nothing new. It is the *forum internum* of Canon law to which Ferrari alludes. And it is the individual Hindu defining his own *dharma* as described by Menski.

A SUMMING UP

At the risk of seeming over-ambitious, I shall attempt to sum up this final chapter, and the issues to which this volume is devoted:

a   Taxonomy is not necessarily useless as a way of organising knowledge.

b   When organising, one should choose the most relevant taxon for classification.

c   Taxa should be applied successively and not simultaneously.

d   The most relevant taxon when dealing with laws is their source – the form under which they are produced.

e   Classifying laws as religious describes one of their material sources, not their formal sources.

f There are six main formal sources, producing respectively individual acts, case law, custom, legal science, legislation and revelation.

g Of the so-called religious laws, some, such as Christian, Islamic and Jewish laws, had *in their original state* revelation as their main source. Others, such as Buddhist, Confucian and Daoist laws, had legal science. Yet others, such as Hindu law, had custom.

h With the development of state-power and the ensuing triangular competition with religious power and societal power, various outcomes are possible. They cover the spectrum of solutions from (1) the apparently complete incorporation of revelation into legislation exemplified by the French *Code civil*, (2) a state controlled system which pays lip-service to revelation, as exemplified by colonial Algeria, (3) a provisionally mixed system where no source has yet emerged as dominant, as exemplified by present day Palestine, to (4) a purely 'religious state'.[24]

i From a radical pluralist point of view, any taxonomy of laws cannot tell the whole truth, since each taxon must necessarily exclude the rival sources which simultaneously bear down on a given individual.

j As a comparatist, I believe firmly in the value of taxonomy. As a pluralist, I believe taxonomy cannot tell the whole truth about how social conflict is resolved. My reconciliation of these two views may appear more like a pirouette than a pas de deux: Legal taxonomy, like law, is a construct of the mind which belongs to the realm of thought. Radical legal pluralism refers to law in a different sense, which belongs to a different level of reality. Always assuming that there is such a thing as reality! On this ontological crux the world's religions have more to tell us than the world's laws.

NOTES

1 I have my doubts as to their capacity of ever bringing that process to a satisfactory end. See: Jacques Vanderlinden, *Anthropologie juridique* (Paris: Dalloz, 1996).

2 I avoid the phrase *comparative law*, as it designates something which does not exist. I prefer to speak of *comparison of laws* or *comparing laws*; hence the title of my contribution to that approach of the laws of the world: Jacques Vanderlinden, *Comparer les droits* (Bruxelles: Kluwer, 1995).

3 B.Z. Tamanaha, 'A Non-Essentialist Version of Legal Pluralism' *Journal of Law and Society*, 27: 296–321 (2000).

4 Perhaps Tamanaha's proposal would work for Canon law, if we assume that *ius* may be adequately translated as *law*. Silvio Ferrari's chapter challenges this assumption.

5 H. Afchar, 'The Muslim Conception of Law' 84–106 of ed. R. David *International Encyclopedia of Comparative Law, Vol. II – The Legal Systems of the World, Chap. I The Different Conceptions of Law* (Tübingen: Mohr, 1975), 86.

6 N.J. Coulson, *A History of Islamic Law* (Edinburgh: Edinburgh University Press, 1964), 2.

7 J. Schacht, *An Introduction to Islamic Law* (Oxford: Clarendon Press, 1964), 1.

8 My comparative and historical analysis of law began in fall of 1953. I was privileged to present my findings at SOAS in the spring of 1974, as holder of the Belgian Chair in the University of London.

9 Under the heading 'The structure of legal systems', this topic has been put on the agenda of the XVITH INTERNATIONAL CONGRESS OF COMPARATIVE LAW to be held in Brisbane in 2002; this author has been designated as general reporter for that subject.

10 *The Shorter Oxford English Dictionary* 3rd ed (Oxford: Clarendon Press, 1965).

11 See further: Vanderlinden, *supra* note 2, at 365–366.

12 For an expanded treatment, see Vanderlinden, *supra* note 2, at 311–337.

13 This typically involved complainants jumping from a palm-tree after having clamoured their grievances before the assembled villagers.

14 Two of the contributors have been colleagues and friends for decades now. I shall try to avoid bias in favour of their chapters.

15 His chapter makes several other noteworthy points. His presentation of Americano-European comparatists' and other scholars' views of Hinduism and Hindu law is the most devastating indictment of a certain legal science one could make. Needless to say, I fully subscribe to it and could cite several depressing parallels from my own field of African laws.

16 G. Steir, 'Source of Law and the Issue of Legitimacy and Rights' *Middle East Journal* 42: 436–446 (1998).

17 Art. II of the Constitution of Libya reads 'The Holy Qu'ran is the constitution of the Socialist People's Libyan Arab Jamahiriya'. according to T. Ehrhardt (ed.), Libya, in A.P. Blaustein & G. Flanz, gen. ed. *Constitutions of the Countries of the World* (Dobbs Ferry: Oceana, 1984), 10.

18 His discussion of the origins of the American constitution is compelling, and could be applied to many other fundamental documents.

19 David, *supra* note 5, at 84 (footnote).

20 The Christian inspiration of socialist laws is an especially provocative concept.

21 I insist on the word network rather than field which is often used by other pluralists for the reason that the latter has in my view a spatial connotation which (a) is too much linked to a territorial view of society, which (b) precisely would not apply to universal societies such as the "religious" ones.

22 'Informal law' is one of many deprecatory terms by which positivist lawyers identify those norms or mechanisms of adjudication which were not incorporated in the State-controlled positivist model of law.

23 It may well transpire that my competing social networks can be analysed as the three sides of Buskens' or Menski's normative triangle.

24 This volume has not disclosed an example of a state where religious sources prevail completely. Possibly Iran (1979–1988), which French literature referred to as 'the ayatollah state', was one such. So possibly was Tibet (1480–1950) under Dalai Lama rule.

INDEX